THE MOST FABULOUS TREASURE

*The marvelous
Grimoire of Abraham the Jew*

Copyright © 2025 RICHARD TOUITOU

DEDICATION

To all those who dream of hidden treasures, magic and adventure.

To those who wish to attempt the pursuit of the extraordinary.

Come and immerse yourself in this exciting quest for the Absolute, for which thousands of seekers have dedicated their lives out of thirst for gold and their crazy dream of living for eternity.

ACKNOWLEDGMENT

*In memory of my late wife Annie
without which I could not have written my book.*

TABLE OF CONTENTS

Dedication	3
Acknowledgment	4
Prologue	7
Chapter 1	10
Chapter 2	19
Chapter 3	33
Chapter 4	53
Chapter 5	65
Chapter 6	86
Chapter 7	103
Chapter 8	111
Chapter 9	119
Chapter 10	136
Chapter 11	149
Chapter 12	167
Chapter 13	170
Chapter 14	182
Chapter 15	189
Chapter 16	206
Chapter 17	213
Chapter 18	223
Chapter 19	236

Chapter 20 242

Chapter 21 247

Chapter 22 268

Chapter 23 272

Epilogue 283

PROLOGUE

"I see the wonder of which I am amazed"

Paris, September 11, 1397

The old man strolled nonchalantly through the deserted alleys of the Parisian cemetery. The Charnier des Innocents was bathed in the soft light of the full moon, casting reflections of the starry night on the scattered puddles left by a recent rain. The atmosphere was gloomy, not the ideal setting for a nocturnal stroll in these uncertain times, yet the peaceful figure showed no fear. He clutched a bag under his right arm, the contents of which seemed precious. Dressed in a scarlet cape and with his head covered by a Phrygian cap, he had an almost doll-like face adorned with a long white beard. His lively, mobile eyes shone with a brilliant light.

The old man calmly crossed half of the central aisle, deserted at this late hour, before stopping in front of a recently erected mausoleum. On the facade of the monument, a painting of an all-black man faced a laconic inscription: "I see the wonder of which I am amazed." At the base, a second, smaller inscription was discreetly engraved in the stone: "Perrenelle 11 sept. 1397."

Much more mysterious was the message engraved on a banner above a strange figure, which held an hourglass in one hand and two spheres in the other: *"I hold the agent in my dexter, Sun and Moon in my sinister*

And the nice Mercury too, I know how to join them together

That however I can it seems to me to live healthy and rich."

The man knelt as best he could on the marble plinth, oblivious to the damp chill seeping into his knees. With both hands clasped, he meditated for long minutes, then piously crossed himself. His faithful companion had been resting in peace in this final resting place for only a few hours. The old man was moved; tears slowly flowed from his eyes, forcing him to wipe them frequently with the back of his hand.

He rose without haste, having collected himself, and walked around the monument with a slow but resolute step. On the other side, in the form of an arcade, mysterious figures were engraved in the stone. Without hesitation, he walked toward a metal plate apparently sealed in stone. It was wrought iron—or perhaps cast iron—and bore a beautifully chiselled capital letter "N."

Opposite the facade, another very similar plaque bore the letter "F."

"N" for Nicolas and "F" for Flamel.

Nicolas Flamel!

What was the famous Parisian alchemist and writer doing in this sinister setting, in the middle of the night?

The alchemist reached into his bag and extracted a hammer and mason's pick. He approached the "N"-stamped plate and gave a few sharp taps to the edges of the metal. The plate—surprisingly not firmly sealed—came off without difficulty, revealing a tiny hidden cache. Flamel reached into his satchel once more to pull out something resembling a book. He gazed at it for a long time under the moonlight, as though to engrave the image of it forever in his memory. He sighed deeply before finally taking a large velvet cloth from his pocket. With great care, he wrapped the mysterious work, placing it gently in the small alcove.

The public writer searched his bag one last time and withdrew a glass jar sealed with a large cork. He removed the cork, placed it on the floor, and spread the strange paste-like contents on the back of the metal plate. After dutifully smearing what looked like glue, he pressed the metal plate back into place, applying firm pressure to secure it. He waited patiently for the cement to harden before closing the vial and returning his tools to the bag.

Satisfied with his work, he set off again, never looking back, as calmly as he had come, the satchel once more under his arm.

In the following days, the Parisian alchemist busied himself with distributing vast wealth to charitable works. Flamel tirelessly pursued the goal he and his faithful wife had set for themselves some ten years earlier, continuing until his death. Thus, his fortune was used to restore, maintain, and build a large number of churches and hospitals in Paris, as well as several refuges and hospices to house the poor, free of charge.

While countless investigations have been made over the centuries, no one has ever been able to explain the origin of the fabulous fortune of the public writer.

The most famous alchemist of all time curiously disappeared on March 22, 1417—the day of the vernal equinox, traditionally marking the beginning of the Great Work.

CHAPTER 1

Algiers, June 22, 1949

The Hotel Saint George was teeming with people, as it had been every evening since the liberation. Post-war Algeria had become a hub of major strategic importance in the Mediterranean, and the largest hotel in the Mediterranean capital was regularly overrun by the personalities who landed in Algiers. As a direct consequence, there was almost a permanent shortage of rooms. The palace had become the privileged venue for international meetings due to its strategic position in the heart of the city. The headquarters of the Allied Forces had established itself there during the landing in North Africa, and a large American delegation still occupied an entire floor.

The French colony was not a tourist destination, with only a few hotels available for visitors in the white city. Other establishments resembled dens of iniquity or places of debauchery more than havens of rest, limiting the options for travellers in transit.

On this hot summer night, a mysterious gathering was taking place in a discreet salon on the mezzanine floor of the palace. It appeared to be reserved for a wealthy local elite. On the door, hanging from a tiny hook, was a curious wooden painting, in surprisingly bright colours, showing a salamander roasting in a furnace. In the ribboned speech bubble surrounding the illustration, a strange, barely legible Latin inscription read: "Azoth & Ignis tibi sufficiunt."

Was there a scent of sulphur floating in the corridors of the Hotel Saint George? Certainly not!

Twelve respectable individuals had gathered in the guest room around a large round table. The Grand College was in full session that evening. The table had just been cleared after a very local dinner, and the butler had asked the floor staff not to disturb the guests in the room any longer.

In this very "Art Deco" style private room, the atmosphere was agitated to say the least. One might have thought they were in a tumultuous schoolroom, abandoned by a teacher in despair at being unable to restore order.

An imposing man stood up, resolutely determined to speak. He was chairing the current session. Dressed in a midnight blue satin djellaba, with a white saroual belted with a scarlet ribbon, he wore a large turban on which was pinned the emblem of his tribe: the Southern Cross. He had removed his veil early in the evening. His long, coppery face, with bluish streaks, seemed sculpted by the Sirocco. He wore a neatly trimmed short beard with dignity, topped with a thin moustache. This fascinating character seemed to have stepped straight out of a Hollywood production.

His Serene Highness Ahmed Ranzi el Sahraoui, Prince of the Targuis, eyed the effervescent assembly with severity, and, pretending to be exasperated, cast an icy gaze toward the turbulent members who were discussing at random. He tapped his glass a few times with his teaspoon, hoping to silence the more talkative guests.

The Grand College had very strict rules, established by former Freemasons. Had they ever been enforced? Certainly not. The traditionally unruly Mediterranean spirit inevitably resurfaced, requiring frequent calls to order.

During this brief moment when the prince was striving to bring silence, he had a thought for the creators of this noble secular institution, the Grand College, which, like the Invisible College founded in Europe at the very beginning of the Renaissance, brought together great initiates—the heirs of Templar knowledge and Sufi wisdom. All these initiates were true scholars who secretly pursued the same quest. Shadow researchers who met regularly in this place to share their passion, exchange ideas, develop new theories, and also perpetuate the tradition by adding new links to this long, unbroken chain that had persisted for many centuries.

The prince hesitated, visibly moved. This evening, he would announce his intention to go into exile far away, for an indefinite period. It was a decision he had long considered. By embarking on a long pilgrimage, Ranzi believed he could finally escape the remorse that had tormented him since the tragic death of his wife and the child she was carrying.

The Targui composed himself after these few seconds of hesitation.

He liked his brothers in arms, all of them, with their qualities and their faults. This assembly was a big family because powerful bonds had been forged over time in a country torn apart by centuries of conflict. Its members truly saw themselves as brothers.

Noting that silence had finally settled, and satisfied with the atmosphere, Ranzi continued with a brief speech in impeccable French. Only his close companions could detect the sadness that modulated his voice. He made one final effort and then smiled.

"Brothers," he announced solemnly, "I declare the summer session open. We were treated, as usual, to an excellent dinner, during which you had plenty of time to converse among yourselves. Now, it's high time to get down to business. I therefore claim your full attention, as I have important revelations to make."

Slowly but confidently, he pulled some typed sheets from a leather briefcase and spread them out on the table. Taking a deep breath, he continued.

"Isaac has just returned from a grand tour of Europe," he said, winking slightly at his right-hand neighbour. "After many unsuccessful searches over the past two decades, he has acquired a legendary grimoire—the one that is believed to have inspired Flamel to write the most widely read of his alchemical treatises: the 'Book of Hieroglyphic Figures of Abraham the Jew.'"

A great silence filled the room, followed by long applause and then a terrible ruckus. All eyes turned to the hero of the evening, whose modesty was being sorely tested.

The news seemed incredible. This manuscript, a true monument of alchemical literature, a unique piece, the esoteric work of a learned rabbi who likely lived in the 14th century, had been thought lost forever.

The president, grinning widely, glanced at the assembly once more and then resumed his presentation after a pause long enough to pique the curiosity of the other members, who were beginning to show signs of impatience.

"Dear brethren, you all know the story of that famous grimoire, I believe?" he continued. "Over the past six centuries, fanciful copies—more or less well-made, largely inspired by Flamel's description—have circulated here and there across Europe."

The news seemed impossible to believe. How could so many scholars and historians have been deceived for six centuries? How many artists or collectors had been misled in the same way?

Questions began to fly in all directions, and poor Isaac didn't know where to start in answering them.

Ranzi, smiling broadly, had fully anticipated the reaction he had just provoked. He caught his breath, waved his right hand for a long while, and held up the typed sheet he was clutching, hoping to assist his neighbour, who appeared overwhelmed by the repeated questions from the other members. Would he finally silence an assembly more unruly than ever?

After a few minutes that seemed endless, calm was finally restored, and Ranzi was able to continue his presentation.

"This is how Nicolas Flamel describes this grimoire," he continued, his voice steady as he began to read, perfectly mimicking the intonations of Old French.

"So, just as after the death of my parents, I earned my living in our art of writing—making inventories, drawing up accounts, and stopping the expenses of guardians and minors—it fell into my hands, for the sum of two florins, a golden book, very old and very large. It was not made of paper or parchment, as others are, but appeared to be of loose bark, perhaps from tender shrubs. Its cover was of fine copper, engraved with strange letters and figures. As for me, I believe they could very well be Greek characters or another ancient language.

"As long as I didn't know how to read them, and I knew very well that they weren't notes in Latin or Gallic—because I understand a little of the latter.

"As for the inside, its bark leaves were engraved, and with great skill, written with an iron chisel in beautiful and very clear coloured Latin letters. It contained three sets of seven leaves, the seventh of which was still without writing...

"On the first of the pages, there was written in large golden capitals: 'Abraham Jew, Prince, Priest, Levite, Astrologer, Philosopher, to the Nation of the Jews, by the wrath of God dispersed at the Gaulles, Salut. D.I...'

Then, resuming his presentation after a brief hesitation, he specified:

– I wanted to read you this extract that you know well, so that you can realise for yourselves the inconsistencies that can be noted between the description Flamel gives of the book of Abraham the Jew and reality, since we have the original.

The manuscript in our possession consists of a total of twenty-four pages, not three sets of seven leaves. The cover of the original is not copper, but thick leather. The work includes twelve pages with beautiful illustrations and colourful illuminations, alternated with twelve pages of text in Hebrew.

The illustrations in the manuscript are all noticeably different from those described to us by the Parisian public writer. Finally, the grimoire is made of parchment, not papyrus. Fulcanelli was, therefore, correct in asserting that the grimoire could not have been written on a medium that had been abandoned for centuries and was no longer current in Europe.

All these gross errors make us think that the very famous Parisian writer of the 14th century deliberately falsified reality. We need to solve this puzzle.

Flamel could not read Hebrew, which justifies the trip he made to Santiago de Compostela to consult a Jewish translator and cabalist. You know that, at that time, in France, the Inquisition had chased the Jews beyond Les Gaulles.

Fulcanelli dwelt at length on this pilgrimage. He speculated that Flamel's initiatory journey was allegorical. Without contesting the possible metaphorical or allegorical interpretation of the great master, I remain convinced that Nicolas Flamel indeed undertook the pilgrimage to Compostela in order to elucidate the enigmatic inscriptions of the marvellous grimoire, as he could not count on any help in France.

There is a strange similarity between the discovery of this manuscript by Flamel and that of the same masterpiece by Isaac, six centuries later. Both acquired it for a pittance.

Failing to show you the original this evening, Isaac will present you with some very fine colour reproductions, taken by a professional photographer. I recommend that you take great care of them and return them to their owner at the end of the session.

He added, not without irony:

– They certainly cost more than the original, my friends! Know that we will not fail to return to this same place to present our discoveries to you, as soon as we have deciphered the old grimoire, of course.

He paused for a long time, allowing the photographic prints to circulate from hand to hand, then announced in a monotone voice reflecting great sadness:

– Now, dear brothers, know that I am about to leave the country to undertake a long pilgrimage. I would like my position as a permanent member to be left vacant until my return.

Voices rose in the room. The Targui waved his hand, as if to preempt certain questions he did not wish to address.

– Please, my friends, please, he begged, do not ask me anything more. My decision is irrevocable. I will return as soon as possible. If you don't mind, we will now move on to various questions and set the next agenda before electing the future president.

There are two candidates for the presidency of our noble assembly. You have the choice between the honourable Dr Kaleb Boutelja and our esteemed brother Isaac Yakobi.

The various questions being debated and the agenda for the future session fixed, the members of the Grand Council proceeded to vote in a serene atmosphere, contrasting with the usual joy, undoubtedly because of the announcement of the forthcoming departure of the Targui.

Isaac Yakobi was elected unanimously, minus one vote.

After the usual congratulations, the new president declared the meeting adjourned.

The room quickly emptied.

It was almost midnight when Isaac and the Targui found themselves in the great Government Square, sad and deserted at night, in the damp coolness of the sea breeze.

They approached the heavy and unsightly cast iron railing of the waterfront rather briskly, when Isaac, visibly embarrassed, slowed down and then suddenly stopped.

– You're still determined to go into exile, you won't change your mind, will you, Ranzi? When will you return to the country? he finally asked, with an emotion he couldn't hide.

"As soon as my wounds heal, Yssic. I miss her terribly, my brother," confided the Targui, very affected by the disappearance of his wife.

Isaac replied with a mock-irritated look. How many times had he asked him, but in vain, not to use this nickname his father had given him when he was a child.

– Stop calling me Yssic, will you? Then, changing his tone, you should pull yourself together, he said. The Eternal called her back to Him. His ways are impenetrable.

And take good care of yourself, Prince of the Dunes, recommended Isaac, a tremolo in his voice.

The Targui put his hands on Isaac's shoulders, looking him straight in the eyes.

– Watch over your family, little brother, and may the Lord protect you all. Kiss Rachel and Sarah for me, will you? I will certainly not have the opportunity to greet them before I leave.

Ranzi hesitated for a few seconds, then continued in a slightly muffled voice:

– I will send you regular updates from Yssic, by any means at my disposal, I promise.

After a long silence, they gave each other a long and fraternal hug before parting.

CHAPTER 2
Khenchela, April 1954

Perched on one of the largest plateaus of the Aurès mountain range, Khenchela is unlike any other village in Algeria. It is certainly distinguished by its atypical houses, constructed in traditional masonry, with cracked walls that are sometimes whitewashed. The tiled roofs, nearly all crowned with chimneys, often emit smoke every winter—when they are not obstructed by storks' nests.

Khenchela! What a peculiar name for a village. It is a name difficult to pronounce for those unfamiliar with the chouïa (Berber dialect), though certainly easier to bear than its Roman name, Mascula, given when the first stone was laid over two thousand years ago.

Located in the southeast of Algeria, Khenchela sits 48 km southwest of Aïn-Beïda. The city lies at the foot of the Aures massif and is dominated to the west by Mont Ras Sardhoun, which stands at 1,263 metres. To the east, it is bordered by the Baghai wadi. Khenchela is said to be named after the daughter of Queen Dihya (Kahena). It is also referred to as Khenshala or Hansala in various documents. "Khen" or "Hen" means dove, bird, or hen, while "chela", "shala", or "sala" means peace. Hence, Khenchela translates to the "announcer of peace".

This small, isolated village is nestled in the heart of an arid, mountainous desert, covered with pebbles. Yet, scattered in places, are frail shrubs whose roots reach deep into the earth in search of the moisture necessary for survival.

Khenchela is difficult to access, with only old buildings, one or two storeys high, separated by narrow, straight streets, often of beaten earth. These streets are occasionally traversed by mule-drawn carts and riders whose irregular gaits raise thick clouds of dust in summer or leave deep tracks in the mud on rainy or snowy winter days.

To the west, Mount Chabor rises above the village. This rocky peak towers over the plateau, just a few hundred metres from the village's edge. At its summit sits a curious little cubic building, devoid of a roof, with walls pierced by multiple loopholes. No one seems to recall who built it or against which invaders it might have been used.

The great mountain range of the Aurès extends approximately 250 kilometres wide and about 100 kilometres deep. In its centre lies the Némemchas, an ancient volcanic region of which Khenchela has long been the capital. When approaching the village via the national road, it is wise to avoid the rocky path that climbs up on the right, as it leads directly to the city of the troglodytes, dug into the hillside and still inhabited by a tribe of Chaouias, an authentic Berber people of the Aurès.

Khenchela is not a gourbi! The paved road branching left should be followed to reach the heart of the village. This road leads to a narrow avenue, shaded and lined with magnificent leafy trees that provide much-needed shelter on summer days, when the blazing sun scorches the maquis at midday or during the frequent violent hailstorms.

A few kilometres to the west, on the road to Timgad, another legendary Roman city, lies a large spa complex at the top of a hill. These ancient facilities harness hot waters flowing through an extinct volcano in the eroded massif; these are the thermal baths of Fontaine Chaude, or Hamam Elsalhin. An ingenious hot water network supplies two large outdoor swimming pools—one circular, the other rectangular. Almost boiling water springs miraculously from the basalt rock, where it is collected by aqueducts and skilfully distributed throughout the complex.

Surrounding the swimming pools, the Romans constructed a dozen stone bathtubs, now housed in rustic millstone buildings and used as bathrooms. The village teenagers frequented this magical place, often walking there through the Habor or cycling along a chaotic track. Once near the complex, they would undress in unison, running and shouting, racing to dive into the large rectangular pool or, a little further, the smaller, but far more entertaining, circular pool.

Even in the middle of winter, the children bathed in the surreal warmth of this place, where warm mists rose from the water's surface. The few remaining centimetres of snow surrounding the pools could not deter them.

The souk, Thursday, April 1, 1954

Every first Thursday of the month was market day in Khenchela. Early in the morning, as if by magic, entire caravans of camels, carts drawn by weary mules or rustic draft horses, and old trucks in various states of disrepair, would emerge from the dusty void. Mechanised vehicles, mostly rusty and without number plates, were a common sight, as the laws of the metropolis had no bearing here. Despite their dilapidated appearance, these vehicles somehow continued to function.

Caravaneers arrived from all corners of North Africa—Tunisian borders to the east, Biskra, the southern Sahara, and the west. They would gather the day before on a plateau below the village, pitching their tents to shelter families and servants. The vacant lot next to their camp would house cattle that could not enter the town.

The Grand Place, dominated by the town hall, barely accommodated the fairgrounds. Camels and draft horses were parked alongside motorised vehicles, further down in open ground beside the church.

An incredible and free spectacle unfolded before the eyes of onlookers, as the travellers unpacked their bundles in chaotic, yet strangely disciplined, fashion. Onlookers could sense a deep serenity emanating from these weathered faces, their skin tanned by the scorching sun and deepened by sandstorms and long treks to the borders of the Sahara. The showmen, clad in thick, enveloping woollen burnous, remained unfazed by the elements. Merchants, sporting traditional turbans or red chechia, displayed a myriad of products on their stalls—everything from old recycled electrical equipment and wool skeins, to leather saddles, jugs, truck rims, and sand roses, prized by the few tourists. The display was a chaotic mix of vegetables, citrus fruits, dried fruits, prickly pears, and bags of colourful spices, their aromas permeating the air.

On market days, you could admire the large, colourful tents, impeccably aligned in front of the town hall. They housed the counters of important traders and wholesalers of all kinds, whose transactions involved goods from all over the world.

This great souk was also the hub of the animal trade, which had developed over an immense territory extending beyond the great massif, encompassing more than half a dozen countries. Transactions had been carried out calmly for two millennia, far from hazardous speculation and excessive inflation.

The participants in this great fair were unlikely to feel out of place. Real mobile kitchens, mounted on tricycles or pulled by hand, served grilled meats cooked over a wood fire, merguez sausages and mechouis, or dishes with very spicy sauces made from chickpeas, broad beans, or beans – the authentic local loubia. The natives also appreciated the tender and hot pancakes cooked over a charcoal fire in a *canoun*, a small brazier made of terracotta that was light, practical, and easily transportable.

At noon, during mealtime, perfumes that were inconceivable elsewhere but customary here mingled with the scents abundantly distilling from domestic animals.

What an exotic shambles!

Wandering through the stalls, you risked encountering the tooth-puller, hard at work in his open-air office. Nearby, the apothecary shaman offered remedies in the form of powders or granules with disturbing colourings, along with dried plants, henna, sticks of wood licorice, and good old chewing glue – probably the ancestor of chewing gum.

A little further on, seated on the ground, the copper-faced and fully tattooed fortune teller, an old *guezana* (fortune teller), was doing her best to draw cabalistic signs on the sand just to impress curious passers-by. She claimed to be able to read the future, whether on molten lead, in tea or coffee grounds, or on the lines of the hand...

Thursday was also a day off from school.

It was almost eleven o'clock already. The sun was gently starting to warm up beneath a beautiful, spotless blue sky. Fortunately, the hailstorm season had not yet started.

Dror was returning from Fontaine Chaude, where he had spent part of the morning with his classmates. They had gone there together on foot just after sunrise to avoid the hot weather. A short hour of swimming, alternating with dives in the large swimming pool, was more than enough for them to perk up and bicker. What could be more normal for these energetic young people!

That day, the group, consisting of a dozen teenagers, returned to the village around nine o'clock. It broke apart as soon as it reached the marketplace, about an hour and a half later.

Dror waved to his friends, then called out to his friend Millot, who seemed undecided.

"Accompany me to the souk, Michel," he said insistently. "I'd like you to help me choose stones to complete my collection. Be nice, please."

"Impossible, Dror. I'm late. I have to take care of my little sister, Lydie; I'm babysitting today. I'm sorry, but maybe that's for another time. I hope you don't mind," the teenager said simply, holding out his right hand reluctantly.

"Ciào!" he added, walking off.

Dror, disappointed, shook his friend's hand and watched him walk away in silence. He resigned himself to starting his rounds on his own in the big market. The boy, passionate about mineralogy, spent his spare time looking for rare stones, which he had been collecting and conscientiously cataloguing for years in his room. The day before, his father Isaac, who was not unaware of his passion, had informed him of the arrival of particularly interesting minerals at the next souk. He had advised him not to miss such an opportunity at any price, slipping a small note discreetly into the pocket of Dror's grey apron.

The teenager was lively and smart, much more so than other kids his age. Dror was soon to celebrate his thirteenth birthday. He had the privilege of being the youngest of three children, which naturally made him the family's favourite. At school, he was top of his class in all subjects, and his friends were not jealous of him because there was an aura about him that everyone respected and admired.

Brown, wavy, and shiny hair and steel-grey eyes, Dror was dressed in a cotton shirt with black and white checks, a fashion imported from France, and khaki shorts. He proudly wore a bush hat that matched the shorts, and like a paratrooper commando, he sported genuine Pataugas.

Strolling at a leisurely pace through the stalls he knew so well, Dror passed a dealer in jugs and then a peddler selling roasted corn and peanuts. He was tempted for a moment by the enticing smell of grilled corn but changed his mind immediately when his gaze was caught by a pile of the most unusual objects. On the floor lay an incredible collection of spare parts—perhaps from a car graveyard or surplus from the last war. He studied the rusty, gutted old engines, connecting rods, a piston with its worn rings, an old crankshaft, a perforated radiator, and an intact Jeep windshield with its wipers. He wondered who could possibly be interested in these old cuckoo clocks.

Then he thought of the games he loved in magazine comics, one of his few distractions: "Find the odd one out," he thought aloud, almost laughing at the absurdity of it, admiring the brand-new windshield.

After passing the centre of the square, he paused for a moment and watched the snake charmer perform, contorting himself to the rhythm of his jouhak, a kind of flute with a flared end. The head of the royal naja swayed slowly from side to side, in perfect synchrony with the movement of the flautist, who the snake never seemed to take his eyes off. Dror knew that the snake – from which the venom had been extracted – was deaf and insensitive to the sound of the wind instrument. This scene no longer held any fascination for him.

He quickly lost interest in the spectacle, which he had certainly seen dozens of times, and ended up stopping in front of the large tent of a merchant who was offering superb gold jewellery, pearl necklaces, and curious minerals, all neatly arranged on the counter. This must be the new arrival announced by my father, thought the teenager.

Dressed in an ecru djellaba with midnight blue stripes and sporting a short, slightly graying but perfectly trimmed beard, the merchant, seen up close, did not look like a Chaouia at all – that is, the Berbers from the Aurès mountain range – not even a Mozabite, and certainly not an Arab. He was very tall, easily six feet, and had a Mauritanian appearance, though with much finer features.

He must be a Targui, thought Dror.

The merchant's face seemed familiar, but Dror could not place where he had seen him before, which intrigued him for a moment. Targuis were not so rare after all, the young man reasoned, and since Khenchela was at the crossroads of the main roads, it wasn't surprising. The teenager began mechanically to observe the individual, who was wearing a large turban of immaculate white. His djellaba likely concealed the traditional Tuareg saber, and an aura of authority emanated from the man, whose fixed and penetrating gaze never wavered.

Without realising it, Dror stared straight into the merchant's eyes—a mistake that should never be made when speaking to an adult in this country. Well-educated, the teenager quickly recovered, lowering his gaze as if to apologise. It was then that he noticed the huge gold signet ring on the merchant's left ring finger, topped with a bucranium that resembled a terrifying devil's head. Dror had never seen anything like it, and he moved closer to examine the mysterious object.

"This is a Baphomet," the merchant told him pleasantly, in impeccable French, without the slightest accent.

Surprised, Dror didn't know how to respond.

"A Ba-Baphomet?" he stammered, somewhat taken aback by the Targui's announcement.

Exactly, this represents a Baphomet, insisted the merchant. It was the emblem of the Templars. The pretext for which they were all arrested, tortured and then murdered in the Middle Ages in Europe, young man. The ring I wear on my left index finger comes from the commandery of Almagro in Spain. It comes to me directly from the great master of Calatrava, who lived until 1421 in the medieval city of Almagro, the capital of La Mancha and the land of Don Quixote, continued the merchant with a very falsely sententious air. He seemed to be having a great time intriguing the young man.

The Targui paused, looked to the right, then to the left, gave a knowing wink towards Dror, then continued his explanations, lowering his voice as if to confide an important secret to the young interlocutor.

– Do you know that, according to legend, twelve identical signet rings were cast with alchemical gold? Two of them were intended for the Spanish commanderies. The others were distributed among the commanderies of France, Malta and Jerusalem. During the Inquisition, only the members of the Order of Calatrava were spared. The Spanish royalty protected them out of duty or interest; who knows?

– So it's a pagan emblem; it looks like a devil's head, the kid replied brazenly, and I, who believed Muslims were monotheists...

– How dare you call me a pagan, you presumptuous young man. You deserve a good blow from the felaka (braided ox sinew, used as a whip by the masters of Koranic schools to call unruly students to order). This emblem is a symbol that perhaps conceals the greatest secret of all time. It is not the head of Satan or Beelzebub to whom all the Templars would have sworn allegiance as the Christian priests decried to find a good reason to burn or massacre the dignitaries of the Temple in France and Italy. This was the only and true pretext to eliminate them in order to seize all the fortune of the Temple at a good price.

I really like this kid, the merchant finally admitted to himself, pretending to get carried away, just enough to test his reaction. He then raised his voice, taking on a threatening air.

– Baphomet, according to a great metropolitan philosopher of the beginning of the century known under the pseudonym of Fulcanelli, symbolizes in Alchemy the baptism of Meteus or Metis, which is the conventional representation of the Moon of the philosophers. It also reveals the most mysterious operation of Hermetic Philosophy, which concerns the capture of the Universal Spirit and the condensation of the Secret Fire. It is, in a word, the Secret of Secrets.

Continuing to watch the reactions of the adolescent, he continued calmly, in a much friendlier tone this time, even more amused.

– The Templars were great men and not bloodthirsty warriors. They created true Freemasonry, this army of frimasons who built all the Gothic cathedrals. The Templars were humble knights who had taken a vow of poverty. Eager for knowledge, they did not hesitate to learn Arabic and Hebrew as well as Latin or Greek in order to acquire a thousand-year-old and hidden know-how, that which was possessed by the great learned alchemists of Alexandria at the beginning of our era or the Byzantines in the 10th or 11th century.

Dror couldn't believe his ears. How could a simple merchant, a Bedouin to boot, have such erudition? It still seemed strange to him that a Muslim could praise those who were accomplices of the Crusaders and who perpetrated horrible ethnic massacres during the eleventh and twelfth centuries in the name of their holy faith.

The teenager dared to make a remark. Dror remembered a recent history lesson on the Crusades; he wouldn't be short of arguments this time.

"Noble Targui, praising the Templars seems rather out of place to me. Have you forgotten that the Crusaders massacred tens of thousands of Jews and Muslims in the name of the Holy Cross, with the exception of those, a few, who agreed to convert to Christianity?" – The Crusaders were murderers, barbarians of the worst kind, I grant you that, but not the Templars. The latter had carefully kept themselves away from the war. I can assure you of this thanks to archives in my possession that leave no doubt on the subject. They were invested in a secret mission that they hid even under torture before the Inquisition decimated them.

In his heart of hearts, the Targui was pleased with the liveliness of his young interlocutor, noticing this spark in the steel blue gaze of the adolescent, a gleam that seemed very familiar to him.

The sheik slowly raised his left hand so that the boy could better examine the large gold signet ring.

– Look closely at my ring, young, impetuous one; what does this face shape remind you of?

Dror widened his eyes to better see the hand that the merchant was holding out to him. The horribly misshapen head resembled that of a devil with its jaws wide open.

– Um… it vaguely resembles a triangle with a big deformed mouth? He said, just in case.

"Excellent!" replied the merchant, laughing under his breath. This noble triangular face is a clue that the wise have kindly left to their disciples. It is the symbol of Water, the Water of the Philosophers, the Mercury of the Sages, and not the vulgar flowing mercury, as some fools who are more greedy for wealth than for wisdom think. It is the dry Water that does not wet the hands. Inverted, the triangle becomes the symbol of the secret fire.

Dror was increasingly perplexed. It seemed to him that the Targui had just crossed the line with all this incoherent gibberish. Was his interlocutor making fun of him by any chance?

"I've never heard anything more absurd, Targui! Water that doesn't wet your hands, what is that? Ice?"

"Enough joking around, will you!" the merchant replied dryly, pretending to be offended.

The Targui realized that he was going a bit too far and that his young and lively interlocutor would eventually lose patience. He decided to change the subject.

"Now," he said, pretending to be irritated, "are you going to tell me what your name is, you cheeky young fellow?"

"Dror, Dror Yakobi," the teenager replied without flinching, intrigued but not in the least disconcerted.

"By Allah!" exclaimed the merchant, laughing heartily. "So, you're from the tribe of the venerable Kahéna—the great lineage of Cohanim and Yakobi. I knew your grandfather well when I was your age. He once taught me Kabbalah."

"How could my grandfather have taught Kabbalah to a Muslim? I don't believe a word of it!" Dror replied cheekily.

"By the Grand Architect of the Universe, I feel that I will truly regret not having felaka with me, young presumptuous one. In return, I taught Arabic and the Qur'an to your father, Isaac. Your family still lives on rue de Paris, on the first floor, just above the Bazar des Aures, right?"

The boy realised that he had just overstepped the boundaries that governed relations between adults and adolescents in this country. Clearly, his interlocutor knew his parents very well. Dror suddenly recalled who this mysterious Targui was—he had seen him many times with his father, both at home and in the company of his father, a long time ago...

He then decided to adopt a more respectful tone.

"Yes, yes, hami (my uncle)," Dror replied, lowering his head in an apologetic gesture.

But the merchant did not give him time to explain or apologise.

"Then inform your honourable father that Si Ahmed Ranzi el Sahraoui, his foster brother, has returned and wishes to visit him later today."

Dror could hardly contain his surprise. His father and this Targui were indeed foster brothers—his memories were now rushing back.

"Foster brother!" he repeated aloud. "It will be done according to your wishes, hami."

Dror, feeling embarrassed, suddenly felt an overwhelming urge to slip away. He had just realised that his father had sent him to the Targui for a specific purpose, but what could it be?

The merchant appeared to be greatly enjoying himself. It was clear this young boy amused him more and more.

He chose an almost black stone with metallic reflections streaked with white and yellow markings.

"Wait a bit before running off!" called out the Targui, still smiling.

Dror retraced his steps and gave the merchant a look of surprise.

"What do you want from me, Uncle Ranzi?" he finally asked.

"How old are you, Dror?"

"Nearly thirteen, uncle."

Si Ahmed Ranzi, all smiles, handed him the black stone, punctuated with white and yellow spots.

"Here, accept this modest gift, for your collection, if you will."

"Galena?" Dror asked, recognising the stone's composition. He then shook his head, adding, "I can't accept."

"Know that it is indeed a sulphide, a secret mineral. In our sacred language, this mineral is called *El kohl*, and some attribute magical properties to it. In the Middle Ages, European scholars gave it all sorts of names, but 'Alcohol' suits it better. Take it, I tell you—you can't refuse. One day, you will certainly learn to recognise all its properties."

"You can go now," the Targui concluded, waving his right hand as if to say goodbye, without appeal.

Sitting curled up on the ground behind a nearby tent, a native dressed as a beggar had observed the entire scene without being noticed. After young Dror passed just a few steps away from him, the beggar closed his eyes, pretending to fall asleep.

CHAPTER 3

Thursday, April 1, 1954, around noon

The whole Yakobi family was gathered around the table, enjoying a succulent mahjouba. This specialty, passed down through generations, was one of Rachel's—Dror's mother—own recipes. It consisted of a thin pancake, fried in olive oil, and had a melt-in-your-mouth texture. It was generously stuffed with a rich onion coulis and strips of beef, slow-cooked to perfection. Delicate herbs from the maquis added the finishing touch. A true masterpiece of local cuisine.

Dror, eager for dessert, waited patiently. His mother often made him a delicious ginger or melon jam pie. After wolfing down his portion of dessert at breakneck speed, under the watchful eye of Sarah—his older sister, who seemed to scrutinise every move—he asked, "Dad, Sir Ahmed Ranzi el Sahraoui will come and meet us tonight at home."

Rachel knocked over her glass in surprise, while Sarah and Nathan seemed almost giddy with excitement.

"My old friend Ranzi the Saharan is back," Isaac replied with a smile. "What great news. But how do you know?"

Dror, fully aware that his father had planned the whole thing, responded ironically, "I think you expected me to meet him, Dad. I took your advice and went through the market this morning on my way back from Fontaine Chaude, looking for a stone for my collection. Remember, you said there'd be a new shipment of rare stones? Well, I stopped in front of a display with magnificent objects—gold and silver jewels, as well as superb precious stones."

Sarah, suddenly interested, interrupted, "So what?"

"That's when I found myself face to face with the Targui, Si Ahmed Ranzi," Dror continued, his tone unchanged. "He wore a very strange ring on his index finger. He explained the origin of his signet ring, then asked my name. He immediately deduced who I was and claimed to know all my family, including grandfather. He also gave me a kohl stone. I wanted to refuse it, but he insisted so much that I was afraid to offend him. Look!" Dror said, showing off the black ore.

"Ha ha! Our youngest is shopping like an adult now, though he hasn't done his Bar Mitzvah yet!" Nathan teased, enjoying the moment as much as he liked playing the protective older brother.

"And thus, one squanders the family funds by buying trinkets at the souk," Sarah added. "It deserves a good spanking... unless you're planning to offer jewellery to your big sister? How nice that would be!"

"Dad, can you tell me who Sir Ahmed Ranzi is?" Dror asked, ignoring his brother's remark and his sister's teasing.

Isaac paused for a moment before answering. "His Serene Highness Sheikh Ahmed Ranzi el Sahraoui is a prince—the last Grand Sheik of the Blue Men tribe of Touat, a region of the Sahara from which we also hail. He is also my foster brother. We were raised by the same nanny, and the ties between us are as strong as family bonds."

Isaac's voice became more animated as he continued. "Ranzi wrote to me recently to inform me of his return after a very long absence. That's why I sent you to meet him. I knew you'd find him. You may not remember him because you were little when he decided to travel the world."

Isaac leaned back, clearly enjoying the tale. "Your ancestors, the Yakobi, rubbed shoulders with the Blue Men for centuries. They bivouacked, hunted, and fought together against their common enemies. They traded goods all across North Africa and the Middle East for over a millennium. The Yakobi transported all sorts of goods on camels across the

Sahara, journeying to Baghdad and Constantinople, and returning to Ouargla, Touggourt, or Biskra, where they sold their goods to the Targui tribes. The Saharawis then marketed them across the western Sahara, Mauritania, and Morocco."

He paused, giving his children a chance to absorb the information. "The Yakobi also planted date palms in Biskra—those that produce the famous deglat nour (dates of light)—importing them from Iraq. They also introduced the first lemon trees. They're also the ones who brought dromedaries from Arabia—these mounts essential for crossing the Sahara."

"Our people survived in Algeria thanks to the privileged relationships they maintained with men of goodwill, like Sheik Ranzi and his tribe. Your grandfather and Ranzi's father, may they rest in peace, were inseparable—like brothers. They worked together on many ventures and spread good in the world. Much of their earnings went to help needy families, especially during the last two wars. As notables, they also had the heavy responsibility of administering justice, settling disputes, and handling political conflicts—and they did so admirably. Today, with the French in control, the institutions function almost normally."

"The Targuis have always regarded Jews as allies, even friends. In living memory, there has never been a conflict between our two peoples," Isaac continued. "As for Ranzi, he is a brilliant engineer. He studied at the School of Chemistry and Metallurgy in Algiers. He's also a true Targui—formidable in combat, skilled in martial arts. During the last war, he fought alongside the Americans against the Nazis and was decorated for his acts of bravery."

The story seemed to captivate the entire family, each member listening in silence. Dror, though engrossed in the tale, interrupted suddenly, "And who was the Kahena?"

"The Berbers called her Kahéna or Kahina, but her real name was Cohen," Isaac replied. "She was the queen of a Jewish tribe from the Aurès. Kahéna is the Arabic-Berber transcription of Cohen. Her husband was named Yakov, and all his descendants were called Yakobi—'the sons of Jacob'—to avoid attracting attention from the Islamist hordes. In truth, we are Cohens, and you are indeed a descendant of Kahéna, named Dihya, daughter of Tabet, queen of the Aurès."

Isaac's eyes shone with pride as he continued, "Kahéna led a motley army of Jews and Berbers—Christian and pagan—to fight the Arabs during the great invasion of North Africa. She had the courage to do what many men would not: resist the invader. She held off the opposing army, led by Hassan Ibn Nohman, driving them out of the Aurès all the way to Tunisia. She defeated them in Libya but, out of nobility, refused to wipe them out completely. That decision would ultimately cost her. The invaders regrouped and returned with force, around the year 700 or 701. They attacked the villagers who had laid down their weapons, thinking the war was over. The new conquerors were ruthless, massacring many of your ancestors for refusing to convert to Islam. They assassinated Kahéna in 703."

Isaac paused before adding, "Some dubious historians claim that she and her children converted to Islam to avoid death, but in truth, she was beheaded by the invaders. Her children survived and escaped. And the best proof of this, Dror, is us. We are her direct descendants."

"Now, be nice and say your thanks, so your mother and sister can clear the table."

As was customary on Thursdays and Sundays, Dror took a short nap in the afternoon. That day, however, he had trouble falling asleep, so excited was he by the adventure. What would have seemed mundane for any other child, took on great significance in this mountain town where little ever happened. He had met a real Muslim prince—his father's foster brother. That alone was remarkable. But there was more: Ranzi was not only a scholar, but also a brilliant engineer.

Dror had a sense that Ranzi held many secrets, heavy and possibly dangerous ones. He knew that if his friends learned of this, it would be the talk of the town. But no, Dror was reserved. He wouldn't say anything, of course. If his uncle had secrets, they would stay hidden, as the family code demanded.

Night fell abruptly, as usual for that latitude. The moon, low on the horizon, appeared enormous and glowed a rich red against a clear sky. It was likely caused by a temperature inversion above the mountain range. For a time after sunset, the stars were obscured. But, in an hour or two, the air would cool, and the constellations would be visible again, in a pure and serene sky. From the heights, the Habor would have made an ideal location for an astronomical observatory.

In the early evening, Rachel asked Sarah to set the table and add a place setting for the prince. Without being asked twice, Sarah quickly complied, with Dror's help. The young girl arranged the cutlery tastefully, decorating each plate with daffodils she had picked that afternoon from the banks of the El Arab wadi below. Dror was in charge of preparing cold drinks—lemonade made from lemon juice and grapefruit juice.

The smell of barbouche—a typical Algiers specialty, a spicy couscous—wafted through the air. Rachel had been simmering loubia, a dish similar to chili con carne, with a good piece of beef in the finest spices, while the couscous, sprinkled with cumin and finely chopped mint, was steaming in the traditional way from an earthenware pot filled with a rich vegetable broth.

Isaac owned a busy department store, the Bazar des Aurès, located on the first floor of their house. It attracted customers from across the Sahara, eager to stock up on goods.

Nathan, her eldest son, had recently been assisting her. It was he who would later take over the management of the store. He had an innate sense of commerce and a sharp eye for layout. Thanks to him, Isaac had more time to manage the accounts.

Nathan hadn't yet turned twenty. He was a tall, athletic young man, standing well over six feet, with the build of a rugby player. His brown eyes and wavy brown hair made him the favourite target of the young girls in the village. Always meticulous, he was dressed to the nines under the blue blouse he wore for work, which he took very seriously.

When Nathan walked through the door of the shop at precisely six o'clock, he greeted Ranzi warmly.

"Uncle Ranzi, I couldn't believe my ears when Dror, my brainless younger brother, told us you were in Khenchela this afternoon. Welcome to the Yakobi house."

"Thank you, Nathan. You've grown into a handsome man. By Allah, when was the last time we saw each other?"

"Exactly five years," Isaac replied, moving forward with arms outstretched for his old friend to kiss. "And just four years after the end of the war, when your father and mine—rest their souls—put an end to the quarrels of the parishes, which threatened not only the village but all the Némemchas."

Isaac added, "In my arms, Prince of the Dunes."

The two men congratulated each other at length, as if to erase the separation of years.

"We've all been waiting for you for ages, Ranzi. Where have you been, and what are your new occupations?" Isaac continued.

Ranzi was elegant and striking. No one could have guessed his age—forty, perhaps forty-five. This evening, he wore a large turquoise satin turban, fastened with a gold buckle set with emeralds and rubies, the traditional Southern Cross. Under his white silk djellaba, he wore black satin saroual and a white shirt. A curved-bladed dagger, in its leather sheath, was slung at an angle beneath a wide scarlet sash that tied around his waist, as though to remind everyone that its possessor belonged to a race of warriors.

The only odd detail was that the Targui wore soft, cream-coloured moccasins, not his usual slippers. This need for comfort seemed paradoxical for someone born in the heart of the Sahara, used to walking barefoot on the burning desert sands. His appearance contrasted with that of his friend—slightly shorter, with redder hair and a more stocky build.

Isaac, on the other hand, was dressed in a light grey flannel three-piece suit, a white shirt, and a scarlet silk bow tie.

"I've been around the world, Yssic!" exclaimed Ranzi, unable to conceal his joy at being back. "I had a mad desire to see as many countries and people of diverse cultures as possible before leaving this poor land. I've learned enough now, so I'm quietly returning home to rest."

Ranzi paused. His expression grew more serious, and he leaned closer to Isaac, whispering in his ear.

"We must speak privately later. I have serious things to confide in you."

He then resumed his usual tone.

"I understand that you received my letter, and that's why you sent Dror to me this morning, isn't it?"

Isaac, still reeling from his emotions, waited several seconds before answering.

"You're right. Dror was only eight years old when you went into exile; he might not even remember you. I was curious to see if, in His infinite wisdom, the Almighty Lord would bring you and Dror together. It's extraordinary—it worked, although it did need a little help," he admitted at last.

"Do you want to take a bath to relax after this long day?" Isaac then offered, inviting his old friend out the back door. "Then we can talk over a good cup of mint tea, like in the good old days."

"There's no need for a bath, thank you," Ranzi replied. "I just left the hammam at the corner of Rue de Constantine and even had an excellent massage to loosen up my joints."

"I hope the masseur rubbed your skin vigorously with one of those rough horsehair gloves," Isaac replied, recalling his own experiences with Berber massage.

"I almost forgot," Isaac added. "Are you planning to live in your villa again, Rue Gérôme-Bertania? Fatma has been in charge of its upkeep once a week since you left. I asked her to prepare everything for your arrival."

"Everything was perfect, as usual, Isaac. Ali, my chaouch (valet), took care of it. Please thank Fatma for me."

Leaving Nathan to handle the closing of the shop, Isaac led his foster brother upstairs to the apartment on the first floor.

Sarah, who had heard footsteps on the stairs, hurried to the door to open it, just as the two friends arrived.

"You remember Sarah, don't you?" Isaac exclaimed.

"My little princess of the Arabian Nights, how many times have I rocked you in my arms?"

The young girl, visibly moved, grabbed hold of the prince's hands.

"Uncle Ranzi, you haven't changed! It feels like the last time I saw you was just yesterday. You're still so elegant, I see. You won't go away again, will you? Promise us you'll stay and tell us about all your adventures."

"Come on, come on, Sarah. Stop pestering Uncle Ranzi," Isaac replied with a smirk. "Be nice and serve us some cold mint tea or lemonade instead; you can see the prince is thirsty."

"Let's not exaggerate, Isaac," Ranzi said, settling onto the large couch.

"Aren't you engaged yet, little princess?" the Targui asked. "Haven't you found the chosen one of your heart?"

"Uncle Ranzi, thank God, I have no reason to imitate the young girls of the Sahara who marry at thirteen. I have plenty of time to think about marriage. I'm not even fifteen yet, you know, and I intend to continue my medical studies as soon as my father agrees to sign the necessary formalities," Sarah replied, without blushing.

Sarah was a beautiful young girl, tall and slender, with long, slightly wavy jet-black hair. She resembled her mother, having inherited her grace and appearance, with the same large steel-grey eyes that lit up her brother Dror's face. She had always harboured a passion for medicine. Brilliant, she had finished her last year in the complementary course in Khenchela. But to continue her studies, first for the baccalaureate and then for a doctorate in medicine, she would need to go to Algiers with her parents' indispensable blessing.

"Princess, I brought you a modest souvenir from my recent travels in the Far East," Ranzi said, smiling broadly.

He took a small plum-coloured box from his pocket and offered it to the young girl.

Sarah vividly remembered the time when Ranzi and her father had been inseparable, before the Targui's exile. He had always called her "princess". He spoiled her like his own daughter and never missed an opportunity to give her a gift. She eagerly reached out for the precious box, then rushed over to kiss him tenderly on the cheek.

She lifted the lid and gasped in delight, letting her joy burst forth when she saw two earrings, each adorned with a magnificent bluish pearl. The two beautiful pearls appeared almost identical.

"I caught them myself in Surabaya Bay," he said proudly, "in Indonesia, in a cove where I almost ended up in the belly of one of those huge, hungry great white sharks. I also cast the ring and fashioned the clasp with my own hands. It's not much, I assure you."

"Uncle Ranzi, would you have preferred that they cost you your life?" Nathan quipped, entering the room.

"Who speaks of such serious matters with such levity?" Rachel protested, as she burst into the living room. She was holding a carved copper tray laden with cups and a teapot. "My handsome Prince of the Dunes," she said, "what a pleasure to see you again in the Yakobi house after such a long absence. We're going to share bread and salt, just like the good old days, right?"

Rachel kissed the Targui, then asked him point-blank:

"Ranzi, I heard you had a stall at the market this Thursday. Have you resumed your trading activities in oriental jewellery and rare stones?"

"Not quite, Rachel. Today was my first and my last day. I've decided to give up retail altogether. I've just made agreements with a well-established distributor throughout the northern sector of Algeria, and he will handle the entire distribution of my products. From now on, I'll no longer need to browse the markets."

"It's wonderful," Nathan said ironically. "You're modernising yourself by applying new marketing techniques..."

"Sufficient, Nathan!" Rachel ordered. "Leave our guest in peace for a moment; he's starving, can't you see? Come on, let's get to the table. But where's Dror? Dror, where are you?"

"Here I am, Ma, I hadn't finished my evening prayer," Dror replied, running towards the dining room.

Reunions between old friends always stir intense emotions. Confused sensations at times, but always shared by those who appreciate each other and who have managed to form indestructible bonds, as strong as true fraternal ties. This was certainly the case for these two great families of North Africa, the Yakobi and the Saharawi. Their friendship had endured for at least a millennium, and there was no reason to believe it would ever end.

Rachel had outdone herself once again. She would certainly have earned all the stars from the best gastronomic guides in Algeria had she run a restaurant. The evening meal was enjoyed in silence by the guests, who all honoured the mistress of the house and their guest.

Once the table was cleared, Rachel prepared a very hot tea with strong mint, slightly sweetened. She had made sure to add a handful of pine nuts that Ranzi particularly enjoyed. She was especially eager to ask about Rachida, Ranzi's sister, a few years her junior. Before Prince Targui's temporary exile, Rachida and Rachel had been inseparable. Every Friday morning, they met in the women's hammam to chat and gossip about the latest village news. They also met in their respective homes on other days to have tea or coffee, sometimes at one, sometimes at the other.

Rachida had married a few months before her brother's departure and had moved to El Goléa, where she lived with her husband within the great Sahrawi tribe. The two friends had only maintained an irregular correspondence since then.

When the Targui set down his cup, Rachel finally had the chance to ask about her sister.

"Do you realise, Ranzi, I haven't seen Rachida since she left. How is she? Has she written to you lately?"

"I found some letters from her today, while sorting through the mail that's been piling up in my villa for years. She has two beautiful children, a boy and a girl, by the grace of God. Our tribe is still camped in El Goléa, and I can't wait to join them," the sheikh replied in a deep voice, his emotion evident.

But the Targui seemed very concerned. He was making a considerable effort to hide an obvious anxiety. Rachel had noticed it several times—something indefinable in his voice and attitude betrayed a level of distress quite unusual for Ranzi. Rachel understood that the prince was eager to speak to Isaac privately. He must have something important to confide in him. She could sense these things, her instincts rarely failed her, so she decided it was best to leave the two men alone. She immediately decided to send her children to bed.

"Nathan, Sarah, and Dror, salute his serene highness before heading off to bed; a long day awaits us all tomorrow. I'll do the same, Ranzi, if you don't mind. We'll meet tomorrow at noon for lunch, yes?"

Sarah bowed gracefully before placing a kiss on Ranzi's cheek and slipped away, followed promptly by her two brothers.

Finally alone, the two friends seized the opportunity for a few moments of silence to gather their thoughts.

Noticing his foster brother's prolonged silence, Isaac finally spoke.

"We're alone now, Ranzi. I suppose you have a lot to reveal to me."

With a furrowed brow and a sad look, the Targui finally confessed in a serious tone.

"Yssic, criminals are preparing a dark future for us. People, greedy for power and ambition, without faith or law, who claim to be lovers of justice, or who, under the pretext of seeking the independence of this country, are willing to commit the irreparable."

"You mean that a revolutionary movement is about to take up arms, attempting a coup or insurrection like the one in Indochina?"

"Yes, I found out about it by chance during my last pilgrimage to Mecca. I had the opportunity to meet a high-ranking Algerian dignitary, whose name I promised not to reveal. He even offered me a place in the revolutionary leadership of a movement in formation. There would be several emerging groups, if I believe the rumours. The activists are being supported and funded by the USSR and Egypt. Weapons are piling up on the Tunisian border, and according to the rare confidences my contact was kind enough to share, the training has been ongoing for years, in Tunisia, Libya, and Egypt, in particular."

"This is extremely serious. It could become dangerous for you if you continue to refuse to join their ranks. They may accuse you of treason, and they might even try to eliminate you. Believe me, these people are fanatics."

"I know it," Ranzi replied. "I told my contact that the Sahrawis are a free, nomadic people with no borders. A people who belong to all of the Sahara, from the Atlantic to the Indian Ocean. If the Targuis were to claim land, they would have to fight against at least half a dozen countries. So, it's out of the question for my people to get involved in a revolution, no matter how just the cause may be. This dignitary knows very well that I have at least ten thousand men who would avenge me if something were to happen. Hopefully, that will make the activists hesitate."

"Do you know the date of the outbreak of this insurrection?" Isaac asked.

Ranzi nodded.

"I've no idea, but it will always be too soon. You can imagine, the dignitary was testing the waters, so he couldn't tell me anything too compromising. Either way, I wasn't asking. However, I think it's imminent, and the outbreak of hostilities will probably take place before the end of this year."

Ranzi was visibly disturbed and resumed with a sigh of disgust.

"I can't even warn our college brothers."

The circle, which was largely inspired by the principles set by the Sufi philosophers in the Middle Ages, had twelve members from the three monotheistic faiths and had occult support throughout the country. But their capacity for action had limits, and in the conflict that was brewing, they would certainly declare themselves incompetent.

Isaac took a moment to reflect before formulating his thoughts.

"As you wish, big brother. I am, of course, on your side. We will find a way to warn our brothers at the College later if we have other more specific elements, of course. Knowing that we do not know the exact date of the insurrection, the identity of the other members of the plot, and the extent of the actions envisaged... What more can we do?" he added, a hint of bitterness in his voice.

"Apparently everything's happening overseas right now," Isaac continued. "An unfortunate leak could risk catastrophic proportions and result in repressive measures from the metropolis, from which no one would benefit. We also risk having riots on our hands that could end in a bloodbath. Remember Sétif and Guelma in 1945. And then, if the DST (French counterintelligence office) has no precise information on this matter, there is no need to worry about it for the moment."

However, Isaac continued very slowly, as if thinking aloud, "If I were you, I would immediately inform my people in order to take into account the majority viewpoint of the Targuis. Similarly, I would take advantage of high-level relations with the splinter faction to try to ensure that, if the insurgency were to break out, it could in no way target civilians. Innocent blood must not be shed—this would escalate hatred between communities. When you consider how long it took your father and mine to appease the deleterious climate that reigned in this region just a few decades ago..."

"By Allah, you have come to the same conclusions as me," noted the Targui.

There was another long silence, and the Targui seemed to be lost in thought. His mind was clearly elsewhere, and after a few moments, he shifted topics abruptly.

"I have another request for you, Yssic," he said solemnly. "The time has come to pass on the knowledge taught to us by the elders, and I need a disciple. Leave me Dror on Thursdays and Sundays. It will take me years to train him properly, and I want that done before things get too bad here."

"You also know that our ancestors swore to alternately initiate a child from each clan," the Targui continued. "I was trained by your father, may the great Surveyor have his soul with him. I owe you and your family a debt, and I want to pay it at all costs. Times are uncertain, Yssic, and nothing should happen to me before I have properly fulfilled all my duties."

Isaac seemed moved. His gaze clouded almost imperceptibly. Why these sudden fears? He knew too well the legendary courage of the Targui, who seemed upset tonight—it was not at all in his habits. The Targui, beneath his harsh exterior, was a great sentimentalist.

"Why so much haste?" Isaac suddenly questioned, his throat tight. "Dror is not ready yet; he lacks maturity. Moreover, he must complete his religious training for his Bar Mitzvah, which will take place at the start of the school year."

"Yssic, your argument does not hold water. First, consider the Bar Mitzvah. Your son certainly knows as much as the rabbi supposed to have trained him. He therefore no longer needs to attend Talmud lessons during school holidays.

"On the other hand, when it comes to his maturity, would you have me believe that an almost thirteen-year-old Yakobi is still a baby? Believe me, I saw the flame that shone in his eyes when I told him about Baphomet and the Commandery of Calatrava... Now, if it bothers you for personal reasons..."

Stung, Isaac, after a brief moment of reflection, finally gave in. Dror's learning seemed secondary to him, and he persisted in thinking that the Targui had other, much more serious concerns. Something indefinable betrayed his voice. They absolutely had to talk about it tonight.

"Ranzi, what bothers me, you see, is that you feel threatened. This, I cannot admit. I hope you're not hiding anything else from me. As for Dror's training, you won. We're not going to bicker over such trivial matters. Fix it all with my son, will you?"

"Perfect, you are becoming reasonable, little brother. Now, I am going to leave you. I plan to leave tomorrow morning for El Goléa. I will be back in a few days, by the grace of Allah. Let Rachel know I'm leaving; she'll probably have the opportunity to postpone her invitation. Kiss everyone for me, Isaac."

As they passed through the door, the Targui retraced his steps, looking far more seriously disturbed than before.

"I almost didn't tell you, Isaac, damn it! I think I was followed!"

"How then?" continued Isaac, disconcerted. "You could have said that earlier. I suspected for a long time that you were hiding something serious from me. So my fears were justified."

Isaac thought for a moment, then exclaimed,

"I have an idea! We will solve this problem in our own way by taking the initiative. You will leave here, as naturally as possible, to go to your villa on Rue Gérôme-Bertania. When you reach the end of the block, take the Rue de Constantine on the right. About ten metres from the corner, hide under the large porch of the wine merchant. Wait for your follower to reach your level, then intercept him. As for me, I will follow him like his shadow, and I'll be there to lend a hand if needed."

"It's very basic, but it suits me," said Ranzi, resigned.

The Targui descended the stairs and walked resolutely towards the door at the end of the long corridor. He left the house and quickly turned to the right, not looking back, continuing to look straight ahead. It was dark, with only a diffuse glow emanating from the few lampposts in the narrow street. After about thirty metres, without changing the sidewalk, he turned right, entered Rue de Constantine, and disappeared into the shadows under the first porch.

A man followed him about ten seconds later. He suspected nothing. Isaac followed him discreetly.

Ranzi held his breath. His pulse quickened the instant the man passed the porch. The Targui then suddenly threw himself on the follower, pinning him to the ground, his arm firmly folded around his neck, ready to strangle him at the slightest alarm.

"I see you haven't lost your touch," Isaac said, coming to the rescue with a flashlight in his hand. He directed the beam to illuminate the face of the intruder.

Ranzi released the pressure slightly and spun his opponent on the ground, immobilising his right arm and folding it behind the follower's back with a new hold. Under the beam of the torch, he stared at the individual, who began to grimace in pain. The man, dressed like a Mozabite, wore a long grey blouse over baggy trousers and a braided white skullcap, pulled low over his frizzy hair. His face reminded Ranzi of someone. He seemed to have met him before, but where?

"Who sent you to spy on me, bandit? It's not very polite to follow decent people at night."

The man remained as silent as a carp.

Ranzi and Isaac were under no illusions that the individual would speak easily. If he was a fanatical Berber, he would let himself be gutted rather than unclench his teeth.

"One minute," said Isaac. "I recognize this individual. He's the *chaouch* (valet) of the bachagha Abou Dahrem, a high dignitary. What could that mean?"

The *chaouch* of the bachagha often came to make purchases at the bazaar for his master. Isaac had seen him in the shop on several occasions. The bachagha was a notable, a powerful lord whom everyone feared or hated around here. He had even run for office in the last municipal elections but had been decisively defeated by his more modest, and above all, more honest competitor. What on earth could he be up to now?

The *chaouch* began to tremble all over his body. He thought more about the terrible punishment his master would inflict upon him when he returned than about the present moment.

"Pity, prince," stammered the handyman in Berber, not caring whether he would be understood. "I know who you are, I'm not a threat to you. I was simply asked to follow you and find out where you were going."

Ranzi snapped back in the same dialect, "Who asked you to follow me? Your master, maybe?"

The *chaouch* did not answer.

Ranzi increased the pressure on the Berber's arm, who began to moan even louder, almost screaming.

After a minute or two, feeling that the threats were useless, Ranzi let go.

"I'll spare you this time, *chaouch*. Tell your master that I have been invited to dine with my foster brother, Isaac Yakob. And also tell him that the next time he has me followed, I, Sheikh Ahmed Ranzi el Sahraoui, will come in person to bring him back his henchmen—or rather, what will be left of them."

The *chaouch* took off without hesitation.

Isaac felt that the matter was far more serious than it appeared. The bachagha was almost certainly involved up to his neck in something shady, and it would be interesting to find out who was giving him orders. Isaac was convinced that tonight's incident should not be minimized. Ranzi's return to the country had caused quite a stir, and it seemed clear that many people were intrigued by it.

"Ranzi, it seems obvious that Dahrem is plotting something sinister with his sponsors."

Isaac seemed deep in thought, then stared directly at Ranzi.

"I think it's over for tonight," he finally confessed with resignation. "I'm going to go home, if you don't mind. However, I would like to accompany you tomorrow to El Goléa. I'd like the pleasure of seeing Rachida again."

In reality, Isaac was worried. He sensed that his foster brother's life was in danger, but he didn't want to alarm him by being too insistent.

For his part, the Targui didn't seem concerned. The incident seemed quite secondary to him.

"No, Yssic," Ranzi replied after a brief moment of silence. "Certainly, I understand your concerns, but it's better that you stay here with your family. I leave for El Goléa by jeep tomorrow before dawn, and I'll be well-armed as always during my expeditions. I'll be back as soon as possible, and don't worry about me. Kiss all the Yakobi for me, will you?"

CHAPTER 4

Friday, April 2, 1954

The Jeep pulled out through the main gate of the villa on Gérôme-Bertania Street just as the sun peeked over the horizon. Ali had filled up with gas and water, prepared all the necessary provisions for the long trek into the Sahara, and checked both the tire pressure and the charge of the batteries.

Ranzi leaned over to the chaouch and handed him a folded telegram.

"Send this as soon as the Ali post opens. It's very important."

"Yes, master. It will be done at eight o'clock sharp this morning."

As soon as the Jeep disappeared down the road, the chaouch ran back and swung the heavy gate shut.

Ranzi drove as fast as the rough road allowed. After three minutes, he passed Aïn-Berda, the source of cold drinking water at the northern edge of the village. From there, he veered west, taking the secondary road toward Batna.

His route would take him through El Kantara, Biskra, and El Oued. He planned to stop somewhere between Touggourt and Ouargla—the last town accessible by departmental road—where he would spend the first night of the journey under the open sky. After that, he would decide as needed.

The full trip would cover more than a thousand kilometers, half of which would be on poorly marked tracks, where he could manage no more than 30 to 40 km/h. He had no time to waste.

Luckily, it was early spring. The heat was not yet at its peak, though the temperature could still reach 30 degrees in the middle of the day. In the Sahara, it was the machines that suffered from the heat more than men, he thought.

That first night, he rested peacefully under the stars. He pitched his small tent, then unpacked a brand-new sleeping bag—an item he had picked up during a recent trip to Europe.

His dinner was simple: olives and a round bread that Ali had prepared, washed down with a few sips of goat's milk. He finished with dried dates and, after the evening prayer, lay down to sleep.

Saturday, April 3, 1954

On the second day, Ranzi hit the road again at sunrise, after his morning prayer. He traveled without incident along a good stretch of track to Ghardaïa, where he made a technical stop at the local mechanic-gas station. He instructed the mechanic to refill the fuel, oil, and water and to carefully check the tires and both spare wheels.

Leaving his vehicle in the mechanic's care, he took his travel bag and headed toward the only hotel in the village, hoping to find accommodation for the night.

Ghardaïa was a small, uneventful town with about a thousand inhabitants. Fortunately for the truckers who crisscrossed the main roads of the South, the town had everything essential for drivers and their machines: fuel, water, a post office, a police station, and even a hotel with a decent restaurant.

The hotel manager, a fundamentally hypocritical man whose obesity was poorly concealed by a large, not-so-clean gandoura, was quietly sipping a glass of seltzer water on the forecourt. At the sight of Ranzi, he jolted upright, setting his drink down on a small table to his right before rising to greet him. He had clearly recognized the Sahrawi prince.

"Ahlan wa sahlan, Sheikh Ahmed!" the manager exclaimed in Arabic. "May Allah grant you a long life."

The hotelier was overdoing it, but that was the custom here. Who could possibly be offended?

"Thank you, hotelier. Do you have a free room?"

"I'll give you the nicest room, Si Ahmed. How long are you staying?"

"Tonight only, innkeeper. I leave tomorrow morning at dawn."

The man crossed the hall, went behind the counter, and took a key from the grimy board.

"You have Room Three, the best, Si Ahmed. You are our only customer tonight. Will you have breakfast in the morning?"

"Yes. Tea, hot donuts, and honey, please," Ranzi said as he picked up the key.

He went up to his room, dropped off his luggage, and came out almost immediately, heading for the only bathroom on the landing. After showering in brackish water, he returned to his room, locked the door, said his evening prayers, and went to bed, too tired for dinner.

Ranzi was exhausted from the tough day, but still, he only slept with one eye open when away from home. This habit, formed in his youth in the Sahara, had saved his life many times.

Around midnight, his senses were alerted by a faint noise from the landing. He sat up silently, grabbed his curved dagger, and, like a feline, crept quickly toward the door, barefoot and silent. He pressed against the wall, controlling his breathing and steadying his heartbeat. His years of practicing yoga had proven invaluable in situations like this.

The key was still firmly in the lock, yet something—or someone—was pressing on the other side of the door. The key began to turn, then slowly slid out of the bolt, finally dropping to the tiled floor with a high-pitched tink—bouncing twice, breaking the heavy silence of the night.

Ranzi instinctively pressed himself further against the wall.

Muffled voices came from the other side of the door.

"Yallah, ezreb, ezreb, fissah!" (Come on, quickly... quickly, let's go!) said a hushed voice in Arabic.

Then came the sound of rushing footsteps. One, maybe two people were running down the stairs. Silence followed.

Ranzi flipped the light switch and quickly spotted the key on the floor. He snatched it up, yanked open the door, and bolted after the intruders. Several seconds had already passed since their attempted break-in—precious seconds they had surely used to escape.

He bounded down the dimly lit staircase, moving with agility. When he reached the lobby, he noticed the front door of the hotel was wide open.

"Too late. They're gone," he muttered.

Stepping into the street, he scanned the darkened alleyways, his eyes struggling to adjust. Ghardaïa had no streetlights, and shadows swallowed everything. He was about to turn back when a distinct hum of a diesel engine rumbled in the distance.

They just fled.

The sound indicated that the vehicle was heading toward Ourgla.

Things were starting to take a troubling shape. First of all, he was spied on and followed as soon as he arrived in Khenchela. Then, someone had managed to track him to Ghardaïa and attempted to enter his hotel room in the middle of the night.

At least they hadn't intercepted me in the desert, he thought.

He replayed his journey over the past two days. No vehicle had followed him—of that, he was sure.

But who wanted to harm him? Were they trying to kill him? Capture him? And Abu Dahrem—what role did he play in all this?

Apart from Isaac, only his sister and Ali knew about this trip. Unless…

The postman.

Yes. The telegram could have been intercepted. But which postman? The one in Khenchela or the one in El Goléa?

His thoughts drifted to the innkeeper. If the man had played a role in this, Ranzi needed to confirm it immediately.

The manager lived on the ground floor, his door tucked behind the reception counter. Ranzi stormed around the counter and pounded loudly on the door.

From inside, a string of Arabic curses erupted. The innkeeper, half-asleep, swore at the infidel who dared interrupt the slumber of a righteous man, calling him a son of a female dog and a henchman of Satan.

A moment later, the door cracked open, revealing the innkeeper in his nightgown, barefoot, eyes widening in alarm.

His expression shifted instantly when he saw Ranzi. Shame washed over his face as he mumbled in broken dialect:

"Your Excellency... forgive me, Si Ahmed. But... what time is it?"

Ranzi, genuinely enraged, shouted back:

"Your Excellency will tear you to pieces, miscreant! Give me the names of the bandits who tried to enter my room to slit my throat just minutes ago!"

The innkeeper, trembling, struggled to catch his breath.

"There must be a mistake, my prince. I don't understand. I swear by Allah, I know nothing of this attack! You're the only guest here... so it wasn't hard for them to find your room," he stammered, pointing toward the empty key slots behind the counter.

Ranzi's glare hardened.

"Hotelier, I swear—if you're lying to me, I will come back and gut you myself. You'll go straight to Satan. Word of a Targui."

The hotelier muttered something unintelligible and scurried back into his quarters, visibly shaken.

As Ranzi climbed the stairs back to his room, he paused on the landing. Something had caught his attention earlier.

Lowering himself to all fours, he scanned the floor until he found it—a cigarette butt, lying near the balustrade.

Not a Marlboro, not a Camel, and certainly not a Lucky Strike, he noted. He recognized the distinct pale yellow of the paper immediately.

Gitanes, French Corn Paper Gitanes.

One of the intruders had been smoking them.

Slipping the cigarette butt into an envelope, he sealed it carefully before laying back down.

This time, he fell asleep instantly.

He knew full well that he had nothing more to fear tonight.

Sunday, April 4, 1954

The Targui was awakened, much to his regret, around five o'clock in the morning by the call of the muezzin. He would not have minded sleeping an extra hour or two, but unfortunately, the minaret stood right in front of the hotel.

Ranzi showered, cursing again at the brackish water that refused to lather his soap. He dressed quickly and performed the morning prayer. Feeling refreshed, he descended the stairs four at a time and headed to the dining room, where his breakfast awaited him—a steaming cup of tea accompanied by large Tunisian donuts drizzled with honey.

In the Jeep, a bloodied body slumped in the driver's seat, its head resting against the steering wheel. He approached cautiously. Bruises covered the man's face, and his hands were stained with blood. Leaning closer, Ranzi noticed a sharp, clean cut on the victim's neck—likely from a blade. The gas station attendant had probably had his throat slit after enduring a brutal interrogation.

A wave of nausea hit him. Instinctively, he looked away, but he quickly regained control, forcing himself to examine the victim meticulously.

"Whoever did this will pay dearly," he muttered aloud.

His eyes scanned the workshop with an inquisitive gaze, scrutinizing every corner of the garage to ensure the attackers had not left any traps behind. Reassured, he holstered his pistol and stepped out, disgusted by the gruesome sight.

The Sahrawi knew he had to alert the local authorities. A police station stood at the village's outskirts, barely a hundred meters away. He picked up his bag and walked toward it at a steady pace.

"It's too early for the police station to be open," he thought, "but that doesn't matter."

He climbed the three steps of the white-washed building with its tricolor flag and knocked vigorously on the door. When no response came after a few moments, he knocked again, harder this time.

"Alright, alright, I'm coming, damn it! Stop that racket, or I'll throw you in the cell—by Zeus!" a nasal voice barked, tinged with a thick Alsatian accent.

Still fastening his uniform, the brigadier opened the door, squinting against the first rays of sun breaking over Ghardaïa. He blinked rapidly, tucked in his shirttail, buckled his belt, and looked at Ranzi with a startled expression.

"I feel like I know you," he said, bewildered. "Aren't you Sheikh Ahmed Ranzi El Sahraoui? Forgive me, Si Ahmed, I just woke up," he added apologetically.

The gendarme's accent and fair features—blond hair and blue eyes—stood out in the bled, and many locals found him an unusual presence. Yet, there was something paternal in his demeanor. He quickly motioned for the prince to enter.

"I am Brigadier Stellen. What can I do for you, Your Highness?"

"Good morning, Brigadier. Let's set aside the formalities, shall we? I remember you as well—it must have been over five years ago, at the commemoration of the Armistice on November 11, 1948. You had just been transferred here."

"Yes, that's right," Stellen nodded.

"I apologize for waking you so early, but unfortunately, I have to report a crime that took place last night in Ghardaïa, followed by an attempt on my life."

Ranzi recounted the events of the previous night to the stunned policeman. The brigadier was already dreading how he would explain a murder and an attempted assault in a town where nothing had happened since the last war.

"Sheikh Ahmed," the astonished gendarme finally said, "let's head to the crime scene right away. You can give me the details as we go. A murder in Ghardaïa—this is unheard of! The last homicide here was over twenty years ago, and it was never solved."

The two men set off toward the gas station at a brisk pace. Upon arrival, Stellen examined the small door's lock closely.

"No signs of forced entry. You didn't touch anything when you came in, did you?" he asked.

"No," Ranzi replied. "The door was ajar when I arrived to pick up the Jeep. When I didn't see the mechanic, I entered without hesitation—and that's when I found the body in the front seat. He must have been killed elsewhere and then dragged into the Jeep. Look at the blood trails on the ground."

"I see," Stellen murmured, stepping into the garage.

He approached the body, inspecting it carefully while jotting down notes.

"Look at his face—bruises. And his fingernails... they were torn out. You were right; this man was tortured before being murdered."

The gendarme hesitated for a moment before asking, "Were you in any sort of business with the mechanic, Sheikh?"

"I simply asked him to perform a full check-up on my Jeep—refuel it, change the oil, inflate the tires. That's all," Ranzi answered truthfully.

"Sheikh Ahmed, do you think this murder is connected to last night's attack at the hotel?"

"Most likely, Brigadier. The killers were after me. They must have interrogated the poor mechanic to find out where I was staying and possibly my destination. Maybe they even wanted to search my Jeep. Then they eliminated him to keep him from raising the alarm."

Brigadier Stellen studied him for a moment before pressing further.

"Sheikh Ahmed, forgive my insistence, but do you have any idea why someone would target you?"

"Brigadier, as you know, I have been in the jewelry and precious stone trade for a long time. These bandits may have intended to rob me. But they couldn't have known that I had sold my entire collection before returning to my camp."

"That does seem plausible," Stellen admitted. "Help me move the body out of your Jeep, and let's check if your vehicle is still in working order. They may have tried to sabotage it. I'll call the doctor to perform an autopsy before burial—that's standard procedure. I also need to notify the victim's family."

Stellen caught her breath.

"Sir Ahmed, could you stop by today or tomorrow to sign your deposition?"

"I'd rather sign it right away," Ranzi replied. "I have an important meeting in El Goléa tomorrow."

He paused, suddenly recalling a crucial detail. Turning to the brigadier, he asked,

"Brigadier, can you find Corn Paper Gitanes here?" He pointed to the cigarette butt he had found on the landing of his hotel.

Stellen shook his head.

"No, Si Ahmed, no one smokes that brand in this village. You suspected that, didn't you? Where did this butt come from?"

"Do you want to keep it as evidence?" Ranzi asked, handing the envelope to the gendarme. "I found it on the first-floor landing of the hotel that night, just after the attempted attack."

They returned to the station, where the brigadier offered the Targui prince a hot coffee before taking his statement.

"I really missed having coffee at breakfast this morning," Ranzi said, appreciative. "I usually avoid drinking it in this region—I find it terrible. But yours, Brigadier…"

"I bring it regularly from France," Stellen explained. "Like you, Si Ahmed, I only appreciate pure Arabica."

The gendarme carefully reread the sheikh's statement.

"Ah, you see," he said thoughtfully, "there's still something that bothers me. How exactly did they try to break into your hotel room?"

"It was quite simple," Ranzi replied. "I had left the key in the lock. The intruders must have used a stick or some tool coated with glue to turn it. They pushed too hard, and it fell onto the floor with a clinking sound. They probably didn't expect such a commotion. Realizing they'd been noticed, they chose to flee."

"They would have had less trouble kicking the door down. Luckily for you, they didn't."

"Not necessarily," Ranzi said. "The door seemed quite solid to me. Besides, breaking it down would have made too much noise and likely attracted the attention of the manager."

He glanced at his watch. "I need to get on the road now, Brigadier—I don't have much time. I'll be sure to stop by again when I return."

"Sir Ahmed, one piece of advice—be careful on the road," the gendarme cautioned.

"Thank you, Brigadier. A warned man is worth two," the Targui replied with a wink.

From the porch of the gendarmerie, Brigadier Stellen watched as Sir Ahmed drove off in his Jeep, heading back to the open road.

CHAPTER 5

Luckily, the track toward El Goléa had just been taken the day before by a long military convoy. The effects of the damage would certainly remain until the next rain—that is to say, in a few days or perhaps even a few years. The 4x4 would therefore be able to travel at a suitable speed on this section.

Ranzi had grown suspicious. He constantly scanned the horizon or checked his rearview mirror, wary of any new attempt at aggression. He kept his Luger close at hand on the passenger seat. Questions swirled in his mind, though he knew perfectly well that he would find no answers here, in the middle of the Sahara. Resigned, he pressed down on the accelerator, the Jeep happily swallowing the dust as it sped up to 50 km/h without the slightest difficulty.

Six hours after his departure, he was already entering El Goléa.

The town was built on either side of a single long street—if one could even call it that. In reality, it was merely an extension of the track from Ghardaïa, a path without sidewalks that stretched through to the other end of the town.

The few tiny white houses, with their terraces but no windows—or at least only small slits resembling loopholes—were typical of this part of the Sahara. Thanks to construction techniques perfected centuries earlier, these dwellings, with their thick walls and modest interiors of just one or two rooms, provided what was most rare and invaluable in this fiery desert: shade and an incredible coolness for the occupants.

The Targui camp lay at the far end of the village, just near the large oasis. After traveling less than a kilometer, Ranzi saw the village of a hundred multicolored tents below. He quickly spotted his clan's tent, recognizable by the yellow and green flag emblazoned with the Southern Cross—the princely emblem. His family was certainly there.

El Goléa was the rallying point for all the tribes.

It was here that the long caravans formed and dispersed. These journeys were not undertaken haphazardly; on the contrary, every expedition was planned years in advance. It had to be so, for the round trips stretched over months, given the vast distances to be crossed and the slow, steady progress of the camels.

As the Jeep entered the tent village at a very moderate pace, a horde of yaouleds (young boys) suddenly appeared out of nowhere, their voices rising in excited shouts as they rushed forward, blocking its path. The Targui children had come to welcome Ranzi in their own way, escorting the vehicle to a large gimp. As the Jeep rolled to a stop, Ranzi jumped out, only to find himself, as if by magic, face to face with Rachida, who had come running, alerted by the children's cries.

"The Prince of the Dunes is back after five long years of absence!" she exclaimed joyfully. "Kiss me quickly, Ranzi!"

Her eyes filled with tears as she caught her breath. She wore a beautiful green damask silk dress, and a red veil was tied over her glossy black hair, dark as a raven's wing. On her forehead, the discreet caste tattoo—the Southern Cross—enhanced her oval face, with its delicate yet slightly coppery features, illuminated by a bright gaze.

"You seem to be in great shape. Did you have a good trip?" she asked after a few seconds.

Ranzi was about to answer, but she didn't give him the chance.

"Come quickly! I want to introduce you to your nephew, Saïd, and your niece, Aïcha. You will be very surprised—Saïd is your spitting image! Come," she insisted. "Then I'll make you some good tea while we wait for Bashir to join us."

"Rachida, I went to see our friends, the Yakobi, as soon as I returned to Khenchela. Rachel told me she misses you very much since you left. She asked me to give you a kiss for her and for Isaac."

"I miss her too, you know, big brother," Rachida said as she led him inside the tent. "We had so much in common. I can't wait to see her again."

Inside the tent, the children played on a thick woolen carpet, sheltered from the sun. The air inside was pleasantly cool, several degrees lower than the scorching heat outside, despite the occasional hot desert breeze.

Saïd, the eldest, was not yet five years old, and his sister had just turned three. As soon as they were within reach, Ranzi swept them both into his arms. He kissed them tenderly, then twirled them in the air.

He was happy to finally be home, reunited with his family after such a long absence. A few days earlier, he had felt a similar joy when reconnecting with his second family, the Yakobi. But the past still haunted him. Time had failed to erase the pain of losing his wife and their unborn child. Fate had made him a widower after less than a year of marriage. The midwife had been unable to stop the internal bleeding or save the baby, who had been in a poor position during delivery. At the time, the region suffered from a severe shortage of doctors.

By going into exile, Ranzi had hoped to find peace and forgetfulness. Eventually, he realized he had been wrong. Returning home had done him good, even though he knew that serious events threatened to upset the country's already precarious balance. Still, he was certain of one thing: the Sahara would never descend into chaos.

After a few minutes of play, he set the children down and turned to his sister, who handed him a cup of tea.

"Thank you, Rachida. This will help me wash away the dust from the road. Did you receive my telegram and summon the notables as I asked?"

"Yes, Ranzi. The meeting will take place tomorrow at nightfall. I believe all the elders will be present."

She paused for a moment, then continued, sensing the worry in her brother's expression.

"Ranzi, you're troubled. I can feel it. Something serious is happening—or is about to happen, isn't it?"

"You're right," he admitted. "There are madmen trying to spark a revolution, and there's no way to stop them. But for now, keep this to yourself. If word got out without context, it would only cause unnecessary fear. I will speak about it officially tomorrow."

He deliberately avoided mentioning the assault he had suffered the day before—his sister was already worried enough.

He was about to leave when he suddenly changed his mind.

"Damn, I almost forgot!" he exclaimed, holding up a large, flat case. "I brought you something from my last trip to Indonesia."

Rachida's lips curled into a broad smile as she eagerly took the package from his hands.

"You shouldn't have," she said, feigning modesty, before opening it to reveal a necklace of rare bluish-gray pearls. "It's absolutely stunning!" she exclaimed, kissing her brother before he walked away.

Night fell suddenly over El Goléa, barely allowing the sky—still ablaze with purple and orange—to fade into darkness. The night promised to be cold.

Ranzi took advantage of this moment of respite to tour the bivouacs. He had to greet all his friends, eager to see him again, even if it meant spending a sleepless night.

His rounds did not end until dawn. After greeting the last of the notables, he finally headed for his own bivouac, where he could at last find some well-deserved rest.

Monday, April 5, 1954

It was a beautiful morning for the Targui, a time of rest and meditation. After the morning prayer, he had asked his sister not to disturb him, except in cases of force majeure.

Around ten o'clock, Rachida came to serve tea, accompanied by a dish of honey cakes.

"How do you feel now, my prince?" she asked as soon as Ranzi set down his empty cup.

"Very well, thank you, sis. I think I'd better stretch my legs. Just a little exercise, as long as the sun isn't too high—it would do me a world of good. I think I'll say a few kind words to Caïd."

"Your friend has been waiting for you with infinite patience for five years. Go see him quickly," advised Rachida. "You'll find your saddle at the bottom of the second tent."

Ranzi picked up his saddle, slung it over his left shoulder, and made his way slowly to the horse paddock. As soon as he arrived at the large fence, he saw a speckled white Thoroughbred approaching him at a small gallop. His old horse must have seen or smelled him from afar. When the horse reached him, it shook its mane and whinnied.

"Kingpin!" exclaimed Ranzi. "My faithful thoroughbred, you were expecting me! Come here quickly so I can saddle you. We'll go for a ride, just the two of us, like the good old days."

Caïd let himself be saddled obediently. The Targui caressed his mount's neck for a long moment before nimbly jumping onto his back. The thoroughbred reared up on its hind legs, neighing and shaking its head, before immediately setting off at a gallop.

Ranzi reined in the spirited horse. He didn't want to tire it prematurely. At a light trot, he rode through the large dunes. He was happy to smell the scent of his native Sahara again. He had almost forgotten the sensations of the hot wind on the skin of his uncovered face. Gradually, he picked up the pace.

Caïd began to gallop. What a wonderful sight it was. One could see, in the middle of the desert, a proud Tuareg warrior riding a magnificent Arabian thoroughbred, soaring over the dunes. The horse kicked up a cloud of sand so fine that it seemed to hang suspended in the air, frozen between the azure sky and the golden hills. Caïd leapt from the ground effortlessly, a proud creature, and it was clear that, despite his age, he was still fast. Bent over his saddle, the rider whispered words his mount seemed to understand.

After riding several miles across the arid expanse, Ranzi dismounted and quietly returned to the oasis, holding the reins in hand. He led Caïd to the watering hole, removed the saddle, and allowed the horse to drink peacefully.

The Sahrawi prince regretted living far from his true homeland—the desert. Here, no one cared about electricity, radio, or cinema. Life flowed simply, far from the constraints and demands of civilization. Ranzi promised himself he would return as soon as possible, after completing his last mission.

Suddenly, he felt as though he were being watched. He slowly turned his head to the right and saw a slender, graceful figure serenely drawing water into an earthenware jug. Their gazes met, and the young woman immediately lowered her head.

Intrigued, Ranzi approached her. By Allah, he thought, who could this beautiful woman be?

When he reached the well, he asked courteously,

"I think I know you, young lady."

She didn't speak but kept her head down, almost desperately.

"Please, raise your head so I can see your face," Ranzi implored.

After a few seconds, she complied. She looked much sadder than reserved.

The prince then recognized her. He had not been mistaken.

"It's Leila, of course! The one and only green-eyed desert woman! You don't say hello to me anymore?"

Leila was of Kabyle origin, which explained the color of her eyes. She was beautiful—like an authentic goddess, her light skin contrasting with the clearly darker complexion of the Sahrawis. She had married a wealthy Targui merchant whom she had met in Tizi Ouzou. Alas, her husband had succumbed to a terrible illness two years earlier, a fact Ranzi had not known.

Leila finally greeted him timidly, her head tilted again as if to express her submission.

"May the great Allah protect you, Prince Ahmed. I didn't mean to offend you."

The sheikh, whose memory was remarkable, recalled that she had a little boy who must have been six years old by now. Always pleasant, he replied,

"All in good time. How are Abdul and your son, Mahmoud?"

Leila was surprised to find that Prince Targui still remembered her son's name. She replied,

"My husband died of malaria almost two years ago, Prince Ahmed. As for Mahmoud, he is doing very well, thank you."

"May Allah take care of Abdul's soul. He was a righteous man. I'm sorry, I didn't know that. Life must not be easy for you, Leila. If you need anything, go see my sister Rachida. Don't hesitate—she can help you."

Leila lowered her gaze respectfully, then raised her head. She was too proud to accept any special favors.

"Thank you, Sir Ranzi," she said politely. "The tribe provides us with everything Mahmoud and I need."

Ranzi knew this well. In the Sahrawi tribe, a widow was never left in need. Satisfied, he was about to let her leave with her jug, now no doubt full of water, when he suddenly changed his mind. She was so beautiful, so sweet. He felt a sudden urge to see her again. It was time to tempt fate, he thought.

"Leila," he began, "would you agree to share dinner with us tomorrow evening under Rachida's tent? And of course, bring your young son along. I would be very happy to see you again before I leave."

"It is a great honor, Prince Ahmed. We will be there as soon as the sun goes down," Leila replied without hesitation, to the great surprise of the Sahrawi.

Ranzi gave a faint smile. He was both moved and surprised. She didn't accept out of politeness, just because I'm the sheik, he told himself. It was spontaneous, I'm sure.

The current had passed between them, and he wondered then if he was behaving like a schoolboy.

He gently took the jug from her hands.

"I'm going to accompany you, Leila. Let's get Caïd. If you don't mind, we'll bring him back to the enclosure together. Don't worry—he's very docile, you know."

After leaving Leila in front of his tent, the Targui spent the rest of the morning pampering his horse while whistling. Once the grooming was completed, satisfied, he returned to his bivouac where he took a long nap followed by a meditation session.

At nightfall, immediately after the evening prayer, about twenty notables—the deans of all the great families—came to sit on woolen carpets with brightly colored stripes, which the women had spread on the ground under the giant tent reserved for special occasions.

The notables were recognizable by their traditional attire: saroual and satin or silk shirts, long white woolen djellabas, and turbans in the colors of their tribe. Their faces were veiled up to their eyes, and they would only uncover their faces for dinner.

The women outside were busy preparing the feast in a delicate nocturnal ballet. They were preparing a gigantic mechoui.

The guests had a great time. It didn't take much for them to feast in the middle of the desert—all they needed was a piece of spit-roasted lamb or mutton, a pitcher of lightly fermented camel or sheep's milk, or a bowl of tea, all accompanied by a hot pancake, olives, and dates for dessert.

Murmurs were heard here and there in the assembly, for rumors circulated as always in such gatherings. No one knew the purpose of this extraordinary meeting, and the guests had to wait patiently until the end of the mechoui to get answers to the many questions that were on everyone's mind.

There had not been such an assembly for more than five years.

Ranzi had chosen his best ceremonial costume for this memorable evening. Dressed in a cream djellaba with large golden stripes, he wore a black-and-white wild silk turban. The precious yatagan, a gift from his old friend and great initiate, the Turkish General Ameur Pasha, was tucked under his wide scarlet silk belt.

He removed his veil, straightened up slowly, and scanned the assembly with a long panoramic look, as if to greet his audience. Finally, he decided to speak in a voice charged with emotion.

"My brothers, noble and worthy representatives of the Saharawi people, I am delighted to be here among you after these long years of exile. In Mecca, just two months ago, I met an Algerian dignitary who suggested that I join the ranks of an organization recently formed with the goal of winning the independence of our country through violence. Perhaps, behind this secret army, there are lawless people preparing to ignite a large-scale rebellion under false pretenses."

This announcement had the effect of a bombshell. Obviously, no one here had expected such a revelation.

A voice rose from the first row reserved for the deans and silenced the murmurs as if by magic.

"Prince Hamed, all colonies yearn for independence. No one can stop the course of history!"

"I don't think these people want to start a revolution for our good and that of all our Si Hussein compatriots," Ranzi replied deferentially. "Well, maybe not all of them. But those I'm speaking of are, above all, thirsty for power. They want to replace colonialism with the worst kind of ancestral feudalism. Just look at what has happened in other countries where democracy has completely disappeared, and where corruption and injustice now reign. As for our country, I tell you bluntly: we are not yet ready to stand on our own two feet. Those who promise us independence and freedom will certainly offer us chaos."

"I find it hard to believe that all separatists behave like bandits," objected a second dean, rising and turning to face the assembly. "But it's true that recent examples tend to show that the new leaders behave like dictators, which is hardly reassuring for our future."

Ranzi turned toward the speaker, arms outstretched, palms turned to the sky.

"The revolutionaries ask us to join their ranks by offering us freedom, Sheikh Malik, but freedom we already have. We are free like the Sirocco. We have been traveling for millennia with the sandstorms, from one end of the Sahara to the other, without ever worrying about borders. Should we kill thousands of innocent men, women, and children, terrorizing a piece of land?

"I am for the voice of dialogue and consultation. I refuse to take up arms. Not that I fear the outcome of the fight—I remain convinced that we could achieve more through wisdom and negotiation than by force.

"I defer to you, honorable deans. You, who are the conscience of our people, will decide tonight if we should join this movement," Ranzi concluded.

The deans were to deliberate behind closed doors. If there were differences among them, they would not be aired in public. So, they left the large tent to gather in another bivouac set up nearby in order to debate in peace.

An hour later, they finally returned to the big tent. Silence reigned as the eldest of the notables, Sheikh Abdullah, finally spoke.

"Sahrawi people, the Council of Elders has unanimously decided to observe a cautious neutrality. This fight is not that of the Targuis. In any case, if we were to get involved in a process of emancipation, we would rather choose dialogue over arms. No demand justifies violence in our eyes. Accordingly, we will firmly oppose any attack on civilians in this region, regardless of faith. Sheik Ahmed Ranzi will be our official spokesperson with the revolutionary authorities, if there are any, to make our position known."

Ranzi's face beamed with satisfaction. He had never doubted the outcome of the deliberations of the Council of Elders.

He addressed the deans:

"You wise ones, my elder brothers, thank you, for you have made the best choice. May the Great Architect protect us and our descendants, and may He testify that on this day the Sahrawis have chosen peace. Should a conflict arise, we will observe strict neutrality unless openly attacked."

The Targui paused. He hesitated. Was he finally going to mention the assault he had suffered two days earlier? Although he was not certain, he was convinced that there was a link between his attackers and the revolutionary movement that was preparing.

"I must also inform you that they tried to assassinate me yesterday in Ghardaïa," he finally admitted, "and I don't know the reasons."

This declaration had even more impact in the assembly than the previous one. Ranzi struggled to contain the cries of anger that erupted from all sides. Dozens of Targuis rose, crying for revenge and brandishing their swords. No one could attack their sovereign with impunity.

It took him several minutes to restore calm.

"I did not want to speak of it before the vote, to avoid it influencing your decision," he said, addressing the notables, "because I do not know if there is a link with the revolutionary movement. Wretches tortured and slaughtered an innocent. They tried to reach me twice. Are these assaults related to the conspiracy that is being prepared? I'm not certain, as I don't have any specific information. However, I will settle this matter in my own way as soon as I return to Khenchela. To carry out this task, I wish to have a small escort. I will need four well-trained volunteers for an indefinite period, as well as a second Jeep in good working order."

The old man who had reported the Council's decision a few minutes earlier raised his right hand to ask for the floor.

"Si Ahmed, your people are distressed by the events you have just reported to us. In the name of all the deans of this assembly, I give you full powers to carry out this mission. We must put all our adversaries out of harm's way as soon as possible."

"Thank you, Sheikh Abdullah. If no one has any questions for me, I declare the meeting adjourned. Let the young people join us for the festivities."

The evening ended with a grand celebration in honor of the prince, under Bengal lights and the blank firing of old rifles, all punctuated by the powerful ululations of the women who had spontaneously lined up in a circle around a large bonfire.

After a mock raid that lasted nearly an hour, much to the delight of the young teenagers, traditional camel races were then organized, followed by jousts on horseback and a contest of spear shooting at skins filled with sand.

The party took place under the glow of a majestic, almost full red moon and did not end until an hour or two before dawn.

Tuesday, April 6, 1954

Rachida had just cleared the low breakfast table. Bachir and Ranzi exchanged their views on the major events of the second half of the twentieth century. They had diametrically opposed visions, but that didn't matter. The prince was more pragmatic and less idealistic than his brother-in-law, who was unusually kind. Bachir was an honest, dynamic, and efficient man, a graduate of an accounting school. Here, in the middle of the desert, his role as manager was crucial. He oversaw all stewardship issues and was able to provide the tribesmen with what was necessary to ensure their survival in this land of fire and sand.

Before leaving the tent, Ranzi called out to his sister.

"Rachida," he said, "I have a special request for you."

"Ah yes, my prince. It's going to cost you a lot, you know."

"You're welcome," he replied. "Stop laughing at me once and for all, or I'll spank you. I'm your older brother, after all!" he said jokingly. "I would like to receive two distinguished guests this evening. Do you think you can organize a sister's dinner for me?"

"No question of talking shop here! If it's a business meal, there's an excellent eatery in El Goléa!" Rachida replied seriously.

"But no, little sister, it's not about work. I invited a couple of friends," he finally admitted, looking a bit embarrassed.

"Oh yes? And can we know who they are?"

"Uh... you know Leila, don't you? I met her yesterday at the well. We chatted for a long time, and one thing led to another. I thought it might do her some good to break free from the loneliness she's felt since Abdul's death. So, I took the liberty of inviting her to dinner here with her son."

"And you say you've invited a couple? Holy joker! But of course, it will give me the greatest pleasure, my prince. I am very happy to see that the natural course of life is regaining its rights. Leila and her son are always welcome in the Sahrawi home."

Before leaving, Rachida added, "She is very beautiful, Leila. You have very good taste, my prince."

Ranzi spent much of the morning receiving the volunteers. Practically all the able-bodied men in the camp wanted to help; they had lined up in single file in front of the bivouac, impatiently waiting to be selected.

He went to the four best candidates, whom he had chosen according to very specific criteria.

"I know you all, my friends, and I am proud to welcome you to my little shock commando," he said.

He turned to the youngest volunteer, a young man just out of his teens. He was barely twenty years old. Tall and thin, he was perfectly determined.

"Amin, your father was the bravest of the Targui hunters. We once tracked lions on the southern edge of the Sahara. You will undoubtedly honor his memory. You will need money for your travel expenses. Take this, young warrior," he said, handing him a purse.

Then, addressing the two volunteers on the left, he stared at them for a long time, a smile on his face. He remembered a certain tournament where they had become adversaries for a day, and he had come out a big loser. The two men were nearly the same age, probably just over thirty. He threw them two purses, which they caught on the fly.

"Mouktar and Idriss, more than five years ago, you both gave me a crushing defeat at the camel tournament by taking insane risks. It was only a game, but this time I recommend extreme caution. There will be no quarter."

Finally, he approached the last volunteer, the oldest of the four. In his forties, he hid an imposing musculature beneath his midnight-blue burnous. Khaled was the most skilled of the Targui at handling pistols, rifles, or shotguns, as well as throwing knives.

"Khaled, my faithful lieutenant, you are always ready to sacrifice yourself for noble causes. I thank you for offering me your precious help. Here is your purse."

The prince then addressed the whole small group.

"Khaled, your eldest, will be the commando leader. He will report to me whenever necessary. I charge you with overseeing the stewardship. We will be traveling in two Jeeps. I will provide mine, which is in perfect condition, so prepare another vehicle. Fill up with gas and water. Provide additional reserves in two or three jerry cans of twenty liters, drinking water, food—everything necessary for three to four days of hiking in the desert.

Add two pairs of binoculars to your list, as well as two walkie-talkies. A good piece of advice: check the state of the batteries before we depart.

For armament, bring daggers, well-oiled pistols or revolvers—beware of the sand—one or two precision rifles, a supply of cartridges, as well as a few offensive grenades. We never know. All artillery must be camouflaged as best as possible in the Jeep. You will find this material in the batches of military surplus the Americans left us before their departure. Solve these issues as soon as possible with my brother-in-law Bachir.

We will leave tomorrow morning, as soon as everything is ready. No rush, everything must be carefully checked before departure. Khaled will pick me up at my bivouac."

The Targui took leave of his men and headed for the enclosure. Along the way, he congratulated himself on being able to count on devoted men, ready to sacrifice their lives to defend their sovereign.

He wanted to see his thoroughbred one last time. Upon arriving near the enclosure, even before he had whistled two notes, Caïd galloped down, very happy to find his master.

Ranzi was eager to find Leila. After reluctantly abandoning Caïd, he returned to his bivouac to take refuge once more in meditation. Yoga was, for him, the best remedy. It allowed him to abstract himself from the material world and regenerate his vital energy.

As night fell, he returned to his sister's tent. After taking off his shoes, he removed his veil.

He saw Leila, already seated to Rachida's right. The two women had known each other for a long time and obviously got along wonderfully. Mahmoud sat wisely between Saïd and Aïcha. Bachir stood right in front of the children.

Leila bowed slightly to greet the sheikh. She was radiant, and it was hard for her to hide her joy.

"Si Ahmed," she said spontaneously, "I am delighted to be in the Sahrawis' home this evening. You do me more honor than I deserve."

"It is a joy that we all share here, Leila. Please, call me Ranzi," he replied.

The Targui was happy. He had finally found his family after a long crossing of the desert, and now, a lovely woman sat right in front of him. His gaze alternated between the people present, under the dim light of the oil lamps. He probably would have liked to immortalize this moment.

Rachida smiled silently, looking in turn at her brother and Leila.

The beautiful Kabyle was dressed in a simple, long red and white rayon dress that molded her perfect body. A discreet perfume with jasmine extracts emanated from her delicate skin. A silk scarf was loosely tied around her long, jet-black hair, which waved and shimmered in the lamplight. A large woven woolen scarf enveloped her beautiful, round shoulders. A discreet Southern Cross was tattooed on her left wrist.

Leila did not dare to look at Ranzi. She kept her eyes lowered most of the time, which did not displease the handsome prince.

The dinner stretched on without the guests noticing the passage of time. Bachir, breaking his legendary reserve, recounted in detail the historical moments that had marked the Sahara over the past two decades.

Having finished his presentation, he invited Leila to speak about her native Kabylie. The young woman seemed surprised at first, knowing that few people on earth cared about her country, which was nonexistent on most maps of the time. She spoke, without being asked too much, in a passionate description of the land of olive trees and citrus fruits, her true homeland. She praised the cultured and peaceful inhabitants of her native country, with a hint of nostalgia.

Ranzi then spoke in a soft voice. He recalled some of the many anecdotes that had marked him during his endless journey around the world. He told the story of the pyramids of Egypt and their astonishing similarity to those of Mexico, the beauty and kindness of the Tahitians, and the austere life of the Tibetan monks.

The evening ended in the middle of the night.

Ranzi took the sleeping little Mahmoud in his arms and offered to drive Leila home. Only a hundred meters separated the two tents.

The nights were magnificent in this season, and the stars of all the constellations twinkled in the deep blue sky. After a few steps, the Targui stopped and took the warm hand of the Kabyle.

"Leila," he said simply, "have you ever thought about starting a new home?"

"So far, I have not felt the need, Ranzi. Mahmoud is everything to me. I don't want to ruin his existence out of pure selfishness, especially since your tribe gives us all the support we could wish for. It is a beautiful testimony of solidarity that I am not ready to forget."

She continued after a brief hesitation.

"Besides, I married Abdul for love. Of course, there are no shortages of parties here, but I do not want a marriage of convenience under any circumstances."

Ranzi gazed into her large green eyes, which were highlighted by a light touch of kohl applied to her upper eyelids. He noticed a light dancing in her eyes, under the dim glow of the stars and the full moon.

"Did you accept my invitation to dinner out of respect, out of politeness... Leila?"

Leila lowered her head, surprised by such a direct question.

"Are you always so unpredictable with women, lord?" she responded sarcastically.

The Targui still couldn't pull away from the gaze of the beautiful Leila. He hesitated for a moment, struggling to find the right words.

"I'll make a confession, Leila. I've been trying to run away from reality all these years. The woman I loved died after childbirth, and I could not accept her loss, nor that of the child she was carrying. Yesterday, I met you at the well. You filled your pitcher with the grace of the nymphs and goddesses of mythology. You were beautiful and sad, your slender silhouette stood out against the sandy background. I approached the well to contemplate you closely, to speak to you. Fate has allowed our paths to cross, and I want to know if you have any feelings for me, Leila..."

She smiled for a long time, making a considerable effort to contain her joy. She looked Ranzi straight in the eye.

"Prince of the Dunes, would I have spontaneously accepted your invitation if I had not felt the same confusion?"

"I am very happy this evening, Leila," the Targui replied, somewhat intimidated.

Leila knew the nickname Isaac had given her when they were both teenagers. It's another shot from Rachida! My sister definitely talks too much, thought Ranzi.

He wanted to pull the beautiful Kabyle into his arms and kiss her, but it was not possible with little Mahmoud just asleep. He thought it best to resume the conversation later. After all, there was no rush.

"We have to go home now, Leila. It is getting late for Mahmoud."

He then realized that he would soon leave El Goléa, with no hope of returning for several months. Would Leila agree to join him in Khenchela?

"I have a very busy schedule," he admitted. "In the days to come, I must return to Khenchela. Would you like to join me there with your son? I have a large villa, and Mahmoud can be enrolled immediately at the municipal school. That won't cause any difficulty. If it suits you, you can arrange this trip with Rachida and Bachir; they must also go there very soon. Anyway, I'll let my sister know tomorrow, and you'll have plenty of time to consider my proposal."

Leila's face flushed, and a few tears moistened the kohl on her eyelids. She hoped Ranzi wouldn't notice them in the dark.

"I gladly accept, Ranzi. I also think it will do Mahmoud the greatest good," she added spontaneously, as if to find an excuse.

The Targui could not believe his ears—Leila agreed to follow him. He was just happy. He took her hand and very delicately placed a kiss on the warm surface of her palm, which exhaled a discreet scent of jasmine.

"I'm leaving tomorrow morning," said the prince, looking the beautiful Kabyle girl in the eye. "I will come to greet you before I leave."

Leila was about to go back to her tent when she turned around and approached until she brushed the prince's face.

"Ranzi," she whispered in the Targui's ear, "don't leave me alone tonight. I've been waiting for this moment for so long."

The Targui gently took her hand, without saying a word, and led the beautiful Kabyle girl into the tent.

CHAPTER 6

Wednesday, April 7, 1954

Ranzi had just left Leila at the precise moment when the jeep of the small commando, advancing like a whirlwind, braked, raising a cloud of sand, and came to a stop just in front of the Sahrawi pennant, next to the all-terrain vehicle of the sheikh.

It was already nine o'clock.

The four men who were going to accompany the Targui were dressed in European style: khaki shorts, safari jackets, and pith helmets. They all wore brand-new Pataugas, better boots than Rangers! The stewardship had not skimped on resources, and Ranzi promised himself that he would thank his brother-in-law.

Khaled jumped out of the vehicle and addressed the prince, smiling under his thin mustache.

"Sabbah el kheir (hello), Si Ahmed," he said in Arabic. "Everything is ready according to your orders."

Ranzi returned the salute to his men and thought it was time to unveil his strategy.

"Hello, my friends. You no longer ignore that there was a murder in Ghardaïa, as well as an attempt to attack me. My enemies will not stop here. I have good reason to believe they will try again. Having failed the first time on the outward journey, they risk severe punishment from their sponsors if they return empty-handed. Above all, I hope they don't expect me to return in force, and I remain convinced that they won't dare try anything in town, knowing that all the gendarmeries in the area have been informed of the aggression in Ghardaïa. They will surely plan a bad move in the desert, on our own ground, and that is where we will wait for them."

"I've assessed the number of our opponents," Ranzi continued. "They are three or four at most. They must travel by jeep or 4x4, and they had plenty of time to restock in the area to set a new trap for me."

Ranzi scanned his companions for any questions, then continued his presentation.

"I will explain how I plan to proceed, but it goes without saying that I welcome any criticisms or suggestions to improve my strategy."

"My jeep will take the lead, with one of you four as a companion, followed by the second, who will need to keep a minimum distance of three or four kilometers to avoid being spotted. We will stay in close contact using our walkie-talkies. It would be ideal for the second jeep to follow a parallel course to the first, if possible. This will prevent them from being noticed. If my off-roader is attacked, the other three companions will come to the rescue."

"Then, in the evening, we will set up a false camp to lure the enemy: tents, campfires, etc. We will take care to hide ourselves as best as possible in our nearby sleeping bags."

Khaled nodded in agreement and spoke.

"Yes, Ahmed, I think that if we manage to detect them first, we should immediately go on the offensive to take advantage of the element of surprise."

"This is a perfectly acceptable proposal, Khaled. I will simply add that it is absolutely necessary to spare the leader of the expedition so that we can question him."

"Who would like to accompany me as a passenger and bodyguard, or as a driver?" Ranzi asked finally.

"I, Sir Ahmed," said Amin, the youngest of the four commandos.

"Then let's get out of here without wasting time," Khaled said.

The two vehicles started, kicking up a cloud of sand as they headed toward El Goléa.

As expected, Ranzi's jeep took the lead, while the second vehicle followed a parallel lane, away from the track. This slowed down the expedition noticeably, as Ranzi knew. The instruction was to make a report every half hour and to report any incident along the way, no matter how small. But nothing of note happened during this first day; the horizon remained desperately barren.

They stopped to relax and eat as the sun reached its peak in the sky. It was relatively warm, but the Targuis seemed to be fine with it. No one complained.

The lead jeep stopped at nightfall, very close to Hassi el Abiod, a well-known drinking water well in the region, about a hundred kilometers from Ghardaïa.

Ranzi found a place to bivouac and immediately informed the following vehicle.

There were no enemies in sight.

When the five accomplices were reunited, Ranzi suggested carrying out a reconnaissance round around the camp before setting up a watchtower.

There were no incidents that night.

Thursday, April 8, 1954

In the early morning, a delicious smell of coffee filled the icy atmosphere, waking Ranzi.

Khaled, already up, was preparing breakfast. To resist the morning cold, he had wrapped himself in a woolen blanket. The sun was just breaking over the horizon when the sheikh stood up to greet his bodyguard.

"Sabbah el kheir, Khaled. I see you're making us some good coffee. I will wake up the other companions."

The five men gathered in a circle around the campfire drank their coffee in silence, savoring the first warm, flavorful sips of the day.

Before returning to the track, Khaled carefully inspected the cars. He fueled them up, checked the water and oil levels, inspected the brakes and tires, and finally decided it was time to go. It was barely seven o'clock.

They arrived in Ghardaïa at nine-thirty. The lead vehicle stopped in front of the entrance to the gendarmerie, while the second sped toward the exit of the village. Ranzi had decided to pay the brigadier a courtesy visit. He stepped out onto the sand of the square and climbed the few steps of the perron. The position was open, and he entered the building, immediately walking over to Stellen, who waved him forward upon seeing him.

"Hello, Brigadier. I come to greet you before my return to Khenchela."

The brigadier firmly shook hands with the Targui.

"Hello, Sheikh Ahmed, good to see you again. It's a good thing I have some information for you."

Behind his desk, the brigadier consulted a small file.

"First of all, according to the doctor, Ben-Ali, the gas station attendant, was savagely tortured before having his throat slit. Nothing new, we knew that from day one. Then, I questioned the people of the village, and one of them claimed to have seen two individuals dressed in European style, though they were clearly Algerian men. They weren't locals. They were dropped off by a third thief in a Jeep or Land Rover at nightfall. Unfortunately, no one was able to note the license plate number of the vehicle."

Stellen continued,

"I took the precaution of informing all the gendarmeries in the region to catch them, distributing the limited description I have. Since then, I've had no further news from you, Si Ahmed."

Ranzi took an envelope from his pocket and handed it to the gendarme.

"You did everything you had to, Brigadier. Thank you for that. Here is some money for the Ben-Ali family. After all, I am indirectly responsible for what happened. Please send my sincere condolences to the family of the victim. Unfortunately, I do not have the time to visit them personally, but assure them that I will return to do so. Thank you once again for your assistance, Brigadier Stellen."

The gendarme accompanied the Targui to the Jeep to see him off.

Having taken his leave, Ranzi jumped into the Jeep and drove off.

There were about two hundred and fifty miles of trail left before reaching their next stop: Ouargla. That meant almost five to six hours of driving, not including technical stops.

Ranzi quickly reached the exit of the village, where his lieutenant was waiting for him. Serenely seated behind the wheel, he asked,

"Tell me, Khaled, how was your trip from Hassi el Abiod to Ghardaïa?"

"Not terrible," Khaled replied, waving his hand dismissively. "There are a lot of fesh fesh (very fine sandbanks in which vehicles risk getting stuck) on the course, and I think it will get worse, Si Ahmed."

The Targui thought for a few seconds, then decided.

"You're going to let four or five kilometers slip between us and drive in our tracks. We won't go very fast, and that will give you time to intervene if necessary. You may be at risk of being discovered, but that's better than breaking an axle or getting caught in quicksand. From now on, we'll drive slowly, as if we were tourists. Do all the necessary checks before departure, Khaled. We're in no hurry now."

They resumed the road according to the agreed instructions. They stopped to eat around one o'clock. It was starting to get very hot, necessitating a few additional stops to allow the mechanics to rest or to top up the water in the overheated radiators.

The monotony was broken at the stroke of five o'clock.

Amin was driving as best he could, given the condition of the track. He had to keep in mind that the other vehicle was a few kilometers behind. It was also essential for the two drivers to constantly maintain the right distance for the plan to succeed. Ranzi, seated in the passenger seat, was scanning the horizon when he saw, twice, the characteristic reflections coming from a rearview mirror or window. The lights came from the slope of a huge dune that could be seen in the distance, almost opposite the setting sun.

Lucky I saw it first, he thought, discreetly picking up his binoculars. He saw the Land Rover trying to hide behind a small dune.

Ranzi hunched down in his seat so as not to be seen, holding his walkie-talkie in hand, just in case the adversary had the bad idea to observe him through binoculars.

"Hello, Khaled? We just saw suspicious reflections a few miles to the east, and I spotted their vehicle. There is a good chance we'll be attacked before Ouargla because afterward, it's only the secondary road, and it's too busy for them to set their trap. So we're going to stop and set up our bivouac.

We'll apply the planned strategy: we'll be the hares, and you'll hunt down the hunters. I'll call you back to let you know our position as soon as night falls. Salam alekum!"

Ranzi and Amin busied themselves setting up their tent near a small rocky outcrop.

After evening prayers and a meal of flatbread, olives, and dates, Ranzi and Amin extinguished the campfire and lit a nightlight in the tent.

They slipped out the back and crawled toward some rocks that were twenty yards away. After checking their weapons, they made themselves as discreet as possible, blending into the night. All that remained was to wait for the trap to close.

Silence reigned over the entire expanse, day and night, interrupted only occasionally by the passing of rare motorized convoys. However, one should not imagine that this territory is completely deserted. The reality is different. There is life in the Sahara, and during the night, all kinds of creatures leave their shelters to live intensely. The ground teems with insects of all kinds, rodents, lizards, scorpions, and snakes, all emerging with the first coolness of dusk in search of food. Only the vegetation is plunged into a sort of lethargy that can last for decades until a providential storm brings the water needed to revive the desert—for a minute, an hour, or a day...

The Targuis observed the surroundings of the camp in complete serenity. They knew how to show infinite patience. They knew their desert by heart, and their eyes were trained to decipher the smallest details highlighted by the light of the stars.

Ranzi didn't know where Khaled and the other two volunteers were at this precise moment, but he was sure of one thing: his lieutenant and his two deputies were hiding somewhere nearby, ready to intervene when the time was right.

It was eight forty-five.

Khaled had made a large semicircle to go around the Land Rover from the south.

By nightfall, he had already spotted the tracks left on the sand by the recent passage of the off-roader. He thought that the use of motorized vehicles was a major disadvantage for their opponents because they left too many clues behind. Had they traveled on camels instead of cars, the mounts would have sniffed out their pursuers right away and sounded the alarm, especially considering the wind was blowing from the wrong direction. That's progress, Khaled concluded with a touch of irony.

He spoke in a low voice to his companions.

"Mouktar, Idriss, have you seen the tracks of the Land Rover? They are only a few hundred meters to the east, a kilometer at most. Let's leave the Jeep here and continue on foot in silence. From now on, we speak only if there's imminent danger."

"Here are my instructions:

We approach the enemy undetected and wait. They know where Si Ahmed's Jeep is. We expect them to move. If the three of them leave together, we follow them. But if they separate, we do the same. You two will follow the commando to the camp—don't get too close, but be ready to intervene. As for me, I'll take care of the third thief and join you as soon as possible. Any questions?"

The instructions were simple and clear. The trio began a silent walk of a thousand meters across the still warm sand. Once they got close to the Land Rover, the Targuis lay down on the sand, out of sight, behind a small dune, ready for any eventuality. It was already dark, and the enemy was right in front of their position, plotting inside the 4x4.

After about ten minutes, an individual who appeared to be the leader got out of the vehicle, immediately followed by his two accomplices.

"Yalah, yalah" (come on, come on), he waved. He returned to the off-roader as soon as his accomplices had melted into the background.

Mouktar and Idriss counted to thirty seconds before silently rushing behind the two bandits, on a parallel track. They had no need to rush; they knew where they were going.

Khaled crawled silently to the Land Rover. It took him a full minute. He circled the off-roader and pulled out his curved-bladed dagger. The head of the opposing commando was sitting quietly in the driver's seat, the front door wide open, completely unaware.

With one swift movement, Khaled rushed at the bandit, who had no idea where his attacker had come from. He didn't even have time to react before the steel blade sank dangerously into his neck.

This was enough to silence him.

"Take it easy," Khaled said. "Get down gently from your seat if you want to avoid having your throat cut. Put your hands behind your back. I'll take care of your weapons and tie you up. And heck, I'll even gag you—no need to take risks. Then, you'll move forward silently until I order you to stop."

Twenty and one hour,

The dry cold numbed Ranzi's limbs, as he had lost the habit of Saharan nights. Suddenly, Amin jumped. He had just seen the beam of light from a thin torch swinging in the darkness. Ranzi calmed him with a pat on the shoulder, signaling that he, too, had seen the danger approaching.

The two men, crouched in the crevice, held their breath. Timing was critical, as the enemy was slowly but surely approaching their tent.

They heard a faint murmur. Two perfectly synchronized shadows crept forward, whispering. The thugs were not very discreet, and a slight crunch on the sand betrayed their presence with every step.

Ranzi was now able to distinguish the bandits, who came within a meter of the guitoune. The enemy still suspected nothing.

One of the two men took out a dagger and, without hesitation, cut the two left slings. Immediately, the two assailants dived onto the tent, which collapsed under them. They had the firm intention of neutralizing their victims by diving to the ground, no doubt counting on the element of surprise. When they hit the false beds, padded with stones and sand, searing pain tore through them, causing them to cry out.

Ranzi, still lurking in the shadows with his Luger in hand and ready to fire, called out to them, almost screaming.

"Stop. Get up and throw down your weapons, or you're dead!"

The reaction was immediate. Panicked, the first of the aggressors straightened up and fired at will. The bullet went astray, lost in the dunes. Two other shots were fired simultaneously from the very spot where the assailants had emerged, mortally wounding the two attackers.

Khaled's team had just arrived to the rescue.

"Si Ahmed, is everything okay?" came a familiar voice in the dark.

"Beslama (it's all right), Mouktar. Everything is in order. Nice shot! You got them both. Get closer and be careful—you never know."

"I still have them in my field of fire," replied Mouktar, directing the beam of the torch he had just lit toward the bodies of the bandits.

The Saharan team regrouped in front of what remained of the camp. Only a minute or two passed before Khaled appeared, pushing a bound and gagged man in front of him. The leader, without a doubt.

Ranzi was satisfied. The trap had worked wonderfully. Two of the attackers were easily eliminated, and the third, arguably the most important character of the trio, was taken prisoner. He congratulated his collaborators.

"A big thanks to all of you. You did an excellent job. We're going to bury the two bandits and ask this gentleman a few questions before handing him over to justice. Khaled, send your two lieutenants to retrieve the Land Rover and your Jeep. We're going to camp here tonight; the place seems quiet to me, after all!"

Ranzi pointed his torch at the two assailants lying lifeless on the guitoune canvas and asked Amin to turn the bodies over so he could examine their faces.

"Oh, oh, an old acquaintance," exclaimed the sheik. "Here is the man who followed me last week to Khenchela, the chaouch of Bachaga Abou Dahrem. He did it again, I see, and it didn't bring him much luck."

Turning then toward the prisoner, the sole survivor, the Targui became more threatening. He illuminated the bandit's face with his torch to reveal the assassin's features.

The individual facing him was of North African origin, with no particular distinguishing features, but dressed like a settler, in a safari jacket and khaki shorts. All that was missing was the pith helmet, which he had probably left in his vehicle.

Ranzi looked him straight in the eye, the torch still pointed at his face.

"Filthy scoundrel," he said. "You got together to torture this poor innocent gas station attendant and ended up slitting his throat. I'm going to make sure you don't harm anyone again. I swear by Allah."

Ranzi then proceeded to search his prisoner. Khaled had already disarmed him; it wasn't a weapon he was looking for. He noticed the rectangular bulge on the left side of the safari jacket. He reached into the pocket with two fingers and pulled out a pack of cigarettes, which he examined in the light of his torch.

"Well, well, since when have you been smoking corn paper Gitanes?" he asked.

Friday, April 9, 1954

At daybreak, Khaled, as early as usual, busied himself preparing a morning snack. He was meticulous and didn't let anyone make the coffee for him. No one complained—his breakfasts were appreciated by all. He warmed up some savory pancakes and woke everyone up with the call to morning prayer, clumsily imitating the song of the muezzin.

Ranzi greeted him.

"What's new?" he asked his lieutenant.

Khaled smiled, showing his white teeth beneath his thin mustache.

"The bandit finally sat down to eat, Si Ahmed."

The sheikh smiled in turn. He wondered how Khaled could have obtained such a... spontaneous confession.

"You didn't torture him, did you?"

"I promised to bury him alive here, at dawn, if he didn't unpack everything. I don't think he ever doubted my word."

Amin and his two colleagues came to join the others for breakfast.

Khaled greeted them, motioned for them to help themselves, and continued his story.

"He told me his name is Aziz Abd Elacem. He comes from Algiers and specializes in... very special helping hands. He says he's in the pay of a Khenchelois, a bookseller called Kalifa. The latter asked him to seize your person and an old manuscript written by a certain Ibrahim. If you resisted, he had orders to shoot you on the spot to avoid further complications."

Ranzi couldn't believe his ears. Kalifa! He had known him for years. This bookseller provided him with rare books that could only be found in the big bookstores of Algiers or Paris. What the hell was Kalifa up to? Murder for a book? Was that sufficient motive? There must be something else behind all these aggressions and this violence, the Targui thought, more perplexed than ever.

Ranzi became more pressing:

"Is that all you could get? And about the other individual, the chaouch of Khenchela, what did he say?"

Khaled nodded and completed his report slowly, as if to avoid forgetting any detail.

"He admitted to me that your villa was under almost permanent surveillance by the chaouch we buried last night. As soon as you left your house on the day you left, he followed Ali to the post office and got a copy of the telegram you wrote, through the kindness of the postman. Kalifa, once alerted, entrusted his Land Rover to the group formed by

Abd Elacem and immediately gave all the necessary instructions so they could prepare their coup.

The bandits took to the road an hour or two after you left Khenchela, and they had no trouble catching up with you. They certainly rode for a good part of the night."

Ranzi, thoughtful and intrigued, finally responded.

"The postman just so happens to be Kalifa's nephew. The chaouch we buried didn't work for the bookseller, but for the bachaga. This means there is collusion between the bachaga and Kalifa. We'll have to dig into this lead.

In the meantime, let's return to Ghardaïa to inform Brigadier Stellen and hand over our prisoner to him," concluded the sheikh.

They rushed with three cars. They now knew the course would be uneventful.

A few hours later, the small convoy stopped in front of the Ghardaïa gendarmerie.

The sheikh made a sign to his companions.

"Mouktar and Idriss will return to the village," he commanded. "Their mission is over. They will take the Land Rover, which now belongs to the Sahraoui house, and hand it over to my brother-in-law Bachir."

Ranzi turned to his two collaborators to greet them.

"Goodbye, my friends," he said. "Thank you very much for your help. May the almighty Allah protect you. We will meet again very soon in El Goléa, Inch'Allah!"

The two accomplices echoed an Inch'Allah in unison.

The Land Rover's tires screeched on the gravel of the gendarmerie forecourt, and the vehicle resumed the southern track.

Ranzi led Amin and Khaled a little away from the Jeeps, out of earshot of the prisoner, who was unlikely to overhear their conversation. He explained to them in a low voice what awaited them once they arrived in Khenchela. They would need to closely monitor the residence and the comings and goings of the bachaga. They would stay in the only hotel in the village, which, luckily, was located right in front of the Yakobi house.

He then ordered the prisoner to get out of the vehicle, signaled his companions to wait outside, and walked toward the entrance to the gendarmerie post.

Once inside, Stellen saw Ranzi pushing his prisoner.

"What do I see, Sheikh Ahmed? You're bringing us some good game this time?" laughed the policeman in his finest accent.

The smiling Sahrawi replied spontaneously.

"Very fair, Brigadier. You can even specify gallows game. You have before you the murderer of Ben Ali. It was he who, with two accomplices, cowardly tried to murder me yesterday. Without the help of my companions, you would have had one more murder case on your hands."

Stellen examined the individual from head to toe. He grimaced, as though digging into his memory was torturing his mind.

"What's his name?"

"Aziz Abd Elacem," Ranzi replied. "Can you check if he's on file?"

Stellen handcuffed the thug's wrists and pushed him toward the single cell at the back of the room. After double-locking the gate, he went to his office to consult files arranged in alphabetical order on an imposing turnstile. He finally pulled one out after a few minutes of research.

"This is a very big catch, Si Ahmed!" exclaimed the gendarme, showing the card. "I will ask for reinforcements from the Biskra gendarmerie so they can take charge of the bandit. Come and tell me about your adventure over a cup of tea or coffee. I want to know the smallest details."

The Targui made a precise and complete report. The brigadier was amazed. At each step, he caught his breath and nodded in approval.

Having finished his presentation, Ranzi waited for the gendarme's reaction.

"Si Ahmed, Abd Elacem is a highly sought-after character by all the police in the region. He particularly excelled in smuggling weapons between the countries of the East and North Africa. He is suspected of having maintained close ties with the old gangs of mobsters who wreaked havoc after the war in the Aurès."

Stellen paused long enough to let his interlocutor react. Obviously, the Targui seemed distracted.

The gendarme, a fine psychologist, noticed the sheikh's unease and wanted to be understanding.

"Si Ahmed, we will not trouble you over the disappearance of two bandits in the desert. This is clearly a case of self-defense. As for the murder of the gas station attendant, thanks to you, the case is solved. Additionally, you have arrested a dangerous criminal wanted by the police in both Algeria and mainland France."

For obvious reasons, Ranzi did not want to publicize the case. He needed to stay in the shadows at all costs.

"Brigadier, in truth, I would prefer to handle this affair with a certain discretion, especially regarding my involvement. In return, I will ensure the competent authorities know that all credit for this arrest belongs to you.

It will be good for your advancement. I also have an urgent request, if you will listen."

Stellen cracked a smile.

"Please, go ahead, Si Ahmed."

"Well," Ranzi continued, "it's clear that the sponsors of this attack are at least three individuals. For two of them—regarding the bookseller Kalifa and his nephew—there is no doubt that their accomplice has formally identified them. However, the third character in the case, undoubtedly the most important, risks not being prosecuted by the courts. Worse, he's a notable, a bachaga who resides in Khenchela. We must be very careful with Kalifa and not reveal the death of the chaouch prematurely. It's imperative that we obtain a full confession from the bookseller and, above all, that we don't forget to charge his nephew, the telegraph operator. He deliberately provided confidential information to his uncle by communicating a copy of the telegram I sent to my sister. In short, lock them up before they have the chance to flee, and if you can, call me next week—I'll be at my villa in Khenchela."

"Very well, Si Ahmed. I will inform Commissioner Petit, who is in charge of the Nememcha police. I suggest you go see him as soon as you return to Khenchela."

Ranzi thanked the brigadier and took his leave. He exited the police station like a rocket, climbed into his Jeep, and ordered the departure.

"On the way to Khenchela," he said.

CHAPTER 7

Khenchela - Sunday, April 10, 1954

Around noon, two dusty vehicles stopped in front of the bazaar on rue de Paris. Ranzi turned off the ignition and addressed his two companions, who were traveling in the second Jeep.

"The Hôtel du Chabor is just opposite. Take a double room there for the month. Tell the manager that you are Targis traders who have come to Khenchela for business, make yourselves comfortable, and have something to eat. You'll meet me at nightfall at my villa, number 36 rue Gérôme-Bertania. See you soon, my friends."

He then walked briskly toward the heavy oak door next to the window of the Grand Bazaar. It opened with a slight creak. He crossed the long, dark corridor, quickly passed through the small courtyard, and climbed the steps leading to the second floor, where Isaac seemed to be waiting for him. He had probably heard the two off-roaders stop in front of the door.

"Go quickly take a shower, Ranzi. It will help you wash off all the sand. We'll discuss things after lunch," Isaac said, welcoming his old friend.

The Targui didn't need to be asked twice. He basked for a long time in the hot shower, whistling. Finally, some fresh water, he thought to himself under the creamy foam. He dressed in the personal effects that Fatma had provided and said his midday prayer. Once ready and relaxed, he crossed the threshold of the large dining room where his friends were waiting for him.

After the joy of reunion, he was bombarded with questions from overexcited children.

"Tell us everything, Uncle Ranzi. How was your crossing of the desert in a Jeep? Would you have lost the habit of traveling on the back of a camel or riding Caïd, your legendary thoroughbred?" Sarah quipped.

"Believe me, princess, I would have preferred the camel if I'd had the time, but I was in a hurry. I swallowed half the sand of the Sahara at the wheel of my Jeep, which is not as sober as our good old humped mounts. The road is passable until Touggourt. It's not very busy, but it's imperative to stop and pull over to the side as soon as a truck comes from the opposite direction, otherwise…"

"After Touggourt, it's just tracks, a few chotts, and occasionally feshfesh, which is better to avoid at the risk of getting bogged down. It's hard to cover more than three hundred kilometers in a day, which makes it almost three days of hiking in the desert—two nights spent under the stars, as I did on the way back, or at best, in pathetic hotels when you can find a free room. The daring traveler has every interest in calculating his water and fuel supplies carefully, because he won't find a service station for hundreds of kilometers. The last civilized bastion is in Touggourt. Finally, I'm starting to get old. I had trouble with the huge temperature differences between day and night. After five years of absence, I've softened a little."

"You must have come across a few caravans on your way, Uncle Ranzi?" asked Dror.

"No, no caravans, only a few convoys of trucks. The caravaneers don't take these winding tracks, which often lengthen their route. They prefer to follow other, more direct routes, but they are punctuated by stops at various water points."

Nathan, very interested in the story, asked, "And how do they find each other?"

"Thanks to the stars at night and the sun by day. Further south, we orient ourselves at night according to the Southern Cross, which is the emblem of our flag, the Sahrawis. The caravaneers have other clues. For example, they know the direction of the prevailing winds, like the Sirocco. Today, they all have a compass, and as a last resort, they let the camels naturally direct them to the nearest water points because their mounts can smell water for miles. But a good Targui knows exactly where he is, by instinct, practically anywhere in the vastness of the Sahara. Still, it's complicated, because with the dunes constantly moving, you can't rely on reliable tracking depending on the relief or the landscape."

"How are Rachida and her little family doing?" Rachel finally asked, eager to hear from her best friend.

"Very well, thank you. She's gotten used to the harsh life of the caravaneers. Her children are beautiful and very endearing. She asked me to kiss you. She misses you a lot, especially you, little sister. Rachida hopes to convince her husband to stop off at Khenchela in a few weeks at most."

"Wonderful! I'll cook her a good homemade butter couscous, with that wonderful whey that Fatma prepares for us. Now, kids, his highness needs to rest, and I guess Uncle Ranzi is starving," Rachel said. "Let's sit down to eat."

Sarah finished clearing the table while Isaac poured another cup of tea for his guest. He was waiting for his youngest daughter to disappear into the kitchen to start the real discussion.

Once alone with Ranzi, Isaac, more preoccupied than ever, asked the question that was burning on his lips.

"How was your extraordinary meeting in El Goléa?"

"Very well, much better than I expected," Ranzi admitted with a smile. "The dignitaries unanimously share our point of view. We, the Targuis, must under no circumstances engage in a belligerent process against France. We have little or no criticism of the Metropolis, so what would be the point of a revolution? Anyway, there's nothing that can't be resolved through negotiations. We don't think we are the only ones refusing to go down the path of rebellion. There are other Berber tribes all the way to the North, who are even ready to fight alongside France in the event of an armed conflict. But the best thing for our clan is to observe neutrality to avoid a civil war."

Isaac nodded. The Targuis were responsible people who could be trusted without hesitation; he had never doubted that.

"Wise decision, but please be careful. We have absolutely no idea who we're dealing with."

"I will be careful, Yssic, I promise. I know who I'm meeting, and when the time comes, I'll let you know. But I also need to inform you about the few misadventures that have befallen my burnous, both on the way there and on the way back," Ranzi added, with an enigmatic air.

He then took on a solemn, monotone tone as he recounted the epic journey he had just experienced, omitting no details, and allowing no emotion to show through.

Ranzi's story held Isaac in suspense. Isaac began to think deeply, then suddenly broke the silence.

"There are two possible motives for this attack. The first could be of a villainous nature, which could explain Kalifa's attitude. The bookseller must suspect that you have an impressive library and could be interested in your particular hobby, shall we say, in the 'esoteric' department. You've been ordering extremely rare books from him for decades, and he smells a juicy business opportunity, given your pronounced taste for old works. Add to that the rumors circulating about your fortune... and a question I must ask: where did he get his information about the Grimoire of Abraham the Jew?"

"The second motive is more serious than you think. It could be the F.N.A. behind this, and I'd bet a Tunisian donut against an Algerian zlabïa (honey cake) that the Bachaga set up this scheme by exploiting Kalifa's greed. But do you think he could have acted alone?"

"I don't think so, and I've almost reached the same conclusions as you. Tomorrow morning, I'll pay a courtesy visit to the Bachaga. It's high time I give him my civilities. Like you, I remain convinced that there are others behind this. The bookseller and the Bachaga are, in my eyes, just pawns in a larger game. Well, we'll see."

Isaac nodded in agreement while Ranzi, changing the subject, asked in a deceptively authoritative tone:

"Now, ask Dror to come. We need to talk about his future."

Isaac went into the next room to fetch Dror, asking him to speak with Ranzi, then slipped away, pretending to be busy elsewhere.

Dror, intrigued, approached cautiously. He wondered why the Sheik had suddenly wanted to speak with him. He didn't recall saying anything inappropriate or shocking lately.

"Do you want to see me, Uncle Ranzi?"

"Yes, cheeky youngster. I would like to know if you are worthy of receiving the very special education that our grandfathers reserved for their most deserving children."

Dror didn't like that kind of question at all. Suspicious, he replied bluntly, "Uncle Ranzi, I'm going to disappoint you. I'm only thirteen years old, I still have so much to learn, and can I really be asked to prove myself at my age? It doesn't seem very serious."

"That's exactly the kind of answer I expected from you," replied the half-fig, half-grape Targui. "Your modesty is one of the qualities you need to possess in order to be worthy of the teaching I wish to give you."

"Listen to me carefully," the Sheik ordered. "I will explain in a few words what it's all about. If it suits you, we will continue together until your apprenticeship is complete. Otherwise, you need not agree to sacrifice your leisure time for two or three years."

After a few seconds of silence, Ranzi resumed his explanation in a soft and pleasant voice.

"Our predecessors, grandfathers, and great-grandfathers taught us three disciplines to make us real men. These are the disciplines I propose to teach you.

First, they bequeathed to us the Cabala, an esoteric science whose keys allow us to solve many enigmas.

Secondly, they explored nature in their own way and laid the foundations of science par excellence: Ancient Philosophy. They gave us the means to penetrate the interior of the atom to extract the Quintessence, the Pure Spirit—Pur Purum, as the Latinists say—that is to say, our Purple, the Carbuncle, the composition of which I will teach you later, known as the Secret Scretorum by the Adepts.

Finally, they invented martial arts. Er… it is not certain that your grandfather would have approved of this discipline being part of your education, had he still been in this world. But I'm sure he understands me from the high place he's in now. Evolution constantly transforms our world into a kind of jungle in which predators reign supreme. Beware of those who do not have the appropriate weapons to defend themselves.

You know the main principles now. Do you want to continue this training?"

The suddenness of this proposition, more than its strangeness, caught Dror off guard. He began to think a hundred miles an hour.

What is this special kind of learning? he wondered. What had my father been up to with Uncle Ranzi? The Cabala, the Philosophy—still makes sense. But martial arts? It's incongruous. What's hidden beneath all of this? And what about my hobbies? What becomes of them? Then there's the Bar Mitzvah—its preparation? Not serious, Dror thought. My father must have received similar training. It's all becoming clear. Maybe I shouldn't refuse. But why me and not Nathan? If it doesn't suit me, I can always quit. Uncle Ranzi and my father certainly won't mind.

Finally, the boy blurted out:

"Preparing for my Bar Mitzvah must be questioned, but I assume you've already discussed it with my father. That's fine with me, Uncle Ranzi. When do we start?"

"Next Thursday, at eight o'clock in the morning, at my villa on rue Gérôme-Bertania, number 36," replied the Targui with satisfaction. "From now on, you will be my disciple, and you will call me 'master' each time you speak to me. This is the tradition, and it must be respected. Without tradition, a man is nothing. As for your Bar Mitzvah, don't worry—you can easily pass your exam with flying colors. Your father assured me you were ready a long time ago. You just need to maintain your skills.

Now you may go, disciple. And don't forget to wear sports clothes."

"Well, master, see you next Thursday," Dror said before slipping away.

At that moment, Dror didn't realize that he had just made the most extraordinary decision of his life. This choice would later shape him into an extraordinary character.

CHAPTER 8

Monday, April 13, 1954

Punctual as always, Khaled and Amin rang the doorbell of the villa at eight o'clock sharp. They removed their shoes immediately after entering the hall and were ushered by Ali into the large Moorish salon.

Seated on an ottoman, Sir Ahmed Ranzi El Sahraoui awaited them, savoring a still-steaming cup of mint tea.

"Hello, my friends. Help yourself," he said, gesturing to the coffee table. "You will escort me this morning; I propose we go greet His Excellency the bachaga Abou Dahrem. While I chat with him, you'll discreetly observe the surroundings of his house. Your mission over the next few days will be to monitor all the comings and goings of the bachaga and his visitors. You'll report to me here whenever necessary. Plan for two to three weeks. Then, if all goes well, you will head home."

Ranzi paused for a few seconds, his mind shifting gears. It was better to visit Police Commissioner Petit first, he decided.

"Let's make a quick detour by the police station," he ordered. "I must make a courtesy visit, and I'll take the opportunity to check on a few unresolved matters. We'll meet the bachaga immediately afterward."

They climbed into the Jeep driven by Khaled, and the vehicle came to a stop a few minutes later in front of the main entrance of the town hall, which also housed the police station in its left wing.

As his companions waited quietly in the Jeep, Ranzi strode confidently into the tall white building. At the sheik's request, the officer at the reception promptly informed

Superintendent Petit by intercom. Petit nodded several times before motioning for the visitor to take the stairs on the right.

"Police Commissioner Petit will see you immediately, Sir Ahmed."

Petit was from the mainland, like most police officers and high-ranking gendarmes in the colonies. Slender and tall, he wore a light navy blue suit and an open-necked white shirt that reflected his apparent nonchalance, though it was not without elegance.

Appointed to lead the Khencheloise police two or three years earlier, Petit had never met the Targui before. He greeted Ranzi warmly, projecting a friendly demeanor as he shook the sheik's hand firmly.

"My respects, Sheikh Ahmed. I am very honored to meet you. So, you are back? Definitely, I hope?"

"In Algeria, of course. In Khenchela for a while; I don't know yet because I intend to return to my true homeland, the Sahara."

"Sheik, please excuse me," replied the Police Commissioner, glancing at his wristwatch. "I must meet our mayor in a few minutes. So let me cut to the chase; we'll resume our civilities later, if you don't mind."

"Please Commissioner," Ranzi agreed.

"I am aware of your adventures in the Sahara. I had a long telephone conversation with Brigadier Stellen of the National Gendarmerie last Friday. Don't believe all the gossip about the inter-agency differences. Here, we take pride in cooperation, always returning the favor," he said, winking.

Petit appeared to chuckle quietly before revealing, "I don't know what you did to Stellen; he swears by you. Nevertheless, we arrested and imprisoned Kalifa the bookseller and his nephew Omar—all operations ceased. We questioned them, but of course, they deny being part of a plot to eliminate you. Soon, we'll bring Abd Elacem under good escort to confront them.

Nonetheless, Stellen has Abd Elacem's damning testimony, and since only the bookseller's nephew could have informed him about your departure to the south, they'll have a hard time exculpating themselves."

"Thank you for this valuable information, Mr. Petit. Would you be so kind as to tell me if Abd Elacem has made any other confessions? The motive for this assault seems trivial to me," Ranzi admitted, feigning curiosity; he wanted to know if any other confidential details had emerged in the investigation.

"You're absolutely right; nobody gets killed over a simple book. It apparently concerns a book by a certain Ibrahim," Petit said.

"Ibrahim is the Arabic transcription of Abraham," Ranzi interjected. "It's not just any old book but a six-hundred-year-old manuscript of which there's only one copy, the legendary grimoire of Abraham the Jew. It's worth a fortune, and I have been entrusted with its care. However, I must emphasize that this aggression is absurd—I never travel with my collection of old works; it would be too bulky and cumbersome. I keep these masterpieces safely stored in a strongroom in my villa, and no one has attempted to rob me so far."

"Ha ha!" Petit exclaimed. "So this is Ibrahim's mysterious book. I thought it was a version of the Koran or something similar." He acknowledged, "It is you who are being targeted; there's no doubt about it. By the way, would you happen to know why and who wants you gone?" he asked innocently, frowning.

"Not in the least, Commissioner!" the sheik shot back, maintaining a facade of innocence. "As you know, I've just returned from a pilgrimage after five years in exile. There's no reason for anyone to personally attack me; absolutely none."

"Listen, Sheikh Ahmed," continued the perplexed policeman, "I promise to do everything in my power to unravel this affair. I will contact you as soon as I have any news. Be very careful; these people definitely have powerful allies. You never know what the future holds in situations like these."

"Thanks for the advice, Commissioner. I've been vigilant for several days now, twenty-four hours a day. I'm sure you'll carry out your duties to the best of your ability, and I look forward to hearing from you very soon."

He nearly departed but reversed his decision at the last moment. "Oh, I almost forgot. I came to give you this," Ranzi said, pulling a plastic case from his pocket. "These are the Land Rover papers that Kalifa lent to his accomplices. My men found them in Abd Elacem's pockets, and I hope they serve as evidence of the bookseller's guilt in this case."

"Where is that Land Rover now?" the policeman asked casually.

"In the desert, of course," the Targui replied ironically, "somewhere in the desert."

Ranzi took his leave of Commissioner Petit and quickly descended the police station steps. He hadn't learned anything beyond what he already knew. Disappointed, he joined Khaled, who had parked the Jeep in the shade of a mulberry tree while waiting for him.

The off-roader sped through the western district of Khenchela. Abu Dahrem lived in a large villa on the edge of the village, an imposing structure in an area typically leading to rough maquis. The estate was encircled by a long, high whitewashed masonry wall, likely topped with shards of glass.

Ranzi approached the heavy carved wooden gate adorned with characteristic North African arabesques, a type of moucharabieh common in the region. He pulled the cord attached to a bell and called out two or three times to ensure he was heard. Finally, a chaouch decided to half-open the door and asked in Arabic who he should announce.

"Tell your master that Prince Ahmed Ranzi El Sahraoui wishes to speak with him," the Targui proclaimed proudly, knowing how much titles impressed men and opened doors.

After several bows and respectful gestures, the chaouch hurried inside the villa and returned two minutes later.

"Si Abu Dahrem would like to receive you, Sheikh Ahmed, please come in."

The bachagha was comfortably seated in a large wicker chair cushioned with thick green velvet. Abu Dahrem was obese, struggling to breathe properly; each puff of air rushed in with an annoying hiss through his nostrils. He regularly wiped the sweat from his fat, neckless face, which was buried in a gold-embroidered gandoura.

"Sheikh Ahmed Ranzi El Sahraoui, what a surprise! May Allah bless you, welcome to my humble home."

"Hello, Sir Abou Dahrem. Thank you for seeing me without an appointment," Ranzi replied, stepping forward. "However, I don't want to take up your valuable time, so I'll be blunt. Why did you attempt to have me killed by Kalifa's minions?"

Abu Dahrem paled, beads of sweat immediately trickling down his already moist forehead.

"But you're mistaken, Sir Ahmed! I don't understand a word of what you're saying," he replied, a sneer creeping onto his lips.

"Oh yes! Let me clarify in case you're considering denying this felony," Ranzi said, raising his voice. "You named yourself as a potential culprit. My people will avenge me if anything happens to me. They will eliminate you and all your descendants. Do I make myself clear?"

Fear registered on the bachagha's contorted face. Realizing his interlocutor was serious, he still persisted in denial.

"But this is nonsense!" he stammered. "I swear by Allah that I do not know what you are talking about."

Ranzi began listing the facts calmly, a deliberate strategy to persuade.

"So stop blaspheming! You had me followed by your chaouch last week. I caught him in the act with my friend Isaac Yakobi, and he undoubtedly reported back to you. Then you somehow collaborated with Kalifa, sending your chaouchs after me, in cahoots with an arms trafficker named Abd Elacem, who is currently under Interpol scrutiny, as well as another accomplice whose identity remains unknown. Even worse, your men cowardly murdered a gas station attendant in Ghardaïa after torturing him horrifically. They could not eliminate me, Ranzi mocked. By Allah, they failed!"

The Targui continued his indictment in the same icy tone. "I set a trap for the three bastards you sent after me, you fat pig! With my men's help, we eliminated your chaouch and the unknown accomplice. In the end, we caught the third miscreant, who is now in police custody. Kalifa and his nephew are also incarcerated. You must be aware of this; news travels fast with the Arabic drum, correct?

I won't repeat myself: why are you targeting me?"

As Ranzi continued speaking, he gradually moved closer to the bachaga until he could almost touch him. The color drained from Abou Dahrem's face, and his sweating intensified.

Suddenly, an uncontrollable tremor seized the bachagha as Ranzi feigned a strangulation gesture. The Targui hesitated momentarily; the urge to eliminate the wretched man was profound. However, Ranzi wasn't a killer, and once dead, the bachagha would no longer serve any purpose.

He took a step back, resuming the conversation, having grasped that, for some unknown reason, the bachagha would not speak. It seemed he was more afraid of his sponsors than of Ranzi himself.

"Abu Dahrem, I spare you, but only temporarily," he added hastily. "I know what you're plotting with the F.N.A., even though I'm unaware of the start date for hostilities. On behalf of the Saharawi Council, of which I am the representative, I will dictate the procedure you must follow for the coming years."

On the verge of a breakdown, the bachagha wanted to protest, but Ranzi silenced him with a gesture.

"Let me continue, or I'll strangle you right now!" the Targui shouted, hardening his tone. "You will inform your associates that the Sahrawis will not involve themselves in your criminal schemes, even if you believe you serve a noble cause by killing innocent people. We will remain neutral as long as you do not harm the populations of the Aurès sector and, of course, of the Sahara. By 'populations,' I mean Muslims, Jews, and Christians. All religions and ethnicities included—do you understand?"

He allowed his opponent a moment to breathe. The fat dignitary was nearly gasping for air. Ranzi wanted to ensure the message reached the separatist movement's leaders but also knew that might not suffice to pacify fanatics.

Nonetheless, he pressed on with firmness. "At the first sign of trouble, should you disregard our demands, my Targui have orders to side with the metropolitan forces. They will come armed to the teeth, beginning in the Aurès, starting with you. So relay this message to your fat pig bosses!" he declared, pointing at the bachaga's belly.

Moving toward the door to leave, Ranzi paused to give a final warning. "There's no need to attempt anything against me or my friends, the Yakobis. You won't survive it for more than twenty-four hours. Also, understand that the police are just waiting for my word to lock you up."

Ranzi walked back to the waiting Jeep without hurrying, allowing his anger to dissipate.

Meanwhile, the bachagha picked up his phone to dial a number in advance in Algiers.

CHAPTER 9

Thursday, April 15, 1954

Dror was on time for his very first lesson.

Very relaxed, he activated the bell of the main gate, whistling. After a few seconds, Ali came to open the door, guiding him directly to the basement without saying a word. Along the way, they passed through a domed vestibule with columns chiseled from floor to ceiling. The entrance was imposing, worthy of a maharajah's palace. The floor of the vestibule was completely covered with large slabs of white marble adorned with dark green cabochons. This was the first time young Yakobi had been received in Ranzi's villa, and he was greatly impressed by the striking architecture of the beautiful residence.

The building, large and Moorish in style, was constructed on three levels: the ground floor, the first floor, and the basement. The latter seemed enormous, likely covering an area much larger than that of the villa itself. Several rooms were accessible, distributed on either side of a long, wide corridor. The chaouch opened the first door on the right and let Dror in. The master sat barefoot in the lotus position, deep in meditation. In the nearly empty room, the floor was covered with a thin mattress that seemed quite firm, placed on a slightly raised wooden platform.

Upon seeing Dror, Ranzi exhaled loudly and welcomed his disciple.

"It's a dojo," he said, forestalling the teenager's question. "Take off your shoes and sit down in front of me. We are going to start the first martial arts class. The program for the months and years to come will remain unchanged. We will begin in the cool of the morning with exercises in yoga, judo, karate, or tai-kwan-do. I will explain what all these words mean. Then, we will move on to purely intellectual exercises, concluding with practical work. This will allow you to go home for lunch and enjoy an afternoon nap. Does that suit you, my disciple?"

"Yes, Master."

"Good. You will have to do the yoga exercises every day that the Great Architect does and devote a quarter of an hour to half an hour, if possible. You'll see, at a certain stage of practice, it will no longer feel like a chore. Meditation will become a necessity for you, just like the air you breathe or the food you need to survive. Of course, you can ask me all the questions you deem necessary for your learning during the intellectual exercises and practical work. However, you will be forbidden to speak during martial arts lessons; it's useless and could distract you.

Remember the three basic principles of training: breathing, concentration, and balance. If you master these three principles, you will emerge victorious from every trial."

Dror began to learn basic movements, warm-up exercises, controlled breathing, and balance exercises—repeating them over and over again. After an hour, he seemed completely exhausted.

Ranzi had been watching him for a while and suspended training as soon as he sensed the teenager weakening. It wasn't an endurance exercise he wanted him to undergo.

"We stop the Dror physical culture session. We are entitled to a fifteen-minute break followed by a good shower. Then, may I offer you a drink—iced tea or orange juice?"

"Very sweet tea, Master. I feel completely exhausted."

"It's normal; your body must gradually adapt to physical exercises to which it is not accustomed. In two or three sessions, you will be completely insensitive to pain, and the aches will fade. I am very satisfied with your training. You have good reflexes and an excellent musculature, which is due, I think, to the swimming exercises that you do regularly in Hammam El Salhine, as well as your daily bicycle rides."

At the back of the training room, a door opened onto the hammam. Ranzi had built a real sauna there, imported directly from Finland, attached to a large bathroom with fully tiled walls and two showers. The master and his disciple took a refreshing shower and then returned to the dojo to dry off.

Ranzi struck the gong with a hammer blow. The chaouch appeared as if by magic, carrying a tray generously filled with drinks and delicious cakes.

"Pour us some tea and a fresh orange juice, please, Ali."

Then, addressing his young disciple, he said, "Help yourself, take some cakes—don't be embarrassed above all. While you restore, I will explain to you the reasons why I want to give you close-combat training.

To succeed in life, you need pugnacity, self-sacrifice, ironclad determination, and the ability to accept failures with stoicism. In adversity, you must have unshakeable self-confidence. All these qualities are not innate; individuals are endowed with them in varying degrees. However, anyone can acquire these qualities with proper training.

The sages of the Far East understood this long ago. They have therefore developed all these techniques for one singular purpose. Martial arts teach you not only how to defend yourself against an opponent, but that is secondary. They will teach you to trust yourself in all circumstances. The confidence you will acquire will paradoxically make you less bellicose; you may sometimes come across as a coward when you recognize that fighting is futile and will not bring a solution to the problem you face.

The philosophy lesson is over; it's time to get down to business. We are going to approach the intellectual part of your training," continued the master with a touch of irony.

"Do you know what the Cabal is?" he asked suddenly.

"Master, I know that the Jewish Kabbalah consists of dissecting the writings of the Old Testament to reveal mysterious messages. It is subdivided into three segments. However, one must be over forty to study it without risking madness."

"I meant Cabal with a 'C' and not with a 'K.' With a 'C,' Cabala has a completely different meaning and a very different origin. With a 'K,' it is the Hebrew Kabbalah—from kebalé, meaning tradition—the tool used by Jewish scholars to comment on or interpret biblical texts. With a 'C,' Cabala becomes the art of deciphering the mysterious coded texts that ancient Adepts wrote for other Adepts. I would say the Cabala is a real esoteric language.

This cryptographic art comes from ancient Greece, where it was closely linked to mythology. Greek and Egyptian fables and legends are almost all closely related to the operations of the Grand Magisterium.

"Speaking of languages, what options did you choose at school?" He asked.

"In Khenchela, there isn't much choice, Master—Arabic and English."

"It's very good, but not enough. I will reveal an important secret to you: the keys to open the cabalistic texts are hidden in the Latin or Greek roots of the words used by the great masters."

"Not very rational, is it?" Ranzi said with a knowing wink.

"Master, this encryption system seems to lack precision," Dror pointed out. "This leaves the door open to multiple and even contradictory interpretations. How can one be sure of the transcription in such a context?"

Definitely, thought the Targui, I like this kid; he's just like his father at the same age.

"You're absolutely right," Ranzi replied. "This is done intentionally to confuse the layman. Know that to overcome this difficulty, you need not only a good knowledge of ancient Greek and Latin but also a lot of insight and solid erudition. All of this can only be achieved through long learning and deep meditation.

"The Cabale," Ranzi continued in a confidential tone, "is the language of the initiated and not that of the profane. I'm going to ask Isaac to teach you Latin and ancient Greek."

"I didn't know my father knew these two dead languages, Master."

Ranzi smiled. There were many secrets that he and his foster brother shared. He led young Dror to another room.

"Here," he said, inserting a key into the lock of a very heavy door, "this is the secret laboratory where we will soon study all the practical aspects of Hermetic Philosophy."

The lab looked like a set from a science fiction film.

In this large room, illuminated by many neon lights, the floor and walls were tiled with shiny white earthenware. There was an acrid, indefinable smell, likely due to the fumes from an ongoing experiment.

Not a speck of dust could be found on the white benches, where various devices were spread out. A few balloons topped with coils, some test tubes, and a centrifuge were present. There was a precision scale, a trebuchet in its glass case, and further down, a Roberval, useful for larger weighings. This was arranged on a workbench alongside various tools typically used by blacksmiths and jewelers—pliers, hammers, and crucibles—all neatly stored.

A large ventilated chapel dominated one corner of the room, the indispensable fume hood for conducting experiments that could generate toxic gases. Behind the thick glass pane were an electric oven, a still, and several Bunsen burners. One of them was on, emitting an almost imperceptible blue flame under a Pyrex glass balloon. The contents, a dark magma, were stirred by bubbles escaping from time to time: an experiment was unfolding in silence in this secret lair.

In the opposite corner of the room stood an imposing oven built from refractory bricks, topped by a stainless steel flue. The fireplace, visible through the opening at the bottom, was specially designed to use butane gas. There were four fire ramps that could be lit together or separately, depending on the heating power required. The fuel—a battery of several large gas cylinders equipped with manifolds and a pressure regulator—was placed, for safety, behind a protective wall built to the left of the furnace. This setup ensured continuous heating for several weeks. The floor of the oven was secured with a thick cast iron door mounted on hinges. Small cast iron windows arranged on each side of the door allowed for visual inspection.

To accentuate the surreal atmosphere that reigned in the lab, strange mottos were written in white chalk, in fine, regular handwriting, on a large blackboard fixed to the back wall.

You could read: « *Una Via, Una Re, Una Dispositione* » *(one Way, one Matter, one Vessel),*

« *Si te fata vocant* » *(if the fates invite you),*

« *V.I.T.R.I.O.L.E.U.M* »,

and: « *May the stars of Diana Horned and Venus be favorable to you»*

And finally, a lapidary formula *"RER, RERE"* repeated three times.

What could these strange mottoes mean, impenetrable to the layman, and what special activities could take place in such a laboratory? Witchcraft? Dror wondered, increasingly intrigued, as he continued his exploration with a suddenly heightened interest.

In the center of the laboratory, he noticed an old writing desk made of patinated oak, enhanced with marquetry—an extremely rare piece for which the master had paid a fortune at an auction, perhaps in mainland France. On the large tray rested an old book, bound in full calfskin, adorned with strange colorful illuminations, as well as a notebook in which Ranzi noted his observations.

Driven by a growing curiosity, the teenager was drawn to the unusual appearance of the work. He approached the writing desk slowly to examine the grimoire in detail.

Dror first noticed that it was an ancient manuscript, somewhat soiled by multiple stains of mold, with very beautiful multicolored illuminations on its pages, along with handwritten text. Gradually leaning closer to the masterpiece, he found that he could decipher, albeit with some difficulty, all the inscriptions.

He turned to the Targui. "Master," he said, "it is Hebrew. I can read this manuscript, but I have some difficulty understanding its meaning."

"No wonder, Dror. These are very technical and esoteric terms that you are not yet accustomed to. Isaac, your father, had promised to translate it for me just before my exile, but he didn't…"

Dror didn't let Ranzi finish her sentence. "Master, the monument that appears in the background here, in the illumination, could it not be the Treasure Tower, one of the last standing towers of the Château de Chinon?"

Ranzi jumped. "By Allah! How can you know that? Not everyone recognizes the monument in the background. It is merely a banal illumination that doesn't relate to anything concrete. I've often wondered what this tower might represent. Esoterically, a dungeon can be likened to our athanor, our secret oven. So, there's nothing particularly mysterious about it appearing in an alchemical treatise."

"But no, Master, I am sure. The Château de Chinon stretches out before us, and there are several towers, including that of Jeanne la Pucelle and the Treasure Tower. The illustration is undeniably faithful; I can't be wrong."

The Targui sighed, admitting to himself that he liked this young one more and more. "How can you be so sure of yourself, oh cultivated disciple?"

"Very simply, Master. The day after we met at the market, I asked our history teacher to tell us about the Templars. He devoted two hours of class to a fascinating presentation. When he reached the time of the arrest of Jacques de Molay and the imprisonment of the Grand Masters of the Temple, our teacher showed us images of the castle in which the Templars were imprisoned, where they underwent the Question. These images came from a great encyclopedia, and it was indeed the castle of Chinon. The teacher even mentioned bizarre, enigmatic inscriptions on the walls of the prison that the Templars carved into the stone. I assure you, the image on the cover of this grimoire is indeed that of the Château de Chinon."

Ranzi sighed, as the solution to the riddle began to take shape thanks to this first revelation. "Congratulations, Dror," said the master, very pleased with his disciple's insight.

"You've solved, at least partially, a problem that your father and I have been grappling with for five years! We'll discuss this further later. Now, take a good look around you."

"Ranzi advised. "This is no ordinary chemical laboratory or metallurgical workshop. It's a bit of both. Right here, with your father, we study the secret reactions of old Spagyria, the ancestor of our chemistry. We are retracing the journey that great Adepts like Artéphius, Basil Valentin, or Philalethes made before us. However, I have a secret to share: we have a slight advantage over them."

The master paused to hold his disciple in suspense. "It's simple," he said, smiling broadly. "We have all their works, ultra-modern equipment, and to top it off, I am an excellent chemist."

He let the teenager walk around the room a few times, counting the imposing equipment and contemplating the mysterious reactions that were taking place. Once Dror's curiosity was satisfied, the Targui spoke again.

"You certainly haven't tackled the chemistry and physics lessons in the complementary course yet, have you?"

"But yes, Master, I just started my first lessons this year."

"Good. I will therefore be able to complete your teaching in these two disciplines a year or two ahead of your program. It won't be too difficult; you will see."

The sheik gave the teenager a friendly pat, gently pushing him towards a large glass cabinet. He opened the right door and reached under the middle shelf in the right corner. A slight click sounded, and the entire wardrobe pivoted backward, revealing another room hidden in the basement.

Dror was amazed. He had once again plunged into a new magical universe and couldn't help but let out a whistle of admiration. It was a library—a magnificent one! Oak shelving ran along three large walls, filled to overflowing with books of all kinds and origins. Ancient grimoires protected by thick leather covers, others adorned with splendid metal fittings, seemed to have awaited a reader for centuries. There were thousands of unusual books—apocryphal Latin or Greek editions and reproductions of more recent works well hidden from prying eyes.

The titles displayed on the edges of the books were written in various languages—German, English, Latin, Greek, Spanish, Old French, and even Hebrew. A whole section of the library was entirely devoted to works by Arab authors. This collection was likely worth a fortune—an invaluable historical and scientific heritage. How many generations had managed to amass all these gems of very special literature? Dror wondered, perhaps dozens?

"A few dozen generations of Yakobi and Sahrawi have worked to accumulate these masterpieces of Hermetic literature," Ranzi confided, as if he had read his disciple's thoughts. "The Sahrawis aren't the only owners; this library also belongs to the Yakobi, associated equally, and thus to you by extension."

The teenager found himself speechless. The Targui had just revealed an extraordinary secret, and rather than rejoicing over this fabulous heritage, he pondered how all these successive generations of Muslims and Jews—Sahrawis and Yakobi—had united to create such an incredible compilation. He then realized that he, Dror, might be part of the next generation tasked with completing the library if all went according to his father's and Ranzi's plans.

"Hey, pull yourself together, disciple! This is not the time to dream."

An imposing black Empire-style desk, with finely chiseled gilding on its corners, furnished the back of the room, along with two comfortable seats for visitors. On top of the desk was an all-leather desk pad, crafted in Tuati or Mauritanian style.

"Come, sit down, Dror. What you saw in this secret room is a true treasure. Do you know that the value of all these works is inestimable? On a scientific level, I mean. Now, we are going to devote some time to the history of chemistry, which is also the history of science.

We have to go back to the Bronze Age, around 5,000 years BC—that is, when the first copper alloy objects were created and discovered in Mesopotamia. This marked the beginning of a new era, one that heralded the true rise of humanity with the discovery of the arts of fire. A millennium later, the first antimony vases appeared. Note that detail," insisted Ranzi, "the antimony to Sumers."

Still in the same region, gold purification techniques emerged 3,000 years before our era in Babylonia. The oldest of the purification techniques utilized stibine, the natural sulfide of antimony. This technique was well known to your ancestors, the Hebrews. It is written in the Old Testament and in an ancient manuscript, the Aesh Mezaref, whose title means "Fire of refining." Another technique used for refining early on in Sumers is cupellation, practiced with lead.

"Master, that is metallurgy, not chemistry."

"No, young disciple, metallurgy is a chemical discipline. To transform ores, it is necessary to undergo chemical processes and reactions. Metallurgy is actually more chemistry than physics. Aside from gold and platinum, most common metals do not exist natively. You must go through chemistry to reduce them to a metallic state, and that's where it gets tricky."

Ranzi paused for just a moment, observing his student. He smiled with satisfaction, noticing that Dror was captivated by this initial presentation.

"Indeed," resumed the master. "Take antimony as an example: it does not exist, or hardly exists, in its native state. Its most common ore is a sulfide—you already know that, I think. Here, the natives call it kohl."

The young apprentice seized the opportunity to contribute. "Excuse me, Master. Kohl does mean black in Arabic, doesn't it? My sister told me that Oriental women use very fine kohl powder moistened with their own saliva as a special eye shadow. This practice dates back quite far; the Old Testament even mentions it. Khôl is therefore the Arabic word for stibine. But why does the French word alcohol have a different meaning?"

"Your remarks are relevant, oh illustrious disciple," quipped the Targui. "But beware. Moroccans only use common galena, which they also call kohl; to my knowledge, they do not have any stibine deposits at home. Galena is merely a substitute for eye makeup, but that's where it ends. As for alcohol, that term designates our black stone, kohl, since the prefix al is the Arabic article. Due to misunderstandings in the teachings of the great masters during the Middle Ages, scholars once believed that ordinary distillation was the fundamental operation to obtain the Philosopher's Stone. They distilled wine and called the resulting product alcohol. Since that product exhibited new properties, they thought it was the quintessence.

"Finally, the teaching of history often leaves much to be desired. You may have noticed that antimony was known at least 3,000 years before our era. Despite many pieces of evidence accepted by scientists, some historians claim that the discovery of this metal is attributed to the great Adept of the 15th century, the Benedictine monk Basil Valentin. This is merely because this scientist wrote a book entirely devoted to this metal and its derivatives entitled 'Le Chariot Triomphal de l'Antimoine.' You always need to be wary of stereotypes."

The young disciple was following his first lesson with genuine interest. He was now convinced that the Targui would provide him with a teaching reserved for a privileged class of initiates. He vowed not to waste this opportunity.

"Master, so you and my father are working together to find the Philosopher's Stone, aren't you? In school, we learned that it was a pipe dream, a mad quest that sent half the planet racing in the Middle Ages and caused more drama than the gold rush in America last century. How can such fruitless research still be pursued in the twentieth century?"

"The great line of adepts did not die out with the advent of the Atomic Age, Dror, and it is not a chimerical quest. Be careful not to take everything your teachers teach you at face value. They do not possess all the data concerning the problem, far from it, even if modern theories are beginning to flesh out. Soon you will understand…"

Ranzi preferred to provide his teachings progressively, rather than abruptly. He concluded his thoughts with an understanding look, signaling that the day's lesson was over. "It's past noon; time for you to head home. Can you please ask your father to see me without fail at the end of the day?"

It was well past six o'clock when Isaac pulled the golden chain that operated the little bell. Night would soon fall. Ali immediately opened the door for him and led him into the villa.

The shopkeeper saw Ranzi sitting on the thick woolen rug in the middle of the large living room. He seemed lost in thought over a steaming cup of tea. Isaac took off his shoes before entering.

"Did you ask to see me, old brother?"

"Come on, Isaac, and tell me what you think of these photos," Ranzi said, holding up a stack of color shots. "Help yourself to some lemonade; it's very fresh."

Isaac complied willingly. While enjoying his drink, he began examining the color prints he had had a professional photographer develop in Algiers.

"I don't see anything special," he finally admitted after a few minutes. He knew these photos by heart and did not understand what could excite his foster brother.

"I'm not surprised at you," Ranzi replied teasingly. "Dror immediately found the key to the first figure. Do you see those long fortifications in the background with a kind of tower at the end?"

"Of course, so what?"

"Dror says it's the Château de Chinon and the Tour au Trésor. What do you think?"

"Nothing; I don't know this castle, and neither does Dror. How the hell did he come up with such a thing, I wonder…"

The Targui smiled. "He didn't invent anything. Your son, passionate about the Templar saga, asked his history teacher to give a lesson on the Templars. The professor recounted the circumstances surrounding the arrest of the members of the Order of the Temple in France, especially the imprisonment of the Grand Masters in Chinon. He even shared photographs of the castle from a school encyclopedia with the students."

"Quite by chance, this morning, Dror's gaze lingered on the grimoire of Abraham the Jew, which he leafed through. Upon seeing the illustration of the first key, he immediately made the connection."

"Next?" Isaac asked, seething with impatience.

"Did you notice anything else in the picture, Isaac?"

Isaac's eyes widened, but he couldn't find anything of real importance. "I give my tongue to the cat," he finally admitted.

"It's not easy when you don't know where to look or what to search for," the Targui resumed. "We have the original, so the reference document, by definition. The manuscript's texts are almost illegible, especially on this page, as for the photograph…"

"Yes," Isaac interrupted, "it's impossible to decipher the texts on the photos. That's why someone is trying to recover the original. Especially since anyone who recognizes the castle in the background can hope to reconstruct the message. We must prioritize deciphering the message that accompanies the illustration; then we will certainly have to visit the site to verify all the hypotheses we've made."

The two friends exchanged intense glances, deep in thought.

Isaac finally broke the silence. "In the end," he said, shifting topics rapidly, "what did you get out of your interview with the bachaga the other day?"

"Nothing. He was obviously terrified of what might happen to him if he sat down to eat. My threats were ineffective. He reacted exactly like his chaouch. He knows me too well and knows that I will never act like a common criminal."

"May I know why you haven't had him arrested yet?"

"It would be useless as long as Kalifa refuses to speak; no charges could be brought against him."

"It's a pity; this shady character deserves prison. And as for the manuscript, have you wondered where the leak could come from, Ranzi?"

"Of course. There are only two possibilities. The first is that we are betrayed by one of our brothers in the Grand Council, which I refuse to believe. The second is your photographer. He would make an ideal culprit. He kept the negatives and may have shared them with someone else."

The Targui's face suddenly changed expression as he elaborated on this last point. "Imagine that after five years, he had ample time to study the content of the manuscript through the photographs he kept the negatives of. Do you follow me? Let's also imagine he finally determined what the drawing on the first key represents and discovered that the illustration relates to the Château de Chinon, which has a tower called the Treasure Tower. He even knows that this monument was once the prison of the Templars. However, he cannot decipher the texts, which turn out to be illegible on the photographs. Therefore, he needs the original."

But there's still one thing wrong with my reasoning," Ranzi continued. "You commissioned the work from the photographer. How did he know that the original was in my possession?"

"First of all," Isaac reminded him, "allow me to point out that I had the manuscript sent to you as soon as the shots were taken because the next day, I was leaving for Paris, and I did not want to carry this precious book across the metropolis. Additionally, I asked that the invoice for the color prints be attached to the package for our archives and our accounts."

The Targui still didn't seem convinced.

"Lastly," added Isaac, "the manuscript is worth a fortune, which may justify an attempted theft."

Ranzi nodded slowly and stared straight at his foster brother. "What's the name of your artist?"

"It's written on the back of the photos: 'Studio Mustapha.'"

"He won't be able to read Hebrew, Isaac, with such a name!" quipped the Targui.

"In that case," Isaac continued, "let's go to Algiers tomorrow morning. I'll finally be able to break in my new Citroën DS19."

"Impossible, little brother; it's Shabbat for you tomorrow. I'll go with Khaled, and I'll break in your DS… if you don't mind. In exchange, I'll leave you my comfortable Jeep. It's less sober than a camel, but… it goes faster!"

CHAPTER 10

Friday, April 16, 1954

Khenchela, 12.45

A large, dust-covered black Buick drove into the courtyard of the bachaga's villa. The visitor was likely expected, as the wooden double-leaf gate stood wide open.

Amin was quietly hidden in a nearby grove. Ranzi had advised him to watch the villa and jot down the license plate numbers of any vehicles that entered. He noted the plate number and realized the visitor wasn't from the area; the car was registered in Algiers.

After about ten minutes, the Buick stormed out of the villa, kicking up a thick cloud of dust behind it. It sped right past the thicket that concealed Amin before racing down rue de Paris, likely heading for the north road. Amin managed to catch a glimpse of the driver, an Algerian in his fifties, dressed like a European. He quickly noted the time of departure and the driver's description.

Alger, 15:30.

The Citroën rolled into Algiers. Behind the wheel that day was Ranzi, usually calm but currently fuming with rage. He disliked driving in Algiers, not due to heavy traffic—which was fluid most of the time—but because of the narrow streets, especially the cursed trams and trolleybuses that hindered traffic more than the endless carts pulled by mules or old draft horses.

He arrived at Place du Gouvernement without any issues and wisely opted to leave the car in the garage of the Hôtel Aletty. Once the formalities at the palace concierge were completed, Ranzi and his faithful lieutenant went up to their room to change. They emerged dressed like pieds-noirs, in blue jeans and shirts, espadrilles on their feet. The two men strode briskly toward Place de Chartres, located barely two minutes from the hotel, accessed by a wide staircase of several steps leading to rue d'Isly.

Place de Chartres was tucked in the lower part of the Casbah of Algiers, a bustling commercial spot filled mainly with wholesalers, a few Moorish cafés, and itinerant merchants. From this square, several steep alleys, often marked by long, impassable irregular steps, wound through the indigenous quarter, climbing up to the prison of Barbe-Rousse—the large penitentiary center of the Algerian capital. From this vantage point, one could get a breathtaking view of the bay of the capital.

Ranzi and Khaled had no trouble locating the photographer's shop. The sign read in capital letters: "Studio Mustapha." The storefront, once possibly a shop window, was now completely empty. The only door to the shop was closed, and the metal shutter was locked with a padlocked chain.

As they approached the shop, the two Targuis noticed a small sign hanging on the glass door: "Closed due to death." They were far from expecting such news.

The waiter from the adjoining café pretended to wipe down the unoccupied tables on the terrace. After a moment, perhaps prompted by the need to be useful, he motioned for the Targuis to come closer.

"Are you looking for Mustapha, the photographer?" he asked.

"Yes, we want our negatives back," Ranzi replied naturally.

"He died two months ago," the waiter continued, his strong Algiers accent noticeable.

"Thanks for the information," Ranzi said. "But how did he die?"

"As a result of a long illness. Everyone here knew he was doomed."

"Who has taken over his business?"

"Nobody. He did have a brother, but the latter preferred to liquidate everything; he wasn't in the game."

The Targui took a note from his pocket, which instantly disappeared as if by magic. "Can we know the name of his brother?"

"I only know Mustapha's last name: Amrouche."

"Amrouche, like the city councilor?"

"I don't know," the café owner replied sharply.

"Thank you for the information. Just one more question: Have you seen anyone else take an interest in this shop?"

The waiter hesitated for a moment before answering. "Now that you remind me, there's a funny guy who's been around for a while. We had never seen him before. Here, look on the other side of the square, at the tavern terrace—he's still there. He's playing dominoes with another patron, but I believe he's been watching Mustapha's shop out of the corner of his eye."

"Thank you again and goodbye," concluded the Targui, slipping a five-franc piece into the waiter's hand.

He then took his lieutenant aside, leaning in to whisper in his ear. "Let's approach cautiously, just to chat—quietly, like civilized people."

The duo crossed the square toward the eatery, which was bustling with people as it often was in this commercial area. The two men kept their eyes fixed on the table where the character playing dominoes sat.

Unfortunately, the man had seen the Targuis converse with the waiter. Acting quickly, he got up, accidentally dropping his dominoes and bumping into the crowd. He dashed toward the narrow alleys leading to the Casbah, having likely sensed something suspicious in the Targuis' demeanor. Without exchanging a word, the two companions immediately set off in pursuit.

The fugitive wreaked havoc in his mad rush, knocking over anything that stood in his way. He stumbled into a greengrocer's stall, toppling crates of tomatoes that spilled across the cobblestones, creating a small red tide, and violently jostled an unfortunate old woman in a veil.

Continuing his reckless flight through the Casbah, he barreled into a porter carrying a load of pumpkins in a wicker basket. The pumpkins exploded as they hit the uneven stones, creating a gooey mess on the already slick steps of the alley.

Ranzi and Khaled were losing ground in the maze of narrow lanes with deep rutted steps. The fugitive obviously knew the neighborhood like the back of his hand—he had a definite advantage. However, the pursuers were physically better trained and noticeably quickened their pace, momentarily regaining some lost ground.

Fortunately, the crowds began to thin out as they moved deeper into the increasingly narrow streets, making their progress easier. They had just covered five hundred meters in a matter of minutes—a notable achievement given the daunting terrain—when they saw the fugitive turn around and crouch down with a pistol in hand.

"Khaled! Take cover; he'll shoot!" Ranzi bellowed, darting for the first porch he could find.

Two shots rang out almost simultaneously, missing their targets thirty meters from the breathless shooter, who was clearly lacking in precision. The bullets ricocheted off the cobblestones. Realizing his failure, the fugitive quickly changed tactics. Gun still in hand, he continued his wild dash through the old quarter.

Fortunately, none of the passersby were struck by stray bullets. The few witnesses present bolted into nearby alleys to seek shelter.

Without wasting time, the two Targuis caught their breath and set off again toward the heights of the Casbah. Spotting an alley to the right, Khaled gestured to it, hoping to outflank the aggressor. The sheik nodded and quickened his pace.

The sound of gunshots had driven away the last stragglers, leaving the top of the street completely deserted. They had only a hundred meters left to cover before reaching Barbe-Rousse.

The fugitive was beginning to tire, losing ground with every stride, sweat pouring from his brow. Fearing he'd soon be caught, he opted to stand his ground. He stopped on two steps, precariously poised, raising his weapon firmly with both hands, preparing to fire. He took care to aim slowly to avoid repeating his earlier mistakes, holding his breath. Sweat trickled down from his forehead, gradually blurring his vision. He mechanically wiped his forehead with the back of his sleeve and readjusted his weapon. He realized he no longer saw the second pursuer and felt a twinge of surprise—just as a mountain of muscle crashed into him from behind.

Khaled had just knocked out the shooter with a precisely applied cuff to the back of the neck. He picked up the weapon, a 7.65 Beretta, holding it up with admiration.

"They really have the means, our friends opposite. It's good stuff," he admitted, satisfied with his small prize of war.

Ranzi had time to catch up with him. Barely out of breath, he leaned toward the bandit and searched his pockets.

"No papers," the sheik noted. "Let's take him to the police station; that will be one less criminal on the road."

The main police station was right on Place du Gouvernement, practically next door. After navigating down Ruelle du Cabestan and crossing Place de Chartres in the opposite direction, they took a left onto Rue d'Isly, finally arriving at the bustling Place d'Alger.

The Targui asked to be received immediately by the divisional officer when they reached the police station. Guichard was an old friend whom Ranzi had met by chance during the last war, specifically during the hunt for Nazi spies infesting the country. This occurred just a few months before the landing. Both had arrested dangerous individuals, and since then, they had maintained a close relationship.

Ranzi was careful not to involve his friend in every little thing, but this time he couldn't avoid it. The divisional officer, ceasing all business, rushed to greet his old friend. In his fifties, with his graying hair cut in a crew cut, he had put on a few extra pounds. He approached with open arms, clearly delighted to see the Targui again.

"My old friend Sheikh Ahmed Ranzi el Sahraoui, prince of the Targuis, is back among us! In my arms, your serene highness!" the policeman exclaimed loudly, his Parisian accent ensuring all the officers in the station heard him.

"André, you're always so exuberant, old buddy. This is Khaled, my faithful lieutenant. He has a present for you," Ranzi announced, pointing toward the captured bandit.

Khaled maintained a firm grip on the bandit's arm, bent behind his back. He pushed the gunslinger forward, increasing the pressure until the man began to groan.

Guichard signaled to a policeman on duty to take the bandit behind bars and instructed that a proper interrogation be conducted immediately. Turning to his friend, he invited him into a large, soberly decorated office.

"Take a seat, and Ranzi, tell me everything from A to Z. As for your recent adventures in the bled (the field), I've already been informed by Brigadier Stellen and most recently by Commissioner Petit. I was planning to pay you a visit on an upcoming official outing to Khenchela. So I've taken an interest in your escapades. Are you thinking about returning to service in the national police, Ranzi?"

"Ha ha ha! Very funny! You can't let that go, huh? Okay, enough of the jokes. I hadn't been back on this old Algerian soil for two days before someone was already tailing me. A bit later, there was an attempted assault on me, plus a completely unnecessary murder of a gas station attendant who was tortured to obtain information. Then there was an ambush and another attempted murder on me. Don't you think that's too much?"

"Who are you bothering?" Guichard asked.

"I'm not bothering anyone. You know someone tried to steal an ancient manuscript from me, don't you?"

"Yes, I've read all the reports. You know well that nothing escapes me here. They like you, the local cops—so what have you done to earn their respect? I'm consumed with jealousy. I can't even garner the respect due my rank in this damned police station where I only take care of administrative tasks, you know the kind?"

"Misery! André! Know that I didn't come here to hear you complain—get a grip. Soon you'll retire and all your problems will vanish," the Targui said with a burst of laughter.

"Yeah, you're right. But I'm going to give you some confidential news anyway; it just came across the ticker this morning. Hold on tight: the Khenchelois bachaga, Abou Dahrem, was found dead by hanging, and according to the preliminary investigation, he committed suicide around seven in the morning at his villa. What do you think?"

Ranzi responded without a moment's hesitation. "This isn't a suicide—he was involved up to his neck in cases that concern me. One of his chaouchs in charge of tailing me participated in the murder of that unfortunate gas station attendant, and my men shot him dead in the desert. I met with the bachaga as soon as I returned to Khenchela; I wanted to get the worms out of him, or at least threaten him if I found him on my way. He was terrified, André—absolutely terrified. He wouldn't open his mouth during our meeting; you could see the fear in his eyes. In short, I couldn't get anything out of him. Clearly, he knew too much. I'm convinced someone eliminated him out of fear that he would spill the beans. But I wouldn't be surprising you if I told you one of my men has been keeping an eye on his place all the time, would I?"

The officer frowned. "Well, no. It doesn't surprise me; I know how you are, you devilish Targui. Can we collect his testimony?"

"No problem, André. As soon as I return to Khenchela, I'll ask him to come in for questioning at the police station."

"It's incredible, Ranzi—there are a lot of corpses around you. Do you need some help or a little push?"

"Yes, of course," replied the Targui. "But first, I'm going to explain to you what we came to do in Algiers and share our initial conclusions."

Ranzi calmly resumed the story from the beginning, neglecting to inform Guichard of the insurrectionary plans of the F.N.A.

"Do you really believe that the municipal councilor Ibrahim Amrouche is involved in this affair?"

"To the neck. If he's Mustapha's brother."

"Affirmative," replied the officer. "It is indeed Mustapha's brother."

"Then I'd add that he is certainly the real instigator. Everything ties together. Let me tell you what likely happened two months ago. After his brother died, Amrouche went to take stock of the studio in Place de Chartres for the succession. He must have found a copy of the photographs that my partner and foster brother Isaac—whom you know well—commissioned from Mustapha five years ago, just before my exile. Amrouche probably realized the inestimable value of what was depicted in those photographs, or what the decryption of the texts on the original could yield. The photos were too blurred to be of any use—are you following me? He would have found my address on a duplicate invoice and devised a plan, simple yet foolish, to seize the manuscript."

"I need to let you in on a secret, but only if you promise not to exploit it for personal gain."

"Oh yes, is it a state secret, old friend?"

"No—it's a treasure, a sacred treasure, if my intuition proves true. One of the figures in the coveted manuscript appears to relate to a French castle—specifically, that of Chinon. In this illustration, you can see a particular tower, yet originally, the castle had several. This fort played a significant role in French history. Richard the Lionheart met his end there, after fruitlessly searching for Henry II's treasure in 1190. It was also in this famous castle that the grand master of the Templars, Jacques de Molay, was imprisoned, and where Jeanne La Pucelle met the Dauphin Charles VII in 1429. The illustration in the coveted manuscript unmistakably depicts the Treasure Tower. Are you still following me? According to some scholars… and I doubt you belong to that category… Yes, yes, the Targui insisted ironically, it could perhaps be the treasure of Henry II or even that of the Templars—who knows?"

"Ho there! Ho there!" the divisional joked. "It certainly sounds exciting, but if I keep listening to you, I'm bound to end up with one of those migraines… By the way, what about the prisoner?"

"Let's go and question him, if you don't mind," Ranzi suggested. "But first, could you check with your men to see if they've identified him?"

Guichard leaned over the intercom, pressed a button, and asked, "Tell me Inspector, have you been able to determine the identity of the bandit that Sheik Ranzi brought to us earlier?"

A nasal voice with a strong black foot accent emerged. "He refuses to reveal anything about the boss, but he's tied to organized crime as a suspected accomplice of Aziz Abd Elacem. His name is Rassoul Maklouf."

"Okay," said the divisional. "Put him in the fridge; we're coming."

Major Guichard, followed by the two Targuis, pushed open the fridge door, which in police jargon meant the dungeon. The bandit had plenty of time to collect his thoughts by now, likely wondering what awaited him after his arrest.

Guichard advanced, rolling his shoulders to impress the thug. "Rassoul Maklouf," the policeman asked curtly, "Are you aware that Sir Ahmed Ranzi has previously had your boss arrested in Ghardaïa, and that your operation's sponsor, Amrouche, is now on the run?"

Maklouf couldn't believe his ears. He momentarily felt defeated; his life was potentially at stake. Since the war, arms dealers and killers hadn't been treated lightly. He briefly considered negotiating. "I'll tell you everything if you settle my case."

"I can't promise you anything, Maklouf, but the judge will certainly take your revelations into account if they prove interesting," the divisional officer replied. "Now please speed up; I'm awaiting answers.

First, tell me who got you involved in this and for how long."

"Amrouche, the municipal councilor," the prisoner admitted. "He promised Aziz and me a fortune if we brought back an old book, plus a bounty for the Targui if we captured him alive. Aziz was contacted a few days after the photographer's death—Mustapha's brother…"

Guichard cut him off. "We know about the photographer, but why did Amrouche want this manuscript?"

"I don't know—it must be worth a fortune. He advanced us the necessary cash for our expenses and promised us a hefty bonus once the book was delivered."

"Do you know someone called Kalifa?"

"He's a friend of Amrouche. He was supposed to obtain information on the ground, specifically in Khenchela."

"Who supplied you with the guns?"

"Amrouche. He claimed to have all the necessary arms to stir up a revolution if need be."

The officer hesitated for a moment before continuing his questioning. "What were you doing in Chartres Square?"

"Amrouche tasked me with watching the photographer's shop. He thought someone might come snooping."

"Why did you shoot at Sir Ahmed Ranzi?"

"Amrouche wanted him dead. I was instructed to eliminate him if he showed up at the store."

"Do you have anything else to tell us before we lock you up?"

"Nothing. I've said enough to deserve being chopped down by that devil, Amrouche."

The divisional officer gestured for his friend to exit the cell. Once in the hallway, he gave him a friendly pat on the shoulder. "I'll issue an international warrant for Amrouche and order an immediate search throughout the territory. We must locate the stash of weapons at all costs to prevent them from falling into criminal hands. That's all I can do at this point," Guichard admitted, resigned.

"Hold on a minute, Commissioner—something seems off in this story. Abd Elacem didn't provide the same version as Maklouf; he claimed Kalifa was behind this whole affair. On top of that, Amrouche's name was never mentioned in Khenchela. Doesn't that strike you as odd, André?"

"That doesn't surprise me," the officer replied without hesitation. "Thugs often lie to protect themselves. In this case, he likely blamed Kalifa to shield Amrouche—there's no doubt about it. I'll notify Petit so he can conduct a proper cross-examination."

Shifting topics, he asked, "What does His Serene Highness intend to do now?"

"I'm returning to Khenchela tomorrow; I have a new puzzle to solve," replied the Targui, donning a mysterious air.

Ranzi tightened his grip on the policeman's hand and whispered, "Want to join me for dinner this evening, say around seven-thirty at the Aletty? I hope Béatrice, your lovely companion, will accompany you—it'll save us from any bickering."

CHAPTER 11

Saturday, April 17, 1954

It had rained heavily on the way back, a biting rain as is often the case in this rugged, mountainous region. Ranzi was in a foul mood. Too many things still lingered in the shadows, much to his regret. One thing was certain: a mysterious organization had declared all-out war on him, and he would sell his skin dearly.

The Targui had a deep-seated fear of driving in the rain. He kept complaining about the bad weather and the deplorable state of the road. To be fair, the poorly maintained road meandered awkwardly through the Aurès massif. Worst of all were the large puddles that spread across the lane, capable of surprising even the most seasoned driver as they exited corners. The engineers responsible for constructing this road had simply neglected to develop drainage systems to evacuate rainwater, leading to torrential downpours. A humorous but unfortunate example of budget cuts.

Ranzi braked in front of the gate at 36 rue Gérôme-Bertania. It was around five o'clock. The kids had returned to playing ball in the street as soon as the storm passed.

As he exited the Citroën, the Targui noticed two Jeeps and a Land Rover cluttering the yard. A broad smile of satisfaction spread across his face, and he quickened his pace.

Wonderful! thought Ranzi, Rachida has just arrived.

The villa's door was wide open, and trunks and suitcases littered the floor, forcing the Targui to weave through the hall.

"Are you coming home at this time?" cried a voice the sheik knew well.

"Rachida, I invited you to come and spend a few days in my villa, not years. However, at first glance, considering the number of suitcases strewn on the floor of the entrance..."

"Taratata. You are wrong once again. It's not just my suitcases!" she sneered. "We haven't had time to put everything away yet, you see. We've just arrived, Prince of the Dunes," her sister crooned as they descended the stairs. "Guess who's here?"

At that precise moment, a slender figure appeared at the top of the stairs. Leila, holding her son Mahmoud by the hand, slowly descended to join the Targuis in the large living room.

"Welcome to the house of the Sahrawis, Leila. Did you have a good trip?" Ranzi asked, taken aback.

"Excellent, Ranzi; however, we swallowed a lot of dust, and a good bath wouldn't do us any harm."

The Targui couldn't hide his happiness. She had kept her promise. She had come, and forever, he hoped—fueled by a newfound strength.

"Rachida, take Leila to the basement, and both of you can relax in the sauna. Ask Ali to prepare everything. I'll handle storing all this luggage while I wait. But please, don't spend the night chatting while you take your bath; you and Leila—I need to freshen up after a very trying trip as well."

Two hours later, Leila and Ranzi met in the lobby. The Targui led the beautiful Kabyle toward the large garden behind the villa. Night had just fallen, and the clear sky revealed the moon in all its majesty. At this latitude, the star of the night shone like an immense orange disc, veiled from time to time by fleeting clouds. The scents of jasmine mingled with those of pompom roses and lilac, which bloomed early here. A soft, light wind had picked up on the plateau, making the clammy warmth of the evening more bearable.

Seizing the moment, the prince gently took his companion's hand to confess his feelings directly.

"I love you, Leila. Will you marry me?"

"Ranzi," she said, moved, "I love you too. Nothing could fill me more. Of course, I want to share my life with you, but you don't have to, you know..."

"Understand me, Leila. I was living like a hermit for five years until I finally met you at the oasis. I finally have a purpose in life and have new projects that concern you, Mahmoud, and me. It's very serious. Do you want to start a new home?"

Leila's beautiful eyes clouded over, and tears of joy streamed down her cheeks.

"Yes, yes, a thousand times yes, Prince of the Dunes! Give me time to realize that I won't wake up from a silly dream."

Ranzi hugged her tenderly.

"This dream, Leila, we will make it together," whispered the prince, placing a long kiss on her lips.

Ranzi, on his return from Algiers, had invited the Yakobi family for a modest gathering to celebrate the arrival of Rachida and Leila. So, at precisely 8:30 p.m., the porch of the Sahrawi villa lit up as Isaac rang the bell at the entrance gate.

They were eagerly awaited.

Rachida appeared on the porch like a princess from a tale of a thousand and one nights, clad in a splendid oriental outfit of green silk accentuated with gold sequins. The dress, slightly low-cut, brushed against her ankles. Her bare arms were adorned with heavy bangles that perfectly complemented her coppery, sun-kissed complexion. Around her neck hung the imposing and precious pearl necklace her brother had given her. At her side stood Said and Aisha.

As soon as her childhood friend crossed the porch, she stepped forward to greet her with open arms. Rachel, moved, barely had time to utter a word before her impatient friend embraced her tightly.

"Be careful, they sting," said Rachel, handing her childhood friend a bouquet of wild roses.

Rachida gracefully took the bouquet from her hands. "Here are my two children Rachel," she said, turning her face to Saïd and Aïcha. "We have two other distinguished guests this evening with the Sahraouis; I will also introduce you to Leila and Mahmoud."

In the large Moorish drawing room, richly adorned with hand-woven Bedouin-style hangings, Ranzi and his brother-in-law chatted casually as they sat on ottomans around a low table with two cups of strong mint tea. They both rose to greet the Yakobi family as soon as they saw them in the hallway. Leila stood back, discreetly framed in the double doors, holding Mahmoud by the hand. She wore a flowing ensemble of wild silk in purple and white, with her waist cinched by a chain adorned with golden Louis.

Leila slowly walked towards Rachel who was impressed by the natural beauty radiating from the Kabyle. She embraced her spontaneously and for a long time.

"Leila! That outfit suits you perfectly! Would you give me the address of your tailor?" she whispered gently in her ear.

"Gladly," replied Leila in a soft voice. "Come see me tomorrow. I will take your measurements, and we will go together to the souk to choose the fabrics!"

Turning then to Prince Rachel complimented him. "Oh Ranzi, my handsome prince, I see you've dressed up for tonight as well," she exclaimed, holding out her arms to him.

The Targui smiled and kissed Rachel tenderly on both cheeks. "I am happy to have my entire second family back under my roof tonight. Come in quickly, my friends; we have so much to say to each other."

"You don't kiss your little princess anymore, Uncle Ranzi?" Sarah asked as she walked through the door. "You want to make me jealous?"

"In my arms, Sarah! There's no way you're sulking with me tonight. And as for you, Nathan and Dror, it gives me immense pleasure to have you join our party tonight."

Ranzi then turned to Isaac with a wink. "And you, little brother, should know it's forbidden to talk business here this evening by order of her Highness, Princess Rachida!"

He invited the newcomers to sit on poufs arranged around the large low table, generously garnished with oriental cakes and various drinks.

While Dror acted like a clown to entertain the three children, running and gesticulating through the large living room, the women discussed their gossip, and Nathan conversed with Bashir, seemingly undistracted by the background noise.

Ranzi felt moved. Like a young schoolboy in love for the first time, he struggled to concentrate, so captivated was he by the beautiful Kabyle sitting beside him. He could feel all eyes on him and his enchanting companion, which troubled him.

Leila radiated in her purple ensemble, perfectly relaxed, savoring this moment with immense joy that she could not conceal.

Midway through the evening, the Targui spoke, asking his guests for a moment of silence. "I have excellent news for you," he said, his voice filled with genuine emotion. "Leila and I have decided to get married..."

Cheers and joyous cries erupted in the large living room.

"I knew it! I knew it from the start!" shouted Rachida. "Ranzi could not resist the charms of the beautiful green-eyed Kabyle. Mabrouk! Mabrouk ahlek!" (all the happiness for you)

"Leila, my sister, now you are also part of the Yakobi family," outbids Rachel. "It is a great joy for the Yakobi. Mabrouk! Mabrouk!"

"I am moved and very touched. Thanks to Ranzi, I now have two families," Leila replied, on the verge of tears.

Isaac poured mint tea into all the cups and stood up. "I raise a toast to the future spouses. May the Lord fill you with all his blessings and bless you, Leila and Ranzi," he continued in a vibrant voice. "We are already looking forward to your future union. Mabrouk ahlek!" (congratulations, Leila!)

The party ended at dawn.

As the Yakobi family prepared to leave, Ranzi walked toward Rachel, holding Mahmoud by the hand. "I would like to ask my little sister a favor. Can you take care of Mahmoud's registration at the communal school? I believe you have some contacts here."

"With joy, Ranzi. I will pick up Leila and Mahmoud on Monday morning to complete all the formalities. You can both count on me."

"I'll come with you," said Rachida. "I can't wait to see the benches of our old school again. And then, it will give us a good opportunity to chat—the three of us."

Sunday, April 18, 1954

Khaled and Amin entered the large living room of the villa; it must have been barely ten o'clock. Ranzi was waiting for them over a cup of tea in the living room. Sitting next to him, Isaac was busy examining photos scattered on the table with a magnifying glass.

After savoring a cup of hot tea, Amin spoke. "Sir Ahmed, I would like to inform you about a visit to the villa of the Bachagha on Friday morning. From what I understand, this visit coincides perfectly with the death of Abu Dahrem. It's not fortuitous. I managed to find the brand and plate number of a car registered in Algiers, and I even spotted the driver's face."

"Excellent work, Amin. Tomorrow we will go to the police station to make a statement. Your testimony confirms our suspicions. We are now certain that the Bachagha was assassinated by Amrouche. He must have thought it wouldn't take long to intercept his accomplice, and he had to eliminate a cumbersome witness who likely knew too much. What do you think, Isaac?" Ranzi asked, his worry evident.

Isaac took a moment to reflect, trying to bring order to the sequence of events over the past two weeks. He had carefully analyzed the facts from all angles without finding a rational explanation for the behavior of this gang of crooks. Ultimately, he settled on one hypothesis—the most probable one.

"You see, Ranzi, what bothers me the most is the reason Amrouche wants to appropriate the manuscript. Certainly, there's something we're missing, but I can't pinpoint what it is. We must first try to determine the true personality of Amrouche—who he is and what real purpose he seeks.

We know this character has links with arms dealers and highwaymen. According to Maklouf's testimony, Amrouche possesses a veritable arsenal. Plus, he associated himself with Bachagha Abou Dahrem, a separatist, and Kalifa, a politically committed intellectual whose true motivation in this affair remains unknown. I should mention that, as a regular bookseller, he frequently received many orders from you, which likely informed him of your inclinations toward rare esoteric works.

All of this leads me to believe that, in the beginning, this was merely a case of arms trafficking. Amrouche, due to his privileged position, could smuggle weapons into Algeria while traveling freely throughout Europe and the East, sparking little suspicion. This lucrative endeavor likely allowed him to drive a large American car. It's worrisome because these weapons probably aim to fuel a possible insurrection.

Compounding this is the death of his brother, Mustapha, the photographer. Amrouche stumbles upon the proofs I had ordered from his brother and recognizes the castle in the background of one of the boards. I think this might awaken some memory in him. Was he aware of the fabulous treasure legends, or had he already visited Chinon? Finding the photos blurry and the texts illegible—he could not have known the manuscript was written in Hebrew—he resolves to recover the original for further study. He discovers the invoice copy indicating "Facsimile in color of the book of Abraham the Jew," which includes your address. He has accomplices in Khenchela, but without enough time to prepare thoroughly, he clumsily orchestrates a forceful operation to reclaim the original."

Ranzi expressed his skepticism with a nod. "Very interesting, but you're not quite there. In my opinion, Amrouche lacks the capacity for deciphering the slightest cabalistic or allegorical message. Perhaps he intended to enlist the services of Kalifa, whom he considers a scholar, or to take me captive to force me to decipher the manuscript's contents. However, there is one very simple explanation for Amrouche's interest in our manuscript: its market value. This one-of-a-kind work must be worth a fortune to a collector—perhaps one or two million dollars on the international art market. Kalifa, consulted by the municipal councilor, would not have failed to provide an assessment based on a photographic print. Moreover, he could likely find fences to sell the manuscript in France or abroad, don't you think, Isaac?"

"Okay! But your arguments don't change much about this story as I see it," Isaac replied, his conviction steadfast. "The bets are open."

Feeling out of sorts, Amin and Khaled excused themselves, leaving the two friends to their thoughts. They then fell into a profound silence, each contemplating new hypotheses only to abandon them as improbable or fanciful. They struggled to identify the real motives, which significantly frustrated them.

"Let's start by studying this manuscript," Ranzi suddenly suggested. "Let's put all this speculation aside for a moment and join Dror in the library."

The teenager was deeply engrossed in examining the precious grimoire. He was so absorbed in reading that he didn't hear the whispers of the adults coming from the hallway. Finally sensing a presence behind him, he turned as his father and Ranzi entered the room.

"Uncle Ranzi, I think I've discovered something again!" Dror exclaimed triumphantly.

"Hey there, my disciple! Have you already forgotten your lessons about humility?" queried the Targui, ironically winking at Isaac, as the clergy advised staying humble in all circumstances.

Dror, overly excited, ignored his mentor's ironic reprimand. On the contrary, he seemed increasingly agitated and pulled Isaac into his excitement. "Father, believe me," he insisted. "I think I have translated the texts that accompany the first figure. Look, check for yourself!"

With the exception of the title written in gold letters above the illustration, which was in Old French, everything else was in Hebrew.

Abraham Juif, Prince et Prêtre Lévite,

pour la Nation Juive dispersée au Royaume des Gaulles,

par l'ire de l'Éternel.

« Jewish Abraham, Levite Prince and Priest,

for the Jewish Nation dispersed in the Kingdom of the Gaulles,

by the wrath of the Lord »

Under the title, the first illustration in the background of the manuscript represents the fortified castle of Chinon, built atop a hill or rocky peak. The Treasure Tower dungeon appears to be illuminated by the rising sun, while a lunar crescent, in its first quarter, hangs to the left.

In the foreground, a strange scene unfolds. The artist has depicted a knight in armor confronting a winged dragon. He brandishes his sword and seems to protect himself with a shield.

Surrounding the dungeon are three words inscribed in a circle. Above, the words "Ruah El," meaning the Divine Spirit, and below, "Athanor," referring to the oven.

On either side of the castle, two triangles are present. The first, on the left and pointing toward the sky, bears an inscription in the center: "Aesh," which means Fire. The second triangle, on the right and pointing toward the earth, is inscribed with the word "Maïm," meaning Water.

Below the illustration, here is the poem that I translated :

« Sur le rocher du Lion,

"On Lion Rock,

« Là où les rois ont bâti leur maison,

Where kings have made their homes,

« Gravi les marches de l'espoir

Climb the steps of hope

« Qui mènent à l'étroit sentier du feu,

Which lead to the narrow path of fire,

« Suis la voie lactée jusqu'à l'Athanor,

Follow the Milky Way to the Athanor,

« Sous la cendre le bouclier

Under the ashes the shield

« de David trouveras ».

of David will be found".

– Congratulations, my disciple. We are very proud of you, Ranzi replied, with all sincerity.

"Wait, that's not all," continued Dror. "The initials of each first word of the verses together form the word 'jewel' in Hebrew."

– No, not a jewel, corrected Isaac. An emerald, perhaps, my son—the Emerald of the Philosophers, that which shines on the forehead of Lucifer, the bestower of the luminous ray.

Ranzi clarified immediately after his foster brother.

– Lucifer, in our esoteric language, means Bearer of Light, from the Latin Luci fero, but also the fire of iron in our green language. Everything confirms that we are indeed in the presence of a coded text, my friends.

Ranzi, intrigued by the nature of the message, closed his eyes for a moment and recited the verses by heart. He had an innate gift for auditory memorization that few people possess. He paused for a moment and began to think aloud, staring at his young disciple.

– It's unusual. Stunning, even! But it's important to specify that hermetic messages always have several interpretations. In this case, there are two possible explanations: the first, cabalistic, concerns an alchemical operation, which is easy to decipher. The second is more delicate; it requires knowledge of the topography of the castle to reveal the nature of the message.

Consider the esoteric version. In the illustration, we see two triangles whose union forms the Seal of David and symbolizes the completed Philosopher's Stone—the perfect assembly of Water and Fire. Meanwhile, the expression "Ruah EL," which means "the divine breath," relates to the Universal and Cosmic Way.

Heaven above, Earth below, as this magnificent verse from the Emerald Tablet proclaims, "All that is above is like what is below, just as all that is below is like what is above."

What does lion rock represent? Certainly one of the materials of the Great Work, the one that acts as a male in the difficult conjunction. The narrow road of fire relates to the process of the dry way, the short way in the crucible and open fire—one of the two secret processes of the ancient Adepts for making the Philosopher's Stone.

The Milky Way symbolizes the operational phase that opens the entrance to the second alchemical work. It is the way of Saint-Jacques, which leads to the "Stellar Compost," cabalistically referred to as "Compostelle" or the "Starry

Compost." The scallop shell is the emblem of the traditional mérelle, that is to say, the Alchemical Vase.

The Athanor is our alchemical furnace, symbolized by the Tower, which appears close-up in the illustration.

Finally, what can "the shield of David" mean? This verse does not apply to the process of the Great Work.

"Perhaps it concerns protection for Jews threatened by the Inquisition," Dror suggested, without waiting for permission to speak.

The Targui, amazed, could not believe his ears. Dror had just uncovered Rabbi Abraham's true secret. The kid kept surprising him.

"Excellent, my disciple. Here is the second possible meaning of the message: Abraham the Jew stayed in Chinon during the time when Jews were hunted down like witches or heretics in the Middle Ages. He may even have lived in the Château de Chinon, under the protection of some prince or lord, and he took it into his head to shelter a treasure intended for his oppressed co-religionists, so they could monetize their peace. To do this, he indicated the location of the hiding place in his manuscript, which he wrote in Hebrew as a precaution, to protect it from profane or criminal hands.

In this case, the word jewel leaves no doubt; Abraham, as a true Philosopher, chose an ambiguous term to designate the carbuncle of Hermes. This word may not exist in Hebrew, but remarkably, it derives from the word Jew in English when we consider the root of jewel—i.e., jew.

In summary, Ranzi continued, the encrypted message does have a double meaning. It allegorically describes the operations of the first work and indicates the location of a treasure.

– But then, what was Flamel doing in this story? asked Isaac.

Ranzi answered without hesitation.

– Flamel must have discovered the treasure of Abraham the Jew, that seems obvious. I can imagine the scenario: the Parisian bookseller of the 15th century buys the grimoire from a receiver who was unaware of its value, possibly coming from a larceny. Only the title of the manuscript is in French; all the rest is written in Hebrew. Our scribe is unaware of this uncommon language, so he is compelled to contact a Jew for the translation of the texts and legends. However, Jews are rather scarce in the country of Gaulles, and for good reason—the Inquisition does not stop chasing them to massacre them. On the other hand, it would be unseemly to ask a Jew to translate a text into Hebrew for the benefit of his own torturers, which forces Flamel to travel to Spain. He knows that this country is full of exiled Jews whom the Spanish authorities of the time have temporarily left in peace. Thus, he undertook the famous pilgrimage to Santiago de Compostela. This is the safest way to travel at this time. The route was perfectly signposted, and well-guarded refuges were placed all along the way to ensure the safety, shelter, and food of the pilgrims who journeyed on foot. Our bookseller knew it was worth the trip since it took him almost three months to complete this long journey.

As soon as he arrived in Spain, he met a rabbi-doctor in the town of Léon—a certain Master Canches wrote Flamel, but I would lean more towards Master Sanches. The rabbi then served as his translator, and perhaps even as an initiator. Flamel succeeded in convincing him to go to France with him under a false identity to avoid the Inquisition—Master Canches, a Christian. Sanches-Canches must have had serious reasons for becoming a Christian.

The two friends then embarked on the first ship, in Sanson, bound for Nantes.

Flamel reported that, during the crossing, the poor rabbi fell ill and eventually died upon their safe arrival, though he offered no further details. Flamel claims that he was buried in Orléans, at Sainte Croix. It's incredible; Orléans is located well after Chinon, coming from Nantes.

The most surprising thing is that Flamel would later write that the rabbi died a good Christian. Is it possible that the rabbi converted? I don't believe it very much. Did Flamel want to demonstrate that Christianity was the only valid religion for humanity? We'll never know. Flamel likely sought to exaggerate the mysterious side of his story to accentuate the cabalistic aspect of his epic.

Leaving Chinon, he would pass through Orléans, and it is surely during this stage of the return journey that his unfortunate companion actually died.

In short, Flamel traveled with master Sanches, probably alias Canches, to Chinon. Upon arriving at the castle, he grabs an immense treasure. Upon returning to Paris, he began to distribute his fortune to charities.

My version is, of course, significantly different from the narrative related by Flamel, but it's much more plausible given the revelations drawn from the manuscript.

Dror raised his hand like a schoolchild asking for the floor.

– What reason pushed Flamel to give a version of the manuscript entirely different from the original in his Book of Hieroglyphic Figures?

Isaac pointed his right index finger at the manuscript.

– Reproducing the grimoire would have revealed the origin of the fortune of the Parisian writer, quite simply. You see, Dror, the illustration of the Castle of Chinon could certainly lead the curious directly to the place where the treasure was hidden.

He turned to Ranzi.

– What do we do now, Prince of the Dunes?

– We are leaving for Tours the day after tomorrow. We will take Khaled with us. I will reserve a twin-engine plane in Constantine, and we will fly to France on Tuesday morning, with a technical stop in Marseille. In Tours, we will rent a sedan to drive to Chinon. I'll handle all the reservations tomorrow. No objections, Isaac?

The Targui was renowned for the speed of its decisions, but this time it was impressive. To decide so suddenly on an airborne expedition across the Mediterranean in the blink of an eye was truly a challenge in 1954. But Ranzi was the kind of character who could undertake a world tour on a mere snap of the fingers; he had done so before.

Isaac tried to dampen the Targui's enthusiasm.

– If I have any objections to make, it's precisely this. We have only decrypted the text of the first figure, and we don't even know what the other puzzles have in store for us, Ranzi. What's the point of rushing to a site we know nothing about when nearly the entire manuscript still needs translation? And what's the point of going there if there's nothing left of this hypothetical treasure?

– Don't be so negative, Yssic. The other pages only concern alchemical secrets, not the treasure. Later, the three of us will have the chance to translate them. Right now, we need to ensure the site hasn't been looted by gangsters, if you know what I mean. We must go to Chinon. All business ceases. Then, we'll see when we're there, Inch'Allah... he added, winking at Dror.

"O.K.," Isaac said resignedly. "I see that nothing can change your mind. Let's go to Chinon."

Dror, who had been following the entire conversation with great interest, eagerly awaited the right moment to seize the opportunity. He took Ranzi's words as an invitation to travel.

"I'd love to come with you, Dad!" he said enthusiastically. "It would be a unique opportunity for me to see the ruins of the castle up close. And then," he added to strengthen his request, "I could write a detailed account of this trip for my class when I return. What a great adventure ahead! Say Dad, will you excuse me from school?"

Isaac shot him an unnecessary stern look. Surprised, he replied curtly.

"It's out of the question, Dror. Don't you realize this is adult business?"

The kid was as clever as a young fox. However, he did not admit defeat. Addressing the Targui, he put on a falsely offended demeanor.

"Uncle Ranzi, you and Dad forced me to neglect my Talmud lessons to learn things that aren't even on the school curriculum! Then, as thanks for figuring out part of the old grimoire's riddle, I'm denied a well-deserved reward; visiting the Treasure Tower is unfair!"

The Saharawi disapproved of his foster brother's decision, which seemed final. He pretended to think for a moment, gazing alternately at Isaac and then at Dror. Isaac was wrong to punish the teenager so unfairly, he reasoned. After all, it was nothing more than a whirlwind trip to the metropolis—a very small jump on the plane... a pleasant excursion followed by a return. He discreetly turned to the teenager and gave him a knowing wink once again.

Isaac noticed the characteristic and telling expression on his foster brother's face. He recognized the sneer that had caused him to retreat so many times in the past.

"His Highness isn't going to try that little smile at the corner of his lips to appease me again, is he?"

No need to insist this time; he would not give in. Dror must not skip his classes. And then—exasperated—he added, such a trip was unsuitable for his age. It would be no, no, and no!

For his age. It would be no, no, and no! and no! For his age. It would be no, no, and no!

CHAPTER 12

Sunday, April 18, 1954

City of Bougie, 06.35 Bordj creek

A curious team, pulled by a mule, advanced along the creek, the air still thick with mist. The driver took the dangerously steep path, leaving the road to descend onto the beach. From there, we could barely see the yacht anchored just a few meters from the shore. The driver pulled hard on the bridle, urging the mule to stop with a reassuring, "Ohhh." The wheels of the cart slowly sank into the wet sand.

Suddenly, two men hiding under the straw bales at the back of the cart emerged. After they landed, they exchanged a few words in Arabic with the driver, and one of them handed him a wad of notes. The men wore European clothing, but the swarthy face of the older one betrayed his Algerian heritage.

The duo climbed into a pastera, a small flat-bottomed boat used by local fishermen. They rowed laboriously toward the yacht, struggling against the swell that impeded their progress. Once they finally reached the yacht, their landing was awkward—everything suggested they were inexperienced. They pulled themselves onto the deck and immediately set about mysterious tasks. In the morning fog, their silhouettes were barely discernible.

After several minutes, the characteristic hum of outboard motors filled the air. One of the men busied himself raising the anchor by cranking a handle. Once the maneuver was complete, he rejoined his companion in the cabin. The roar of the engines rose in volume as the yacht surged forward and sped out to sea, vanishing into the mist, leaving the small boat behind.

Monday, April 19, 1954

Ranzi and his two associates walked through the lobby of the Khenchela police station around nine o'clock.

The orderly recognized the Targui and immediately alerted Commissioner Petit via intercom. He then addressed the visitor.

"Sir Ahmed, Commissioner Petit is waiting for you in his office. You can go there; you know the way now."

The door to the commissioner's office was open. Petit rose to greet the Targui and his two lieutenants warmly.

"Hello Sheikh Ahmed. I had been expecting your visit since your interview with Major Guichard. Clearly, you have a good relationship with law enforcement."

"Commissioner," Ranzi replied jokingly, "since I have nothing in particular to reproach the national police, I do not find it dishonorable to associate with some of their members."

"Well said, Si Ahmed! I really appreciate your humor, and I think I lost an opportunity to keep quiet," he said with a smile. "I will therefore begin by giving you the results of our investigations, as per the wishes of the divisional officer.

"First of all, know that Kalifa remains silent as a grave. He must hold secrets of great importance. He is a real tough guy, a fanatic, and I remain convinced that we will not be able to get him to talk.

"Secondly, I must inform you that the roadblocks set up on all the roads from the Aurès to Algiers have not managed to stop Amrouche, who still cannot be found.

"Finally, good news has just come in over the ticker, directly from divisional Guichard. Thanks to information provided by Amrouche's accomplice, a large weapons cache was discovered in the basement of the villa of the former municipal councilor. It seems something significant is brewing behind the scenes, and hopefully, it won't escalate like the riots of 1945."

Ranzi did not register the last sentence; he was bound by an oath he bitterly regretted having taken. Petit hesitated for a moment before continuing.

"There is another detail that the divisional officer asked me to communicate to you. Amrouche has a nine-meter yacht equipped with two 250-horsepower engines, capable of crossing oceans. The Admiralty could not locate it in the port of Algiers, where it was usually moored. It is feared that our man has managed to anchor in a more discreet port or cove, intending to escape by sea if necessary. His boat is called 'Le Samira.'"

"I am grateful to you for sharing this information, and in return, my collaborator Amin will provide a damning deposition against Amrouche. The adviser was seen entering the bachaga estate on Friday morning, at a time that coincides perfectly with the time of his death. He stayed there for about a quarter of an hour and then left like an arrow, passing right in front of Amin, who was hidden just a few meters away. Amin will also provide you with a description of the individual and the license plate number of the car."

"Very well," replied the commissioner, pressing a button on his intercom. "Someone send me a statement in my office. Yes, I said right away, please!"

A voice sputtered over the loudspeaker, producing sounds that were perfectly inaudible to the uninitiated.

"And don't waste time, Giordano! I told you it was for now!" Petit ordered into the microphone, visibly angered.

CHAPTER 13
Thusday, April 20, 1954

The sun had not yet risen in Port de Bouc, casting a muted brown hue over the morning. The weather was cool; the heavy rain from the previous day had dropped the temperature several degrees. At the bow of a yacht approaching the small fishing port, a figure waved a lantern slowly in an agreed rhythm, while on the quay, another individual responded with flashlight signals: a brief flash, two long flashes, one short, two long, and so forth.

The yacht docked at the deserted pier, engines cut. The only sound was the surf crashing against the shore. The name of the yacht was painted on the stern: "Admiral." It was certainly not very original; the owner had no time to rename the vessel and, obviously, he had prepared for the most urgent, contenting himself with roughly disguising the old name of the cruiser.

One of the passengers threw a rope overboard, which a rather suspicious-looking individual quickly caught. Dressed in jeans and a large sailor sweater, he expertly looped the rope around the mooring post to secure the speedboat. The two passengers jumped to the ground.

The apparent leader engaged in conversation with the man who had come to greet them. The European accomplice spoke with an indefinable accent.

"Everything was done according to your orders, sir. I rented a Mercedes in the name of Frédéric Manin, a wine merchant in Bordeaux. It's parked at the end of the pier. I've also reserved a double room for you for this night in Tours at the Hotel de la Gare, where you'll be expected until midnight. A trustworthy man will introduce himself as soon as you collect the keys to your room, number 137. He will whistle the Internationale under your window.

As you asked, I obtained false papers for you. It cost me a lot to get them so quickly. You will find them in the glove compartment of the limo. One important detail: in France, you must fill out police forms at the hotel. You might be asked to present your passports or identity cards. In the Mercedes, you'll also find road maps, chicken sandwiches as you requested, and a bottle of mineral water."

The interlocutor held out a well-bulged envelope.

"Here," he said dryly, "there's more than enough to cover your expenses and compensate you for your assistance."

The small packet disappeared into the accomplice's pocket as if by magic.

"Take care of the boat; fill it up and ensure everything is checked for a long cruise. Go take a break offshore, pretending to fish. You will return each evening to moor at this same quay and wait for us; we do not know exactly when we will be back."

The Algerian paused for a moment before making a new recommendation.

"If you do not hear from us within exactly three days, there's a letter in the envelope I just gave you. It contains all my instructions that you need to follow to the letter."

The two passengers moved away from the platform and hurried into the Mercedes without wasting time.

The Citroën DS19, driven by Isaac, entered the lawn of the Constantine flying club just as the morning mist began to dissipate. The car rolled up to a shed along the track and came to a stop.

Three men and a teenager stepped out. One of the men started gesticulating, clearly very annoyed. Isaac, frustrated with his foster brother, voiced his displeasure.

"First of all, you persuade me to take Dror with us and even manage to convince my wife of the cultural interest of this trip for our son. Then you inform me that you will be piloting this death trap with my son and me on board! Do you think we will accompany you obediently like passengers on a one-way ticket? Traitor! Fake brother! You were careful not to tell me that you would fly without a pilot, fearing I would refuse to join you. It's like a…"

"Calm down, Yssic. Keep your disrespect in check, please. I'm still your elder, aren't I? You know I have a pilot's license with enough flight hours to circle the globe and fly over any country. Do you think I'd risk Dror's life—yours too? If anything were to happen to you, Rachel and Sarah would never forgive me, not even posthumously!"

"Okay, the Targui, we have a mission to fulfill, but I don't think less of this, and I promise I will make up for this felony. Try to find us good parachutes and life jackets, just in case…"

"You don't have to worry. Life jackets are mandatory for all flights over seas or oceans. I'll see what can be done about the parachutes."

This last remark only heightened the merchant's anxiety. Dror and Khaled giggled, finding the scene comical. No one could tell if the trader was serious or if he was simply dramatizing, as was his tendency.

A technician in a white jumpsuit approached the group, cutting off the ongoing argument. He turned to Isaac.

"My name is Ramirez. I'm the flight coordinator for this flying club. Are you here for the Beech E-18S bound for Tours via Marseille?" he asked politely.

"Yes," replied Ranzi, presenting a briefcase containing all the required papers for a private flight. "I am the pilot."

The technician, surprised, stared at the Targui dressed in his traditional attire: a white djellaba and a long brown turban. The outfit would only need slippers to complete the folkloric look. His gaze then shifted to Khaled, also dressed as a Tuareg, and finally to Isaac, in dark European clothing, neglecting the teenager altogether. He thought to himself that he might have spoken to the wrong person.

"You're the one who reserved this aircraft, Prince Ahmed Ranzi el Sahraoui?" asked the man in the mechanic's overalls.

Isaac's anger flared again. He had not yet processed the surprise his foster brother had sprung on him, and now he found a target for his frustration.

"My word, flight coordinator, you don't understand French. Since we tell you that this gentleman is the pilot! He was the one who had that ridiculous idea of renting a plane!" Isaac snapped, pointing an accusatory finger at Ranzi before continuing:

"Does it seem so incongruous to you that such a swarthy native as this gentleman could fly a twin-engined Beechcraft? And who do you think is the real prince here if not His Serene Highness Ahmed Ranzi el..."

"By the Great Architect!" exclaimed Ranzi, whose mood soured. "We are wasting precious time. Let's settle these formalities quickly before I disturb the president of the flying club himself." The Targui pretended to lose his temper, almost biting his lip to suppress laughter.

Then, taking on a more authoritative tone, he ordered, "You will find in this briefcase my pilot's license with all the certifications required to fly a twin-engine aircraft equipped with retractable landing gear, instrument navigation systems, as well as my radio operator and intercontinental flight licenses. Additionally, I am fluent in English and can land on any airstrip, even a pocket handkerchief if necessary. Does that suit you, sir?"

"Oh, I almost forgot," he added with a sneer, "there is a certified deposit check from my bank (you never know) to cover flight costs and insurance. I also have my benefactor's honorary membership card for the Constantine flying club. If that's not enough for you… Am I clear enough? What do you say, Mr. Ramirez?"

"Uh… I sincerely apologize for this mistake, your highness. Please accept my apologies. I've never seen you at the club since I became the coordinator. I'll take you to your aircraft," the technician replied, shocked at being unjustly taken for a racist. "You've just been refueled, and you are in luck because your plane is brand new; it has just been run in. I'm sure you'll have a lot of fun flying it, your highness."

The technician had a valid excuse for his blunder—Ranzi hadn't registered on the flight board for five years, and that had been when the coordinator had just taken on his role. He began filling out a form, handing a duplicate to Ranzi once the latter signed it. He stapled the check to the counterfoil and returned a folder containing the Beechcraft documentation, flight plan, and all required authorizations.

"Have a good trip," he said by way of farewell. "Please go to the end of the runway into the wind and wait for instructions from the control tower."

Isaac, seemingly calmed down, gave one final reminder to the technician. "Don't forget to take care of my Citroën; the keys are on the dashboard. I'll get my car back when we return in a few days."

The four heroes were quick to board the twin-engine cabin. The interior of the Beechcraft was relatively spacious and comfortable, nothing more. Designed for tourism and business flights, it could carry six passengers with a range of nearly three thousand kilometers and a cruising speed of three hundred kilometers per hour, thanks to its two four-hundred horsepower engines. Its five tanks held more than a thousand liters of fuel.

Khaled stowed the suitcases in the small cargo hold at the back of the plane before returning to his seat in front of Isaac. Dror carefully inspected the cabin interior, remaining pensive for a long moment in front of the imposing dashboard, covered with colorful counters, buttons, and various indicator lights. He was not at all worried; rather, he was naturally curious. Defiantly, perhaps, he decided to sit authoritatively in the co-pilot's seat.

Once seated, Ranzi donned a helmet, inspected all the dials, manipulated the buttons, and then started the two engines one after the other. He adjusted the throttles until the tachometers read 1500 rpm and patiently waited for the engines to warm up.

Meanwhile, Dror diligently noted the subtle manipulations of his uncle, storing everything in his brain, convinced that he would recall it when the time came.

A cheerful voice eventually came through the cabin speakers.

"Put on your life jackets and fasten all your seat belts, my friends. We are about to take flight into adventure!" declared Ranzi, beaming broadly.

Just as the plane began to taxi toward the runway, a piercing siren wailed. Ranzi glanced down the lane parallel to the track, bordering the administrative buildings, and saw a National Gendarmerie vehicle racing toward the twin engine.

The plane stopped abruptly. The Targui, who had just cut the gas, unbuckled his belt, opened the cabin door, and swiftly jumped onto the runway. The van's siren ceased, and an officer stepped out of the vehicle to approach the sheik, saluting in the regulated manner.

"Hello, sir. Are you truly Prince Ahmed Ranzi el Sahraoui?"

"Affirmative, my captain."

"Would you mind showing me some ID?"

"Here is my passport, does that suit you?"

"That's perfect, Sheik Ahmed. My mission is to deliver this envelope to you personally," said the officer, extending the gesture as he spoke. "If you could kindly sign this waiver for me, here."

The Targui complied without a word.

"Thank you, Sheikh Ahmed. I wish you an excellent trip."

The captain stood at attention, saluted the Targui again, then executed a U-turn and returned to his vehicle silently.

Ranzi carelessly stuffed the package he had received into an inside pocket of his suit and returned to the cockpit, meeting his foster brother's questioning gaze.

"Well, what?" he asked apologetically. "I forgot to tell you—it was a gift from my friend Divisionnaire Guichard. I spoke to him yesterday about our trip to France, and he was kind enough to send a small note of recommendation for the local authorities, just in case…"

"And you don't find it quite natural that he sent a gendarmerie officer to deliver your credentials?"

Ranzi smiled broadly, displaying his white teeth but remaining silent, content to gaze at the distant horizon.

"Go back to your seat, little brother. We are going to take off."

He repeated the same series of earlier actions, always under the careful watch of the young passenger.

"Hello, control tower. This is Beechcraft Fox-Alpha-Charlie, four two zero, FAC420, departing for Marseille-Marignane. Do you receive me?"

"This is the control tower, FAC420. I read you five out of five, over to you."

"FAC420 at control tower, I request takeoff permission, over to you."

"You are clear for flight to Marignane aerodrome; the weather conditions are ideal. Ground pressure is 1,002 millibars, temperature 21 degrees, with a light South-Southeast wind of 30 km/h. Over the Mediterranean, the sky is slightly overcast, pressure 995 millibars, temperature fifteen degrees."

"Go into the wind at the end of the runway. Maximum cruising altitude authorized is 12,000 feet. It's your turn."

"Here FAC420, well received. I'm ready; I request takeoff permission."

"Permission granted. Fair winds, FAC420. Roger."

It was 7:55 a.m.

Ranzi pulled on the throttle until the engine speed stabilized at two thousand six hundred rpm. The entire structure of the Beechcraft vibrated intensely for several seconds with a high-pitched noise, barely bearable. Ranzi checked his instruments, adjusted the altimeter one last time, and released the brakes. The aircraft picked up speed, then suddenly surged down the runway. The vibrations subsided, and after covering less than a hundred meters, the Targui gradually pulled on the stick, and the Beechcraft began climbing obediently, then faster and faster, like an arrow shooting into the sky.

The pilot then retracted the landing gear.

Isaac felt a knot form in his stomach. He sensed a slight pang, but then nothing, as the plane, after starting a long semi-circle, began flying straight north. He glanced at Khaled, the unperturbed and confident boy, who seemed to be sleeping peacefully. Dror, his eyes riveted on his uncle, could hardly contain his admiration for the Targui prince.

After a few minutes, the twin-engine reached cruising altitude. Ranzi gradually lowered the throttle to stabilize the speed at 330 km/h. The slight vibrations that had troubled Isaac faded, leaving only a soft hum in the cabin. The interior temperature was pleasant; the air conditioning functioned perfectly.

Half an hour after takeoff, the passengers spotted the sea in the distance, buoyed by exceptional visibility.

Less focused on takeoff maneuvers, the Targui broke the silence.

"So, little brother, still mad at me? Want to try the broomstick? You'll see; it's as easy as driving your DS19."

Isaac, sulking in his corner, looked resigned. He had regained his composure; it was rare for him to get angry, as he was usually quite phlegmatic by nature. But he had to admit that the Targui had played a bad trick on him, which he hated.

"Next time, try not to sneak around anymore, please. I risk aging prematurely."

Dror, who had witnessed the entire exchange, was delighted. He turned to the prince.

"Uncle Ranzi, I'm willing to try piloting your plane," he said, a naive smile on his face.

"Of course," replied the Targui without flinching. "I'll explain how to do it. Look at the dashboard first," he said, pointing to each device. "The instruments are our senses and even more. The most important are the compass here, which we call the compass; this is the horizon, which lets us check the aircraft's inclination; the altimeter; and the badin, which indicates flight speed. Here are the fuel levels in the different tanks, tachometers essential for adjusting the speed and power of each engine, an ammeter that indicates battery charge, and four thermometers, two for external and internal temperatures, and one for each engine. Different lights signal faults, engine overheating, oil pressure, etc."

Isaac, suddenly intrigued, moved closer to the cockpit to catch this unexpected flight lesson.

"Now I'm going to show you the different controls," Ranzi continued. "Here is the joystick, used to operate the ailerons and the elevator. Push it forward to descend and pull it toward you to climb. Handle it gently. Here are the two throttles, and there is the brake. The two pedals on the floor are the rudder pedals, which act on the ailerons at the wings' trailing edges to control the yaw axis.

"I'm going to let go of the handle, so it's up to you now."

The plane nosedived almost immediately.

"Take the handle slowly, hold it straight—that's it, perfect. Now keep one eye on the horizon and the other on the compass. Always steer straight north. That's good, bravo little one, keep it up—gently."

Dror felt an intense exhilaration unlike any he had ever known. He couldn't hide the immense joy of being at the controls of this marvelous machine. He felt fulfilled. So many memories to take back to his small village. His classmates would never believe him; they would call him a storyteller or mock him, certainly.

Skillful and perfectly focused, the teenager was doing splendidly, maintaining course and attitude effortlessly.

After about fifteen minutes, Ranzi deemed it more prudent to regain control.

"I'm taking over the controls, disciple; you did really well," he said sincerely.

The Beechcraft was finally soaring over the Mediterranean, having just passed over Philippeville. It glided between air and water like a beautiful silver bird through the sparse fluffy clouds that stood out against a light blue backdrop.

From the heavens, only the white crests of small waves could be discerned, propagating offshore like endless furrows cutting the sea.

Isaac began to appreciate the light-headed euphoria that floating in space and transcending gravity afforded him. He comprehended the allure flying held over so many aviation enthusiasts. To fly meant to navigate in a three-dimensional expanse, a universe nearly devoid of obstacles. What a magical sensation.

Ah, he mused, if it weren't for all those dials and joysticks making the pilot's job seem overwhelmingly difficult, perhaps he too could learn to fly. Ranzi was quite fortunate to dabble in this sport reserved for an elite during the turbulent times of the 1950s. Isaac eyed the Targui; he noticed how effortlessly his brother operated the radio and the onboard instruments. More impressively, he could find his bearings in the air above the sea as well as in the vastness of the desert. Few would believe he had been traversing the Sahara on camelback just five years prior.

Khaled, unimpressed, placed his unwavering trust in his sovereign. He continued to sleep soundly, snoring periodically, the sounds mixing with the engine noise.

After a lengthy spell, Isaac vacated his chair and took a seat in the co-pilot's position, signaling to his son to relinquish the spot. He fastened his seatbelt as a precaution, feeling much more reassured since lift-off.

"Well, Yssic, aren't you upset anymore?" teased Ranzi, half-joking, half-serious.

"I must admit, you're doing very well. You seem to maneuver this machine much better than a camel in the desert. When did you learn to fly, you secretive?"

"It goes back a dozen years. While hunting Nazis and collaborators, I had the chance to move in very exclusive circles with the US Navy. An American aviator who became an excellent friend, Commander John B. McCoy, introduced me to Spitfire training at the base at El Arrache. Within eighteen months, I accumulated several hundred flight hours and obtained all possible qualifications. You should give piloting a try; it offers extraordinary sensations."

"I have other concerns, you see; I have a family."

"Taratata! You play that card every chance you get! Nothing stops you from indulging in some healthy leisure. Your affairs are well managed by Nathan, and you can free yourself whenever you wish. You see, I have long contemplated creating a small airstrip right behind the football field near my villa. There's all the space you'd need. Then we could go on hikes together, like the good old days in the desert, but this time by plane, not by camel!"

CHAPTER 14

It was already noon when the Marseille coast appeared in all its beauty on the horizon. There were just ten minutes left of the flight before landing.

The Targui stretched his limbs, letting out a long sigh. Ignoring the autopilot, he had regained control about an hour earlier, as the wind began to pick up. For several minutes, he was busy correcting their course, the Mistral boldly pushing them eastward. He adjusted the radio and started transmitting to request clearance to land.

"This is Fox-Alpha-Charlie, four two zero, FAC420 from Constantine at the control tower. Do you read me? Beechcraft FAC420 at control tower, do you read me?"

The response took a few seconds.

"Marignane to Beechcraft FAC420, we receive you four out of five, over to you."

"Marignane, I receive you five out of five. Request authorization to land, over to you."

"Authorization granted. South to southeast wind, speed 60 km/h, light gusts, ground pressure 990 millibars, temperature 19 degrees. Come to the small track by northeast and be careful, it's up to you."

"FAC420 at control tower, I am on final approach, landing expected in about eight minutes."

Ranzi used the rudder pedals to initiate a wide turn to the west, leaving Marseille on his right. He executed a broad loop and began a long descent, gradually reducing the throttle. The twin-engine aircraft presented itself correctly at the end of the runway, landing gear extended.

The pilot sharpened his focus to maintain the correct attitude. The Mistral blew laterally in gusts, pitching the plane like a wisp of straw. Ranzi remained composed; he had faced more critical situations while navigating turbulent storms in the Oran sky above Sénia, and had no reason to panic now.

The plane was just a few centimeters from the runway when it pitched up slightly and touched down with a few jerks, which were quickly absorbed. It came to a stop after rolling a few hundred yards. Isaac and Khaled, settled comfortably in their seats, felt their adrenaline levels return to normal as the plane finally came to a halt.

The nasal voice crackled through the radio again. "Control tower at FAC420, welcome to Marseille-Marignane airport. Report to hangar number twelve for customs control."

Ranzi allowed himself a minute's respite before overshooting and taxiing toward Hangar Twelve.

As the passengers disembarked from the twin-engine, they were greeted by the mainland. They headed directly for the checkpoint. Once the customs formalities were completed, Ranzi instructed the ground mechanics to conduct a quick check-up and refuel the aircraft.

The friends then decided to have a snack before embarking on the second part of their journey. They still had six hundred kilometers to reach Tours, which would take just over two hours of flight time, including take-off and landing maneuvers.

At the restaurant, they chose the dish of the day: various appetizers, sole meunière, and steamed potatoes. The meal suited them perfectly, catering to their specific culinary requirements. After finishing dessert, Isaac ordered the coffees and asked for the bill. He felt the lingering effects of adrenaline and seemed quite worried as he finally spoke up.

"It's high time to draw up an action plan, brother."

"What need?" replied the sheik. "We go to Chinon, we invest the castle, and we realize the current validity of the text of Abraham."

Isaac shook his head in disapproval. "Isn't it better to start by gathering as much information and details as possible about the ruins before undertaking in situ excavations? You could check with the town hall or the city's tourist office, don't you think?"

"Yssic," replied the Targui, feigning annoyance—he knew perfectly well that Isaac disliked the diminutive, but he enjoyed calling him that, as it felt more brotherly. "When will you stop underestimating me? I planned everything. We're going to have valuable local help thanks to some occult interventions, if you know what I mean," he breathed enigmatically. "Let's go now; everything has gone well so far, and I don't want the weather to deteriorate on the continent."

The Beechcraft E-18S completed the second leg of its flight without a hitch. It was 4:30 p.m. sharp when the aircraft parked in the hangar of the Touraine flying club.

The club coordinator came to meet the quartet. A badge sewn to the edge of his upper right pocket indicated his name was Martin.

"Hello gentlemen, I hope you had a good trip. I come to take delivery of the device to condition it before your return. A rental car is waiting for you at the Touring Club counter."

"Thank you, Mr. Martin. It's likely that we will be back this Thursday. Can you ensure that the aircraft is ready to take off with the necessary flight plans for Constantine and a stopover in Marignane, just as on the outward journey? We are in a hurry, so please allow us to leave immediately."

The travelers headed for the lobby of the flying club. At the Touring Club counter, Ranzi quickly completed the usual formalities and collected the papers for a midnight blue DS21.

"I'm driving this time," Isaac said, winking at Khaled. He was eager to compare the performance of the DS21 with that of his own car.

"Go through Tours; we are going to greet Commissioner Boulin and present our credentials to him," the Targui ordered mechanically.

Isaac was beginning to piece together the precise nature of the "occult recommendations" that Ranzi had mentioned earlier that morning.

Fortunately, a sign indicated the direction of the police station and the town hall. The flying club was only a few kilometers from the city center, and it took no more than ten minutes for the Algerians to reach the police station.

The blue Citroën passed through the large gate leading into the building's interior courtyard and stopped a few meters from the entrance. The uniformed officer saluted the quartet and was about to say a word or two when Ranzi cut in.

"Hello, we'd like to meet Commissioner Boulin, if he is available, of course. Here is a letter of recommendation."

The officer asked them to wait in the entrance while he checked with his superior over the phone. He nodded several times before returning with the envelope Ranzi had given him.

"Here," said the policeman. "You can go there. It's on the first floor; you can't miss his office; there's a plaque with his name on the glass door."

Once in the square, Commissioner Boulin greeted them warmly.

The commissioner, a pleasant character with a bit of a round figure, had a crew cut that made him look more like a military officer than a civil servant.

After the introductions were made, he said amiably, "It is my colleague and class friend, Major Guichard, who sent you. I spoke to him at length on the phone yesterday, and he was full of praise for you. What can I do to help you, gentlemen?"

Ranzi took it upon himself to respond. "We are conducting historical research on Chinon and its medieval castle. We want to verify some things in situ, and we don't know anyone who can assist us there. Would you be so kind as to let us know if you have any contacts?"

"Nothing could be simpler. Go see the mayor directly on my behalf; he will give you the warmest welcome. Mr. Chamberlin, the current mayor, knows the history of Chinon better than anyone, and he's currently undertaking renovation work. Hold on," the commissioner suddenly changed his mind, "we'll do it another way. I'll call him right away."

After a few minutes of waiting, the commissioner managed to get through.

"My respects, Mr. Mayor, Commissioner Boulin speaking… yes, thank you, and you? I have a small favor to ask of you; can you spare me a few minutes?… thank you. I'd like for you to take charge of three of my friends and a young man. They are interested in your castle and its history. They've made a long trip to satisfy their curiosity and need a competent guide… Affirmative, they are in my office now and will spend the night at…" Ranzi wrote a note on a sheet of paper and showed it to the commissioner. "… at the inn de l'Oise, yes, in Chinon… You will greet them tomorrow morning at nine o'clock. That's perfect; just ask for His Highness Prince Ahmed Ranzi at the reception… Yes, affirmative, Prince Ahmed. He will be waiting for you for breakfast. My respects and thank you again, Mr. Mayor."

Boulin hung up and fixed the Targui with his warm gaze. "It couldn't be simpler. Are you satisfied?"

"Thank you very much, commissioner. You have just done us a great service. If you pass by Khenchela one day, Isaac and I would be happy to welcome you. With your permission, we'd like to take our leave immediately. We wish to be back in Chinon before nightfall."

It took nearly an hour to cover the forty-five kilometers separating Chinon from Tours. The state of the county left much to be desired; it wasn't just the roads in the settlements that were poorly maintained. Ranzi observed as Isaac strained to avoid the potholes.

The DS21 pulled up alongside the sidewalk in the alley.

The Auberge de l'Oise stood at the entrance to the small town. The building had its back to the large rock upon which the castle ruins emerged. As they arrived, the friends could see that only three towers remained standing, out of the original five from the fortress's heroic past.

Ranzi had reserved three rooms on behalf of Algeria, thanks to the organization of the Touring Club to which he belonged. The small inn had just a dozen rooms, which made it particularly friendly.

The hotel owner welcomed the four tourists with a broad smile, her superb accent rolling the "r."

"Good evening, gentlemen. Did you have a good trip? I've reserved our best rooms for you; we're not yet in high season, you see. Would you like to fill in the forms while I take care of your luggage?"

"No need, ma'am, don't bother," Isaac replied politely. "We only have a small suitcase each, and we can't wait to rest after freshening up."

"Of course! Here are your keys: King Richard's room, with two double beds for Mr. Yakobi father and son, and those of Joan of Arc and Henry II for the other two guests. We name our rooms rather than numbering them here; it feels more personal. All three are upstairs, and if you need anything, just ring the bell."

"Thank you very much, ma'am," Isaac said. "Could you prepare a meal for us this evening? Something light—fish or eggs, no pork or meat—and a hearty breakfast for five people tomorrow morning at nine o'clock. We have a distinguished guest."

CHAPTER 15

Wednesday, April 21, 1954

Mr. Chamberlin was a punctual person - crossing the hotel lobby just minutes before nine o'clock struck.

Short and rather skinny, he wore rimless glasses and a cap that certainly concealed early baldness. He was only in his thirties, yet seemed much too young to be doing this job. He appeared like one of those intellectuals still pure and naive, a perfect boy scout available in all circumstances. He was dressed in a navy blue blazer with gold buttons and wore a smart casually tied club tie, aiming to look rather casual.

The mayor found the Algerians on the terrace of the restaurant where he was warmly welcomed by the Targui who stood up at the same time as his two companions and the young Dror.

The weather was glorious, with a pure blue sky and a temperature rise that made it easy to forget the gloomy and windy weather of the day before.

"Hello Mr. Mayor, allow me to make the introductions," - said Ahmed Ranzi el Sahraoui, with a smile - "I am Ahmed Ranzi el Sahraoui, this is my brother, Isaac Yakobi, my faithful secretary Khaled, and my nephew, the young Dror Yakobi. Do you want to share breakfast with us?"

The mayor nodded in approval.

"Thank you very much Sheikh Ahmed," - replied the mayor - "Gentlemen, I welcome you to Chinon. In order to guide you in your investigations, I have released myself from all my obligations for the morning, and even for the afternoon if necessary, as I promised my friend Superintendent Boulin yesterday. I'm listening to you."

Ranzi motioned for the innkeeper to serve.

"We want to verify some information that we have deciphered on an ancient manuscript from the 14th century," - said Ranzi - "First of all, can you confirm that the illustration in this photograph corresponds to that of your château? But above all know that it is to the young man sitting opposite you that we owe this astonishing discovery."

The mayor looked at Dror with surprise at the involvement of a teenager in a case that immediately seemed more than mysterious. He took the photo Isaac handed him and studied it with undiluted interest. After a minute or two, he spoke up.

"This is our castle," - said the mayor - "The tower we see there is that of the Clock, formerly the Treasure Tower. There are still three or four towers in more or less good condition, including that of the Moulin and the Donjon. What are you looking for in particular in these ruins?"

"Mr. Chamberlin," - replied Isaac deferentially, "to be frank we have no idea. You have seen the illegible texts at the bottom of the page, these are poems written in Hebrew by the author of the manuscript, a certain Abraham the Jew. He was apparently persecuted by the Inquisition in the middle of the 14th century. He bequeathed the manuscript in question to his co-religionists. We have good reason to believe that he lived or sojourned here in the fourteenth century. Here is a translation of the text that interests us, know that we also owe it to my young son."

Isaac began to recite the poem he had memorized the day before:

"On Lion Rock,

"Where kings have made their homes,

"Climb the steps of hope,

"Which lead to the narrow path of fire,

"Follow the Milky Way to the Athanor,

"Under the ashes the shield of David will find"

"What do you think, Mayor?" - asked Ranzi, without much conviction - "Does it awaken something very special for you?"

"Perhaps," - finally admitted the mayor, deeply intrigued by the mysterious phrases in the manuscript - "But let's not waste time, he said, looking suddenly interested after a few seconds of thinking - let's go to the ruins of the castle and we'll find out. You're in the car, aren't you? We will leave it below the rock, this will save us a long detour on foot."

Before leaving, however, I would like to show you this - concluded the mayor, unrolling an old plan. He pointed his index finger at a tower.

"Here is the entrance," - said the mayor - "You reach it by a drawbridge which leads to an interior courtyard. Several paved paths are laid out to serve the various dungeons as well as the walkway. This old plan is in fact a copy of the original and I use it frequently to direct the restoration work because, alas, as you will see, the castle is in ruins. Let's go now, if you don't mind."

The car was spacious enough to hold five passengers. Chamberlin sat in the front seat, the two Targuis and young Dror settled in the large back seat.

The mayor guided Isaac to the foot of the rocky outcrop. He made her park the car on the low side of the small road, near the ruins and got out first. He began the ascent of the rock by the small path that leads to the castle without even waiting for the other passengers.

The fortification was imposing. It extended over at least five hundred meters in length, which probably made it one of the largest castles of the Middle Ages. Once in front of the large drawbridge overlooking the dry moat, the mayor took over the direction of operations and addressed the quartet who had just joined him.

"Follow me," - said the mayor - "We will now enter the courtyard."

From inside, everything looked different. The relief and the groves of leafy trees completely changed the view that the tourist could have of the monument from the road. The mayor caught his breath. He took out a handkerchief to mop his forehead.

"We are indeed on Lion's Rock," - said the mayor - "since this land belonged to Richard the Lionheart. The castle is built on a rocky outcrop and several kings lived here, including Henry II the Plantagenet. As for Richard the Lionheart, he had come here in the hope of recovering the legendary treasure of his predecessor Henry II. And one!"

The mayor hesitated for a moment.

"Remind me of the rest of the poem," asked the mayor. "Will you?"

Ranzi recited three lines:

"Climb the steps of hope,

"Which lead to the narrow path of fire,

"Follow the Milky Way to the Athanor..."

"The steps of hope lead well to the narrow path of fire," - said the mayor - "The walkway was used, during a war, to massacre the attackers. The besieged hurled boiling oil and molten lead at their adversaries. They maintained several fires to heat the cauldrons, but the castle ended up falling into the hands of Philippe Auguste on June 24, 1205. And two!"

Regarding the Milky Way, the mayor couldn't seem to find the solution.

"True, now it is a question of determining what characterizes the right tower," - said the mayor - "Can someone tell me the meaning of the word 'Athanor'?"

"My brother or myself," - replied Isaac - "But above all, allow us to congratulate you on your in-depth knowledge, it is impressive. I will therefore try to impress you in my turn."

Ranzi continued: "Firstly, what can 'Milky Way' mean? Only a few insiders know these days that this is how the alchemists designate the road to Santiago de Compostela. The scallop shell, formerly called Mérelle de Compostelle, is the emblem of common mercury, whose mysterious appearance during the first work has often been considered miraculous. It is also the sign of recognition of the pilgrim in the same way as the calabash and the bumblebee, which therefore all three have a highly cabalistic meaning."

"Secondly, Athanor means 'the oven' in Hebrew, the Arab alchemists later took up this name to designate especially the oven used for the coction of the Philosopher's Stone. This name became popular throughout medieval Europe," - Isaac added, before continuing - "And this is how we will find the solution.".

The mayor grinned broadly, a gleam dancing in his small gray-blue eyes, clearly relishing the moment.

"Yes, of course, there is only one possibility—the Clock Tower. The one that appears very precisely in the illustration of your manuscript."

"Certainly, we suspected as much," Ranzi replied. "But why do you think so?"

"What a question! Come, follow me, and you will quickly understand."

The mayor led them to a staircase leaning against the wall of the walkway and motioned for his new friends to follow him.

"Be careful, this staircase is in rather poor condition. Watch carefully where you put your feet when you climb the steps."

Once on the walkway, the mayor headed feverishly, with a jerky step, toward the Clock Tower. In the center, a large opening revealed a wide staircase that must have led to the top of the tower, flanked on either side by two massive doors that were apparently closed. He stopped in front of the left door and miraculously produced a huge bunch of keys, probably hung from his belt. After some trial and error, he chose one, stuck it in the keyhole, and turned the bolt. A creak of poorly oiled hinges resounded, and finally, the door opened. He retrieved the bunch of keys and crossed the threshold.

"It's here!" exclaimed the mayor. "You have it right in front of you: here is the furnace of the Souffleurs. That's what it used to be called! And three and four!" he added triumphantly.

"Damn," Ranzi cried, "I can't believe my eyes! Do you see what I see, Yssic?"

"Yes, Your Highness. I see precisely a kind of small tower about one meter sixty to one meter seventy high, seventy centimeters in diameter, and topped with a small hemispherical roof. On the convex surface of the small roof, the artist who produced this masterpiece inlaid the Mérelle de Compostelle, our scallop shell. So it is indeed this that represents the Milky Way of Abraham's message, our penultimate milestone. The whole forms a tiny projecting dungeon. I think that these small doors distributed in height are intended to receive crucibles. The oven has a large opening in the shape of a vault in the lower part, slightly raised, constituting the hearth, with an underlying ashtray, quite naturally."

"Yippee! This is our Athanor!" chuckled Dror, carried away by an unspeakable joy. "There is even a Latin inscription in a semicircle, just around the scallop shell; it is barely legible."

"We just have to find David's shield now," Ranzi said, enthralled by how quickly the veil of mystery had been lifted.

"Hey! It comes back to me now!" exclaimed the mayor. "It is known that the hearth had a cast iron door with seven stars curiously placed on it. The door was damaged and has since disappeared."

"Of course," replied Isaac. "Seven stars—the series of philosophical sublimations, or the seven planetary metals, which comes to the same thing. That is the esoteric meaning of the motif inlaid in the door, but that does not, alas, concern the shield of David."

The Targui approached the oven mechanically and bent down to examine the hearth.

"There's nothing," he said, disappointed, after casting a vague glance at the sole.

"Let's continue to examine the oven from every angle, Ranzi. So far, we have followed the text to the letter, and it has worked quite well, so we must continue our research."

Incidentally, Chamberlin looked alternately at the Targui and then at Isaac. He had certainly noted the ethnic difference between the two men. It was obvious, including the way the Bedouin was dressed, which contrasted with the classic three-piece suit of his brother. He questioned, hotly: "I have a question for you, Mr. Yakobi. You're an Israelite, aren't you? But Sheikh Ahmed is a Muslim?"

"Indeed," Isaac exclaimed with a laugh. "Actually, Ranzi is my foster brother. We were raised together by the same nanny and we consider ourselves two real brothers, you see. Does this answer satisfy you?"

"Absolutely. You will now be able to explain to me what this mysterious shield of David may mean."

"It's simple," replied Ranzi. "The Star of David, or the Seal of Solomon (it's the same symbol), is a six-pointed star made up of two inverted equilateral triangles. From the esoteric point of view, this symbol represents the union of water and fire, the fixed and the volatile. It is the major arcana of the Great Work. It was therefore not chosen by chance."

"You should know that there used to be a trap door that allowed you to empty the ashes directly into the moat, with access from this room," continued the mayor, pointing to the wall to their right. "The door has unfortunately been walled up for a very long time."

"What are we waiting for to go under the moat?" Isaac said.

The mayor let out a satisfied laugh. "Very exciting, this treasure hunt! It's been so long since I had so much fun in this damn town. We have to go around the fortifications if we want to find an entrance. Ahead!" he said enthusiastically. "And long live the adventure!"

Khaled opened the door and was about to politely slip away to let the mayor pass when he noticed a silhouette looming about twenty meters from the entrance to the dungeon, on the walkway.

He sharply kicked the heavy door shut, slamming the mayor to the floor. A split second later, a gunshot was heard—the bullet ricocheted off the thick stone wall.

"It's another 7.65 Beretta," Ranzi observed coolly. "Khaled had the right reflex as soon as he saw the attacker(s). It seems that we are trapped in this mousetrap."

The Targui then approached one of the loopholes, hoping to see the enemy, but in vain—the assailants had taken cover.

"Mr. Mayor, please give me the keys. I will close the door. It seems thick enough to withstand the shots of a pistol. And you, Dror, get away from here; do not expose yourself."

"Here, here is the key ring. I don't think they will take the risk of besieging us for too long. The staff at the town hall knows that I am here with you. My collaborators will worry soon enough if they don't hear from me."

Driven by youthful curiosity, Dror began to carefully inspect the Athanor.

"Look at the inscription in a semicircle around the dome," he said triumphantly. "It is half erased, but I can try to decipher it. Let's see... a word 'NO,' then a triangle pointing upwards, the symbol of Fire. Then a second word 'APERIE,' followed by a triangle pointing downwards, the sign of water. Finally, there is a last illegible word ending in a V or VR; a letter is completely erased..."

"'Non aperie tur,'" whispered the Targui. "In pure Latin, it means: 'It (the door) will not be opened.' And the assembly of the two triangles forms the Star of David—the union of fire and water. Congratulations once again, my dear disciple!"

"Perfectly, Ranzi: 'The door will not be opened.' So we can open it!" Isaac exclaimed without the slightest hesitation, convinced he had found a secret passage.

Meanwhile, violent blows were struck on the heavy door, which seemed to resist the attack very well—but for how long?

Khaled pulled out a short-barreled police P38 and stood watch outside the door.

Dror knelt to examine the inside of the oven. He noticed two rows of four thick steel bars running across it—one row at the level of the first hearth, and the second at the level of the upper hearth. These bars were probably intended to support the vessels for cooking over the fire. One of them, on the lower floor, did not cross the oven from side to side like the others; it lacked a few centimeters to join the internal wall.

He began to play with the steel bar and found that it was not sealed like the others. Moreover, it slid perfectly into its housing. Pulling on it, he heard a slight click. Suddenly, he got up, enclosed the oven in his arms, and, as if by magic, swiveled the Athanor ninety degrees with disconcerting ease, revealing a narrow opening that seemed to sink into the thick building wall.

"Congratulations, Dror! You just revealed the secret passage. Khaled, give me your torch. Quick!" ordered Ranzi, who hadn't looked away from the scene.

The Targui scanned the opening the teenager had just discovered, and the beam revealed a narrow spiral staircase in poor condition that descended beneath the room's floor.

"Let's go," said the mayor. "No need to linger here any longer. And lower your head as you descend the stairs," he added, warning his new friends.

Isaac was the last to take the stairs. After going around the oven, he swung the heavy device in the opposite direction to block access to the aggressors. He made sure the secret passage was properly closed by pushing aside the iron handle that emerged before joining his companions.

After descending about thirty steps, they arrived in a circular room that ended in a small corridor. At the end of the corridor, there was a new staircase—straight this time. It was rather cold and damp, with countless cobwebs hanging everywhere and musty smells wafting through the air. Carefully, they descended about twenty steps to find themselves in a huge hall.

Ranzi spotted torches hanging on the walls. He grabbed one and lit it with his lighter. Luckily, a flame erupted with thick smoke. The fuel—a bituminous grease—had managed to last through the centuries. Khaled did the same with another torch nearby, and the entire hall was miraculously illuminated.

This place had not been explored for several centuries, as evidenced by the thick layer of dust that had accumulated on the badly paved ground, Chamberlin realized, while scanning the imposing size of the secret underground space with his gaze.

"My friends," he finally exclaimed, "you will explain to me later the reason for this sudden attack. But for now, we need to find the exit of this tunnel as quickly as possible to go to the gendarmerie and ask for help." Spreading his unfolded map on the ground, he continued, "Let's see where we landed."

Ranzi illuminated it with the beam of his flashlight.

"We are here," said the mayor, pointing to the map. "We made an almost perfect circle going down the spiral staircase, and we went straight down again through a new set of stairs. So we're under that part of the dungeon, right there." He pointed again on the map. "This room ends with a corridor that crosses this entire area. We will be able to emerge under the drawbridge, exactly here!"

"If I understand correctly, we'll meet just under the bridge we crossed, the same one our opponents must have used earlier," Isaac replied.

"Certainly," agreed the mayor. "And that is where the exit must be."

"Provided it exists," Ranzi added. "Let's go now; we may have the chance to take the enemy from behind. We will try to ambush him while you, Mr. Mayor, go and warn the gendarmes. These men are dangerous. They are wanted by Interpol, and they must be neutralized at all costs before they commit other crimes."

Isaac nodded, adding to Chamberlin, "It is essential that the local gendarmerie immediately get in touch with Divisional Guichard in Algiers on our behalf and inform him that we have probably just cornered adviser Amrouche and one of his accomplices."

They took the long corridor leading to the drawbridge, walking almost a hundred meters in the fading light of Khaled's lamp. The torches, with the smoke now emanating from them, provided only mediocre illumination.

After walking three-quarters of the way to the exit, Khaled, usually very reserved, uttered an untranslatable French curse.

"If Ahmed," he said, regaining his composure, "there's a corpse on the ground there, leaning against the wall."

Dror, standing right behind, instinctively took a step back.

As for the corpse, it was now merely a dusty skeleton, resembling a disjointed puppet covered in multiple shreds of fabric—the relics of its clothing. The tilted skull rested above the bones, and a dagger with a rusty steel blade lay in the middle of what must have been the rib cage. The right arm formed a curious angle, and the index finger of the right hand seemed to point in the direction of the opposite wall.

The mayor examined the remains, as well as the pieces of fabric spared by the centuries.

"This man was killed at least five centuries ago, judging by the nature and style of the fabrics he wore," he noted.

"Over six hundred years ago, and I can even identify the victim," Ranzi corrected with conviction.

"You're going a bit strong, Cheikh Ahmed, don't you think?" replied the mayor, jokingly. "You're not going to make me believe that your mediumistic gifts have allowed you to enter into a relationship with the beyond!"

"Please, call me Ranzi, like all my friends do. I have good reason to believe that the skeleton you see there is that of a Spanish doctor and rabbi named Sanches or Canches. He arrived here with Nicolas Flamel around 1380, intending to recover the treasure of Abraham the Jew. Flamel may have changed his mind about sharing and decided to keep all the loot for himself."

"Call me Charles," replied the mayor, his tone familiar. "You're still going a bit strong, Ranzi. Flamel a criminal? I refuse to believe it! You'll have to produce solid proof."

"That's just a guess at the moment, Charles."

"The end of the tunnel is finally in sight!" cried Isaac, cutting off the controversy. "It looks like a dead end to me."

"No, that's not possible!" the mayor responded. "Listen, leave it to me. I'm familiar with the topography outside, and we should be able to find a hidden door somewhere. Please lend me the lamp."

Chamberlin scanned the wall with the beam of the flickering lamp, hoping to find a clue. After several minutes, he focused the light on a section of the wall that seemed to stand out from the rest.

"It's here," he said finally, relief washing over him. "It must be a revolving door. Look at this small rectangular hole and these rusty metal residues. Check out these traces forming a large rectangle in the wall; there must have been a lever controlling the door's opening. The challenge is figuring out how to unlock the system, of which only dust remains."

Khaled mechanically handed the torch to Dror and walked close to the wall for a careful inspection. He sketched a broad smile and gave the mayor a knowing wink before saying, "If there's nothing left of this mechanism but dust, Mr. Mayor, we should be able to open the secret door without any problem. Please help me. Let's apply a push together on the left side and then the right side alternately to see if the slab moves."

A slight creak echoed in the tunnel. Both Ranzi and Isaac waited in silence, trusting in their lucky stars.

Dror took advantage of the moment's tension to slip away into the dungeon.

"It's moving!" exclaimed the mayor. "Now let's push together to the other side, Khaled," he ordered. "The door is beginning to swing."

Fortunately, the locking system had completely deteriorated after six centuries of humidity. A beam of light finally began to filter through, initially growing weak but then bursting forth in a dazzling display, accompanied by a revitalizing breath of fresh air that invigorated the four men.

Ranzi prevented the mayor from leaving the tunnel just as he was about to cross the gaping opening.

"Charles, let's be careful. There may be a third thief keeping watch outside. With your permission, I will take over the direction of operations. Can you tell me exactly where we are and how to reach our car?"

The mayor took out his crumpled old map, recalled the underground journey they had just completed, and pointed confidently at the drawbridge with his index finger. "We must be here, on this side of the drawbridge. There should be a path allowing us to reach the road without being too visible. The road is to your right; the DS21 is parked just there."

The Targui pulled out the Lüger concealed in the holster under his armpit and motioned for Khaled to approach. "There are about fifty meters to go, with around twenty in the open. Head for the road, and if you spot a bandit on duty, knock him out and put him in the trunk of the car after gagging him. His accomplices must not be alerted. As soon as the way is clear, let out three cries of the crow. Charles and Isaac will head to the gendarmerie while we prevent the mobsters from escaping. Dror will stay safe here."

Charles, clearly unconvinced by the prince's plan, retorted jokingly, "Ranzi, do you really think it's reasonable to play cops and robbers? At your age?" He added, "And how come you two are armed?"

"Have no fear, Charles. We each have a proper port of arms. Know that we've already managed to deal with the rest of the gang in Algeria, the small fry that we've successfully imprisoned. Their leader is here—he is a dangerous criminal wanted by Interpol. He is capable of the worst, and it's absolutely necessary to prevent him from escaping. I ask you to trust us. Moreover, I promise to tell you this whole story in detail as soon as these gentlemen are out of harm's way."

Wasting no time, Khaled descended the slope at an angle to reach the bottom of the thankfully dry ditch. He passed under the drawbridge and climbed the slope with some difficulty, struggling to maintain his balance. He risked being spotted by the potential third accomplice lurking nearby.

Finally at the top, he crouched on the lawn and carefully inspected his surroundings. A Mercedes was parked just behind the DS21, and a man dressed like a European kept watch—he was the third accomplice.

Khaled began to crawl silently, inching forward with the patience of a feline. He needed to reach the old oak tree that obscured the opponent's view and was conveniently positioned alongside the sidewalk.

Only a few meters left, he thought to himself.

The man on duty took a pack of cigarettes from his pocket, retrieved one, and sniffed it several times as if savoring the aroma before lighting it. He took matches from his right pocket and attempted to light his cigarette, using his left hand as a shield against the light breeze that flickered the flame.

It was in that moment that the Algerian chose to pounce on his target. The attack was so sudden that the bandit didn't even have time to take his first puff. Khaled knocked him out effortlessly with a well-placed cuff.

He quickly searched the pockets of the fallen man, recovering a Beretta 7.65, a well-stocked wallet, and the precious keys to the Mercedes. He hastily opened the car's spacious trunk, lifted the groggy man as if he weighed nothing, and tipped him into the rear compartment. He tied the man's hands with the belt he had removed from the victim's trousers, stuffed his handkerchief into his mouth, and carefully locked the trunk. After stepping back and feeling satisfied, he mimicked the crow's cry three times.

Khaled waited patiently, a wide smile on his face. "Here are the car keys, Mr. Mayor. It would be better if you take it to the gendarmerie. There's a large parcel in the back."

Ranzi congratulated himself on choosing the most efficient of the Targuis as his lieutenant. "Well done, Khaled. We've just won the first round, but we must win the second. Let's not waste time; let's take our positions in front of the castle entrance."

Isaac, now called Ranzi, asked the gendarmes to be as discreet as possible when they arrived, especially when surrounding the castle.

The sedan drove off slowly and silently, carrying the mayor, Isaac, and the bandit imprisoned in the trunk. It gradually accelerated toward the village, while the two Targuis carefully crossed the drawbridge for the second time.

"We will wait for our attackers at the entrance, behind these two imposing pillars. We'll let them through the gate and surprise them from behind if possible. We'll knock them out. If we have to use our weapons, let's aim to incapacitate them rather than kill them."

CHAPTER 16

On the other side of the castle, the intruders struggled in vain to break down the door of the tower. It had already been more than a quarter of an hour since they had launched their attack.

"Try to open this damn door for me," Amrouche said angrily.

He stamped his feet furiously, the gun was still in his fist, held in a trembling hand.

"No need to insist," replied his apparently much calmer accomplice. "This door is made of solid oak and is at least ten centimeters thick. The lock is made of forged steel, probably from two centuries ago, so there's no point in pulling on it. I think it's over for today, and we better leave before we get noticed. The shots will attract people. We can certainly ambush them on the way back between Chinon and Tours, don't you think?"

Furious, Amrouche handed him a bent steel rod. "Try opening it with this instead."

The sidekick grabbed the makeshift tool and inserted it into the lock, attempting to manipulate the bolt. However, the old lock remained unyielding.

Unable to contain his anger any longer, Amrouche lost his temper. "Get out of here! I'll show you how to get rid of a stubborn lock," he shouted, exasperated. He selected a simple hook, nervously inserted it into the lock, and made a brutal U-turn. A click followed by a creak echoed as the heavy door finally opened… revealing a totally empty room.

"It's not possible!" Exclaimed Amrouche, gun in hand. "There's no one left in this room. Where the hell did they go? There seems to be no other way out."

"This old castle must have hidden doors, like we see in the movies," suggested the accomplice.

They lingered for a moment, carefully examining the walls of the room, hoping to find a secret passage. The former adviser spotted the athanor and approached it, trying in vain to move the oven, whose mechanism had been locked by Isaac just before their descent to the basements.

"I'm sure the passage is there!" Cried the ex-councillor, consumed by rage.

"Let's get out of here," implored the accomplice. "We will get caught if we delay too long."

The sidekick wasn't wrong. It had been over twenty minutes since their arrival on the walkway, and if the enemies had escaped through a secret passage, they had ample time to alert the police, thought Amrouche, a little too late.

The two aggressors stashed their weapons and turned to leave hastily. They took the walkway in the opposite direction, descending the narrow staircase leading to the courtyard and walking quickly toward the drawbridge.

When they reached the gate a few minutes later, Amrouche halted abruptly, a premonition striking him. He listened, signaling for his accomplice to be quiet. He was a cunning councilman. It didn't escape him that the birds had suddenly fallen silent, and he could hear the distant noise of a car followed by the screeching of tires, apparently coming from a sharp stop on the gravel pavement.

The gendarmes had refrained from sounding their sirens, but the brutality of the braking betrayed their presence.

"Let's get the hell out the other side!" Yelled Amrouche. "The cops are coming!"

They hurriedly retraced their steps.

Khaled, hidden behind the right pillar, was watching the scene unfold. He pretended to pursue them when, with a gesture, Ranzi ordered him not to move. It seemed more reasonable to let the gendarmerie act. They were no longer in Algeria; it was best not to get too involved in this city. Once he ensured the bandits were out of sight, Khaled calmly sheathed his weapon and signaled for his lieutenant to do the same.

"Let's wait for the cavalry," Ranzi said, winking to reassure Khaled, who was confused by this sudden reserve. "It is no longer our business now."

The gendarmerie detachment arrived quickly, led by Chamberlin and Isaac.

The mayor, immediately within earshot, called out to Ranzi. "Are you all right?"

"It's fine, but they heard you coming and fled through the yard. Do you know if there's any other way out of these ruins?"

"Yes, but don't worry, Ranzi, our gendarmes are already there. Without a vehicle, even if they deceive our vigilance, our attackers won't get far."

Ranzi didn't seem to share this optimism; he knew full well what the opponent was capable of. "Don't underestimate Amrouche. This man wouldn't hesitate to kill one of his accomplices in cold blood. Like a desperate wolf, he'll be extremely dangerous. He won't hesitate to fire on the police."

"I'll notify the gendarmes by radio," Chamberlin said. He activated his transmitter and whispered barely audible into the microphone, "Commander, do you read me? Recommend extreme caution to all your men; the enemy is very dangerous. You're facing two armed men ready for anything. Don't hesitate to use your weapons; you're covered by my authority."

He then turned to Ranzi, sharing details on the system in place to intercept the attackers. "We have eight men in total; half are with us, while the other team, led by Commander Védrin, is on the opposite side. There are no other passable exits without special equipment. As you've seen, we're on a hell of a rock, a peak."

"Then," Ranzi suggested, "I propose you move in the same direction to encircle them and cut off any potential retreat."

On the other side of the rock, four gendarmes took their positions as soon as they arrived, loaded assault rifles with fingers on the triggers, ready to fire. They hid behind large trees, prepared to thwart any escape through the second gate.

At that precise moment, Isaac had an unsettling thought. "Dror!" he exclaimed in sudden panic. "But where the hell is Dror?"

"I didn't see him come out of the underground," Ranzi muttered, his worry now palpable. "Dror, he echoed, Dror, where are you?"

"Mr. Mayor," Ranzi urged, "tell the gendarmes not to open fire until Dror is found. Isaac and I fear the worst."

The Targui's recommendations were immediately relayed to the gendarmerie commander, who quickly passed the instructions along to his men.

After what felt like an eternity, Amrouche finally emerged from the darkness of the tunnel, pushing the young Dror ahead of him at gunpoint. He was closely followed by his accomplice, also armed.

Young Dror, however, didn't appear frightened by the menacing demeanor of the former councillor. He had simply followed his master's teachings, controlling his breathing and evacuating any stress. Realizing he was responsible for the trap he had fallen into, he refused to panic.

"I advise you to lower your weapons," Amrouche ordered cynically, "otherwise…"

Ranzi immediately assessed the gravity of the situation while patting his foster brother on the shoulder, as if to reassure him. "They must have discovered the secret passage and intercepted Dror, who recklessly stayed behind. Your son has kept his cool—do like him, don't flinch, and let me handle this."

Isaac nodded in silence, placing his complete trust in the Targui. Despite the dire circumstances, he felt secure under Ranzi's command.

Ranzi turned to his lieutenant and gave her a long look, nodding slightly to signal her to prepare for action. Khaled understood the unspoken message and discreetly retrieved his pistol from behind his back, ready for any eventuality. His hunting instinct kicked in.

"Shoot Amrouche; I'll take care of the accomplice," the Targui whispered to his lieutenant.

Tension escalated, and an eerie silence blanketed the forecourt of the old fortifications.

Amrouche pushed forward again, roughly shoving the teenager as he went. He halted at the edge of the ditch, looking around to assess the situation, convinced it would turn in his favor.

Ranzi realized this presented a perfect opportunity. Without wasting another second, he took action, fully aware of his young disciple's reflexes.

"Dror!" he commanded in Hebrew, "regel yamin ve lekh le smola!" (right foot and go to the left).

The young hero didn't need a second invitation. He delivered a swift kick to the bandit's right foot and leapt to the left, executing a perfect roll.

Amrouche was caught off guard. He screamed, hopping on his left foot, swearing and cursing at the audacious youth. But he had little time to react; Khaled instinctively fired twice.

Both bullets struck true. The third bullet, fired by Ranzi, also hit its target. The councillor and his accomplice crumpled to the ground, dropping their weapons into the ditch. Moments later, the gendarmes rushed towards the two bandits, who lay motionless.

"There's one dead; the second is seriously injured, Mr. Mayor," noted the brigadier, leaning over the still bodies.

Ranzi ran as fast as he could, bending over Amrouche's bleeding form. A barely audible whisper escaped the dying man's lips. "Vi…ve l… revo… lution alg…" (Long live the Algerian revolution).

Amrouche never finished his sentence. A thin trickle of blood escaped his mouth as he breathed his last.

"What did he say?" Asked Charles.

"I didn't understand anything," Ranzi lied, opting to keep certain details private. "He just took his last breath."

The mayor then turned to Khaled. "Well done, Khaled. That was a very nice shot."

Turning back to Ranzi, he asked, "Do you recognize these two men?"

"I don't know them personally, Charles," Ranzi replied. "But that one, I've seen in a photo at the police station in Algiers. It's Amrouche, no doubt. As for this one, he seems European; I wouldn't say he's French. He's likely the intermediary in the arms deal. Maybe he's Italian? After all, there are too many Berettas involved in this story."

Dror felt shame wash over him for having broken the elementary rule of caution. Realizing he had just escaped serious danger, he hurried to join his father, who, still in shock, glared at him. Isaac changed his demeanor and hugged his son, overwhelmed with relief at the happy ending of this ordeal.

"Congratulations to you, dear disciple," Ranzi told the teenager. "Your father and I are proud of you, but try to be more careful in the future…"

The gendarmerie commander gave final instructions to his men before rejoining the group consisting of the mayor and his four new friends.

Chamberlin immediately made the introductions. "Commander Védrin of the National Gendarmerie, allow me to introduce to you his serene highness, Prince Ahmed Ranzi el Sahraoui, and his, ahem, private secretary, Mr. Khaled Essoufi. You already know Isaac Yakobi, right? This is his young son, Dror."

Védrin, standing at attention, spontaneously saluted the Algerians. "Gentlemen, you've just performed a great service to our country by helping us end the actions of these two bandits and their accomplice. The mayor informed me that your schedule is quite full, and you're preparing to leave early tomorrow morning. Can you spare me half an hour to take your statements in our van? We will not bother you any further."

Ranzi and his two friends accepted graciously, understanding they could not escape the police routine.

CHAPTER 17

The commander had kept his word. In no time, the testimonies were duly recorded in triplicate by the sergeant, who tapped his two fingers on the keyboard of an old black Remington, the rattling of which annoyed Isaac. Once the formalities were completed, the three friends took their leave, quickly exiting the dark van to finally welcome the light of day.

The mayor waited impatiently in front of the police cell van on the sidewalk, gesturing with delight upon spotting his new friends. "I'll make my statement later or tomorrow," he said eagerly. "I can't wait to find the underground passages of the castle to complete our exciting investigations. Not you?"

"What enthusiasm, Charles! You've certainly caught the virus of the treasure hunt," exclaimed Isaac, surprising himself with his familiarity with the mayor. "So what are we waiting for?"

The mayor displayed two large flashlights and a camera with a flash, tossing a lamp to Khaled, who surprisingly caught it in mid-air with remarkable skill. "I asked Commander Védrin to lend me all this equipment. We will certainly need it for our excavations. I also asked him to station two gendarmes at the entrance to the castle so we aren't disrupted by overly curious tourists. Now I take command of operations under the authority granted to me."

"Hey there! Not so fast; it's an abuse of power, Mr. Mayor. Don't forget that we are the inventors of this treasure hunt," joked Ranzi.

"But this is my Ranzi territory," replied Charles playfully.

It must have been around noon when the four men, along with young Dror, returned under the drawbridge at the main entrance and climbed the slight slope to the secret passage. With the two powerful flashlights, they illuminated the vast corridor that ran beneath the fortifications.

Barely arriving at the spot where the skeleton was discovered an hour or two earlier, Isaac knelt to examine the remains more closely but was immediately interrupted by Charles.

"Wait a minute, please, Isaac," said the mayor, stepping between him and the skeleton. "At least give me time to take a few pictures before touching anything."

He took three shots from different angles along with a close-up of the dagger before finally motioning for Isaac to proceed. The Pieds-Noirs (French people from Algeria) noted that the dagger had been inserted into the belly just beneath the rib cage. The victim had indeed suffered a slow agony before giving up the ghost. He withdrew the weapon, blew off the dust and rust accumulated over six centuries, then gestured for Khaled to come closer with his lamp to illuminate the object, which he examined minutely while slowly rotating it. After a few moments of hesitation, he finally spoke.

"It looks like an old gatehouse dagger from the 15th century, it seems…"

"That poor wretch can only be Master Sanches," Ranzi replied confidently, cutting Isaac off.

"Hey! How do you know it's the rabbi?" said Isaac.

Ranzi leaned over the skeleton to take a strip of fabric that had come off the costume, which revealed a large leather belt, burnt by the centuries and equipped with a strange buckle. "We can guess the Iberian origin by the nature of the clothing scraps that have miraculously remained after so many centuries, and this buckle, finely chiseled in bronze and now fairly blackened, is a typical ornament of the Spanish Basque Country. We'll leave it to the specialists to confirm the nationality of this corpse, but for me, there is no doubt, Charles."

Meanwhile, Isaac seemed distracted. In reality, he was intrigued by the bizarre posture of the victim. He knelt closer to the body to check a detail that had struck him from the start. "Let's stop bickering unnecessarily," he said. "Just observe the right arm of the deceased; it's frozen in a sort of contortion, his hand clenched and his index finger outstretched, seeming to want to show us a direction."

Isaac stood immediately after making this startling observation. What could the last gesture of a man who knew he was doomed mean? Did he want to indicate a point in the basement or leave a posthumous message?

Dror, breaking the silence he had maintained thus far, interjected, "As you know, I came to examine the place while you were waiting for the gendarmerie outside," he admitted. "Just before being surprised by Amrouche and his accomplice, I followed the direction indicated by the dead man's index finger and noticed a curious niche on the opposite wall, barely visible. On top of the niche, there is a perfectly circular medallion, about eighty centimeters in diameter, finely carved in stone, with a splendid six-pointed star."

"It's David's shield!" Isaac exclaimed. "But we'll need an explanation when we get back about your reckless running away, Dror," he added dryly to the teenager.

Ranzi couldn't stand his foster brother's stern attitude toward Dror. In a dry tone that cut off Isaac's remonstrances, he ordered, "Behind this wall, there is certainly a secret room. Help me discover it."

The beams of the powerful lamps moved almost simultaneously to the indicated spot. The inside of the niche was not very deep; however, the spiders had not been shy about weaving their webs, which had thickened over the centuries.

Khaled came to the rescue. He retrieved a torch hanging from the opposite wall, lit it, and carefully cleaned the niche's wall with the flame. Once the crevice was cleared, Charles took a step back and snapped a new shot.

Ranzi approached the niche and discovered that some of the cornerstones were chipped and showed abnormal signs of wear. He concluded that there must have been an opening system, a mechanism similar to those found in two separate locations earlier that morning. Sure enough, he spotted an iron ring sticking out of the wall halfway up. This ring appeared intact and, unlike the one on the other door that opened outward, it had not suffered too much from corrosion. The Targui pulled on it slowly at first, then with all his might, which unlocked the heavy door. He then leaned with all his weight on the left side of it, causing it to pivot slowly.

"We are there," he said quickly, aiming the light at Khaled.

"If you don't mind, I want to go in first," Charles said, brandishing his camera. "I want to take a few shots before you mess up the whole interior. Would that be alright, Ranzi?"

The secret chamber was rectangular, about three or four meters wide and five meters long. Strange accessories were strewn across the ground: crucibles, a broken still made of terracotta, a few glass containers, and a pile of coal that was crumbling to dust in one corner. At the back, facing the door, there was another oven, more squat and much less sophisticated than the one above. To the left of the oven, a stone trough seemed to contain small pieces of coal or some black ore in fairly large quantities.

This secret room was likely used both as a storeroom and for the melting of ingots and the liquefaction of ore, which consisted of fusion intended to eliminate the gangue. The Targui thought it was certainly storing valuable goods as he continued to sweep the room slowly with the beam of his torch.

After nearly completing his scan, the torch beam stopped short on the left side of the room as Chamberlin was attempting to frame new shots. Ranzi had just discovered a second corpse, covered in cobwebs, lying on the dirt floor, hands clasped over its abdomen.

Breaking the silence, Charles attempted a joke in rather dubious taste.

"It's a settling of scores, it seems. No need to alert the coroner; the death was caused by this dagger."

Associating the gesture with the word, he leaned toward the second corpse to extract a thin dagger with a gilded and finely chiselled hilt, noticing that initials were engraved on the handle. "'N' and 'F!'" he added, intrigued by his discovery.

Isaac replied instinctively, "N.F.? Like Nicolas Flamel, for example?"

"What could this second macabre discovery possibly mean?" wondered the Targui.

Chamberlin ventured a hypothesis. "It seems there was a third thief, someone who may have been bribed to grant access to the secret underground—a guard, probably."

"I have another hypothesis, Mr. Mayor," Isaac continued. "The guard could have surprised our couple while exploring the basement. He first attacked Master Canches and stabbed the unfortunate rabbi. But Flamel must have surprised him as he thrust the dagger into the rabbi's abdomen. The Parisian writer couldn't intervene in time to rescue his friend and found himself in mortal danger. Faster than his opponent, he stabbed him and dragged his body into the secret chamber to camouflage it."

"And Master Canches—why did he leave him outside?" wondered Dror.

"It's probable that Flamel thought he could save his friend, but the wound was mortal; he could do nothing, alas," suggested Ranzi, taking a moment for the victim of the Middle Ages. "I suggest we continue our exploration, my friends. We can return to the causes of this tragedy later."

On the right wall, there was a shelf arranged in a niche dug into the stone the entire width. A whole row of small vials containing indefinable contents was visible, all sealed with wax. On the opposite wall, in a similar niche, Charles noticed that dozens of triangular-sectioned ingots were neatly stacked, all covered in a more or less thick layer of grayish dust accumulated over time.

"Can someone describe to me what is in this room?" Chamberlin asked.

Ranzi, visibly moved, did not expect such an important discovery. He took a first look at the contents of the secret room and finally confessed to his new friend,

"We have finally reached our goal, Charles. Take a good look—what you have in front of you is the fabulous treasure of the Templars, or that of Henry II, or at least what remains of it after Flamel's passage in 1370."

"A treasure? What treasure?" Replied Charles, decidedly incredulous.

"What treasure?" Echoed Dror, equally bewildered.

Isaac, much more excited than the Targui, immediately came to the rescue. He approached the shelf of the left niche, took an ingot that must have weighed about twenty kilos, and placed it on the ground. He hesitated, walked along the wall, closely inspecting the other bars, and finally picked up a second ingot that seemed lighter than the first, though of similar size, placing it beside the first. He blew on the metal bars to remove the dust accumulated over the centuries and polished them meticulously with his handkerchief. Then, he exhibited the two shiny ingots with metallic reflections under the mayor's nose. "And what do you think this is?" he asked the mayor sarcastically. "Lead, maybe? If I'm not mistaken, there must be about three hundred kilograms of gold and nearly as much silver in this niche!"

"In my humble opinion," Ranzi countered, aiming a little higher, "there was certainly ten times more before Flamel came through here. He probably didn't have the chance to get everything back; after eliminating the guard, he must have been in a hurry to leave…"

Faced with so much ringing and solid evidence, the mayor could only yield. "I believe you now. My congratulations, my friends; you will become rich."

"We're all going to be rich," Ranzi corrected. "You see, Charles, there's so much gold here that we don't really know what to do with it. Since it's thanks to your valuable help that we were able to unravel this case, a third of the treasure naturally goes to you."

"I cannot accept. The treasure is yours by right; it is the law," replied the mayor.

"Your refusal would be the worst vexation to us, Charles," said Isaac, feigning indignation.

"So be it, and thank you, my friends," the mayor said after a brief hesitation. "But only a quarter of the booty. Let's not forget Khaled," he added, looking at each of his new friends with gratitude. "This generosity honors you, and it's difficult for me to refuse. But what are we going to do with all those old flasks and instruments lying on the ground?" he asked, pointing to them.

Isaac then approached Chamberlin and whispered a few words in his ear. Charles nodded two or three times, then, giving the Targui a knowing wink, said,

"Ranzi, you hid your talents as a chemist from me. Isaac just told me that you have a large modern laboratory in which you conduct amazing research. So these vials naturally come back to you, although their contents must have suffered after so many centuries."

Prince Targui smirked. Isaac played his cards well, he thought. That little guy is damn clever. What the hell had slipped into the mayor's ear?

"My turn to thank you, Charles," Ranzi finally responded, half fig, half grape. "I'm eager to analyze their contents. I also want to take away the black pebbles that are in the stone trough."

"Of course, Ranzi, although I doubt it's worth it."

"About these discoveries," Ranzi stated confidently, "it is agreed between us that you alone will bear full responsibility. We will swear, if necessary, Isaac and I, that you are the one and only inventor of this treasure. For our part, and especially thanks to the insight of my nephew Dror, we've only made our humble contribution in interpreting an old text written in Hebrew and a modest historical expertise, that's all. We also leave it to you to handle all the administrative paperwork. As soon as all the formalities are settled, we will return to collect our share of the treasure."

Chamberlin, touched more by the elegance of the Targui's gesture than by the precious gift, looked at Ranzi and then at Isaac for a long time. Deeply moved, he finally blurted out, "This gift is more important to me than all the gold in the world. It will lead to substantial benefits for the recognition of the renovation work on this site, which I have tirelessly pursued for years, as well as for my future career. But all the credit goes to you, and out of intellectual honesty, I must say I cannot accept."

"Disagree, Charles," Isaac replied. "Without your help, nothing would have happened. You led us directly to the treasure. Our only merit is that we communicated the translation of a poem. Moreover, for very specific and confidential reasons that we may revisit one day, it's imperative that Ranzi and I remain anonymous."

"I don't believe a word of it… But it's already past one o'clock," observed the mayor, mechanically consulting his watch.

He then continued in a more solemn tone,

"Will you please pay attention to me? By virtue of the powers conferred on me, I hereby make you all four Honorary Citizens of the city of Chinon."

Chamberlin embraced each of his new friends, all surprised by the spontaneity of his gesture. "Congratulations, my friends," Charles continued. "This is the first time this has happened to me since I became mayor," he confided, overwhelmed with emotion before adding cheerfully, "Now let's get down to business! I invite you to lunch at a marvelous site on the banks of the Loire. One of my relatives had the brilliant idea to transform an old watermill into a gastronomic relay. I hope you all like fish."

The mayor had not exaggerated. The chef, an outstanding cook, had prepared a beautiful salmon trout, caught the day before in the river, simmered meunière style, adorned with a coulis of shallots and fine herbs, all paired with a delicate white wine from the Loire. Set by the waterside, the venue rivaled the charm of the most beautiful paintings by Renoir.

Weather permitting, they had lunch on the shaded terrace, close to the riverbank and slightly away from the other customers seated in the large room. Surprisingly cheerful after a few sips of chilled wine, Charles began sharing the funniest stories circulating in the metropolis.

Upon returning to the castle around three o'clock, they spent a good two hours clearing the secret room of all its contents under the bewildered gaze of the two gendarmes on duty.

After several trips, the precious ingots were loaded into the DS21 for transfer to the basements of the Caisse Municipale d'Escompte, where the mayor served as administrator and honorary president. The twenty-two small bottles were carefully cleaned, wrapped in straw, and placed in a wooden box.

Chamberlin unearthed two sturdy burlap sacks from his cellar to carry the mysterious ore that seemed to interest Ranzi so much. Finally, around six o'clock, the secret room was completely empty.

Before leaving, the mayor addressed his new friends.

"You are cordially invited to the dinner given in your honor by Madame Chamberlin. I informed her via radiotelephone from the police van earlier. Our good friends, the Védrins, will also be present. I'll pick you up at 7:30 sharp at your hotel."

CHAPTER 18

The arrival of Ranzi and Khaled at the Chamberlin villa was nothing short of sensational.

Both were adorned in traditional Tuareg clothing; the prince wore a midnight blue djellaba paired with a large matching turban artfully wrapped around his head. Exuding ultimate refinement, he also sported a veil that concealed everything but his striking black eyes. That evening, the takouba—the Tuareg sword—was absent, replaced instead by a beautifully designed dagger with a curved blade, which emerged from a wide, pearly handle tucked under his white silk belt.

The quartet was greeted warmly by Madame Chamberlin, a charming brunette dressed in a black evening gown with a wide back neckline. Her smile widened as she noticed young Dror, who held a large bouquet of roses. Clearly intimidated, the teenager quickly handed it over to the mayor's wife without uttering a word, visibly relieved to dispose of the cumbersome package.

Commander Védrin and his wife were already in the living room, and beside them sat a calm young blonde girl on the sofa, waiting patiently. The mayor made the customary introductions after leading his new friends into the living room.

"My friends," he said, "allow me to introduce you to Madame Alice Védrin and her daughter Martine, as well as my wife Simone, who has just welcomed you." The commander, not wanting to be outdone, added, "Ladies," he began, his tone surprisingly kind, "I have the grand privilege of introducing you to His Serene Highness Prince Ahmed Ranzi El Sahraoui, his... um... secretary, Monsieur Khaled," he finished with a hint of irony, gesturing toward Khaled, and concluded with, "and Mr. Isaac Yakobi, accompanied by his remarkable young son, Dror—the real hero of this unforgettable day."

Upon hearing his name, Ranzi lifted his veil and, like the quintessential gentleman, kissed both wives' hands twice in succession, leaving them dazzled not only by his charm but also by the elegance of his gesture.

Once the introductions were out of the way, the two Tuaregs revealed themselves for the remainder of the evening, adhering scrupulously to the Sahrawi protocol. The evening commenced smoothly, filled with an amiable atmosphere. The hostess had demonstrated culinary prowess, achieving an impressive spread while respecting the strict dietary rules of her guests.

Dror naturally settled beside the young girl, pleased to finally find someone his own age. Ranzi found himself positioned between the two wives, while Isaac and Khaled sat on either side of them. The arrangement of guests seemed meticulously planned, Ranzi thought, particularly as he faced an avalanche of questions from the two ladies. Yet, he responded with infinite patience, maintaining a polite smile throughout.

In France, most people knew little about the lives of the Tuaregs, the Pieds-noirs, or the various Berber and Kabyle ethnic groups of North Africa. Communication between the colony and the metropolis was poor, leaving much confusion in the minds of the French. Ranzi answered their diverse and surprising questions with total candor, untroubled by the ignorant taboos upheld by many in his homeland. At times, he allowed Isaac to do the talking, either out of modesty or to take a moment to gather his thoughts.

The two eager ladies were about to inundate young Dror with questions when Charles intervened. "Let's leave the young people in peace," he said with a smile. "Shall we have coffee in the small living room?"

Seizing the moment, Martine gently took Dror by the hand and led him away. "Let's go to the next room, Dror," she said with a smile, "we will have more quiet to chat." Dror needed no further invitation, and they slipped away together.

Settled comfortably in an armchair before the other guests in an opulent living room, Ranzi took a sip of the hot drink, relishing its full-bodied aroma. He allowed himself the luxury of finishing his cup slowly, eyes half-closed, before turning to the mayor, locking eyes with him.

"Charles," he began, "you were curious about what brought Isaac and me to Chinon, as well as the reasons behind the attack we endured in the castle ruins, weren't you?"

His story began five years prior, when Isaac, during a trip to France, purchased an authentic 14th-century manuscript, known as the legendary grimoire of Abraham the Jew. This exceptional work, unique in its kind, had been extensively commented on by Nicolas Flamel in a work known only to a select few specialists called "The Book of Hieroglyphic Figures of Abraham the Jew."

Upon returning to Algiers, Isaac hurriedly arranged for color photographs of this precious manuscript to be taken by a professional photographer named Amrouche.

"Amrouche?" Védrin interjected, raising an eyebrow. "Like the city councilman?"

"Yes, sir. He was actually the brother of the man shot down earlier."

Ranzi continued, "Shortly after obtaining the photographs, I embarked on a lengthy trip around the world. After five long years, I returned to Khenchela, my second home.

That's when my troubles began. On the very day of my return to the village, I was followed by a valet associated with one of Amrouche's accomplices—a man who was not particularly discreet. I quickly realized that I was being tailed. Isaac and I intercepted the valet, demanding to know the reasons for his surveillance, but he refused to speak, fearing reprisals from his master. Regretfully, we released him after advising him to cease his lurking.

That night, we had no inkling of the seriousness of the situation awaiting us.

The following day, I intended to visit my people who were camping in El Goléa on the edge of the Sahara. During my journey there, they attempted to eliminate me twice— once on the way there and again on the return.

Later, I learned from one of my assailants—who we managed to capture alive—that the leader of these bandits sought possession of the grimoire of Abraham the Jew.

"How could your attackers possibly know about this manuscript?" Védrin asked, puzzled.

"Excluding Isaac, the photographer, and myself, only ten members of a prominent Algerian cultural club were aware of it. We had just shown them the photographs of the manuscript the day before I left. Everyone in the club was aware that Isaac was the genuine owner of the book. Anyone had ample time to act against him long before I returned home.

Who else could possibly know of the grimoire's existence and attribute ownership to me? Isaac reminded me that, for practical reasons, he had given my address to the Algiers photographer so he could send me the original manuscript along with the invoice for the photographs. The photographer had held the grimoire in his hands. But, it seems, he was an honest man—had he chosen, he could have seized the manuscript back in 1949 instead of returning it to us after taking the ordered pictures.

The situation took a significant turn when Dror recognized the castle of Chinon from the illumination painted on the cover of the old manuscript. It then became clear that an important secret might be concealed within this grimoire. Are you following me so far?"

Védrin's brow furrowed further, and he interrupted again, still unclear on one point. "But how did you manage to find Councilor Amrouche?"

"I was getting there. After many discussions with Isaac, we deemed it imperative to visit the Algiers photographer to resolve this matter. Was anyone else privy to copies or negatives? Certainly. This was the only person who could connect the dots with the castle and potentially harm me."

I traveled to Algiers with Khaled to investigate this case personally. Upon our arrival, we learned of the recent passing of the photographer, who had succumbed to a long illness. However, his brother—a former municipal councilor—had inherited the shop and all its contents. Tragically, this very man was shot dead today by the gendarmes.

Having been informed of the multiple attacks against me, ex-Councilor Amrouche had placed the shop under surveillance. He ordered his henchmen to remain vigilant, and we were quickly spotted by a lookout as soon as we arrived at Place de Chartres, where the photographer's shop was located. Fearful upon seeing us approach, the lookout attempted to flee, prompting us to chase him through the narrow alleys of the Casbah. Fortunately, after a brief pursuit, we managed to subdue him and had him imprisoned in Algiers.

"Wasn't that a dangerous endeavor?" Madame Védrin asked, visibly perplexed.

"Indeed, dear madam," Ranzi replied, "but I believed it better to take the initiative to outmaneuver my opponent than to remain idle and await another violent attempt on my life."

"But how on earth could Amrouche know about the castle?" the mayor interjected, switching topics abruptly.

"The former councilor was the universal heir to his brother's estate. When he took possession of the shop, he stumbled across a second copy of the manuscript photographs by chance. He recognized the Château de Chinon as a location he had presumably visited and noticed the strange, blurred, illegible inscriptions on the photos—which were nearly erased on the original manuscript. Yet he never considered they might be written in Hebrew. He concluded that the manuscript and its contents were of immense value.

In the envelope, he even found my address on the counterfoil of the invoice, all this just weeks or days before my return to the country."

Charles attempted to interject the conversation, but Ranzi held up his hand politely. "I haven't finished, Charles," he continued. "While we were in Algiers speaking to the photographer, Amrouche travelled to Khenchela to eliminate an accomplice who was terrified and likely ready to disclose information to authorities. This accomplice was the bachaga Abou Dahrem, and his murder was disguised as a suicide. We had no doubt Amrouche was at the helm of this plot, or at least among the conspirators.

All police in Algeria were placed on high alert. Unfortunately, the criminal managed to escape on his yacht, anchored in a secluded cove along the Algerian coast, safely beyond the sight of authorities.

During a thorough search, police discovered a substantial cache of weapons in the former councilor's villa—enough to outfit an entire army, it seemed. Additionally, there was the troubling presence of a European at his side, wasn't that right, Commander?"

"We managed to identify the individual through a portrait provided by Belino," Védrin confirmed with a slight shake of his head. "He's a dangerous thug named Giorgio Biazzi, known for dealing in arms to extremists and revolutionaries around the globe. Cheik Ahmed, you and your associates have enabled us to eliminate two significant threats and arrest one of their accomplices, who is now imprisoned. I take this opportunity to pass on the prefect's congratulations."

"Who is this accomplice?" Madame Védrin asked.

"He's a minor thug—Mr. Khaled adeptly neutralized him and locked him in the trunk of a car. He only played a minimal role in all of this," her husband replied.

Ranzi still had not finished his narrative, and he pressed on. "A lingering question remains: what was Amrouche truly after? To me, it seems he aimed to kill two birds with one stone: by seizing the manuscript, which is invaluable to wealthy collectors, and simultaneously acquiring a treasure sought after since Richard Coeur de Lion's stay in Chinon. He likely needed the funds to finance his arms dealings. So now you know the entire story in meticulous detail."

"But you haven't yet concluded your tale, Ranzi!" the mayor interjected suddenly.

"How so? Is my story not complete?"

"Yes, yes," Charles insisted, "But what happens to Nicolas Flamel in all this?"

"Flamel?" Isaac interjected, eager to continue. "Let me elaborate, as I have reconstructed the entire journey of the Parisian alchemist.

This writer, renowned by the end of the 14th century, became known for distributing vast wealth in donations to various institutions, hospices, hospitals, and churches. Why all this generosity? One might speculate that he had something to atone for, yet the most perplexing aspect was that no one knew where he amassed his fortune, which has sparked countless theories over the past six centuries.

He dedicated years to studying alchemy, and rumors circulated that his immense wealth stemmed from the Philosopher's Stone. In his first book, he claimed to possess a manuscript penned by a Levite prince named Abraham, which he acquired for the meager sum of two florins. The grimoire he referenced in this book enabled him to discover the Philosophers' Stone.

This manuscript was intended for the Jewish diaspora persecuted by the Gauls and hunted by the Inquisition. However, Flamel presented a description that significantly diverged from the original we possess today, presumably to deflect suspicion regarding the source of his wealth.

Going back in time a few years, unable to decipher the grimoire, the esteemed writer embarked on a journey to Spain in search of a Kabbalist who could translate the manuscript—there were not many Jews left living in France at that time. Upon his return, he was met with immense prosperity, and rightfully so! Returning from Spain, he made a stop in Chinon where he uncovered the fabulous treasure hidden in the castle dungeons, with the secret cache and access method discreetly indicated on the cover of the manuscript of Abraham the Jew."

Isaac took a few handwritten pages out of his pocket to read.

– Here is what Flamel wrote about this trip, I read you some excerpts:

"Having lost hope of ever understanding these figures, I made a vow to God and to St. James of Galicia, to ask for the interpretation of them from some Jewish priest, in one of the synagogues of Spain...

"... So, in the same way I set out, and finally I arrived at Montjoye, and then at Saint-Jacques, where, with great devotion, I fulfilled my wish. This done, on my way back I met in Léon a merchant from Boulogne, who introduced me to a doctor, a Jew by nationality and then a Christian, who lived there, and who was very knowledgeable, called Master Canches. When I had shown him the figures of my extract, delighted with great astonishment and joy, he asked me for news of the book from which they were taken...

"... We decided on our trip, and from Léon, we passed to Oviedo, and from there to Sanson, where we put on sea to come to France...

"...When we arrived at Orléans, this learned man fell extremely ill, afflicted with very severe vomiting, which remained to him of those he had suffered on the sea.

"...Finally, he died on the end of the seventh day of his illness, for which I was very grieved. As best I could, I had him buried in the church of Sainte Croix in Orléans, where he still rests"..

– Flamel's story does not align well with the facts. No doubt once in Spain, the writer benefited greatly from the invaluable assistance of a Kabbalist rabbi. This rabbi, after translating and commenting on the Hebrew texts of the manuscript, accompanied Flamel on his journey, posing as a Christian to avoid the Inquisition. This is likely the reason he identifies himself as Canches. When they arrive at the castle of Chinon, the duo manages to enter the chamber where the athanor is located. It seems plausible that they easily located the secret lab at that time, possibly by bribing a few guards. They then discover the secret passage and eventually seize the famous treasure.

What happens next? An intruder, perhaps a guard, catches Sanches-Canches watching in the underground and stabs him.

Another hypothesis can be considered. The individual found stabbed in the treasure room may have been a third thief recruited by Flamel to facilitate access to the castle's basements. This unreliable accomplice might have thought to monopolize the entire treasure. He initially attacks Master Canches, mortally wounding him with a dagger. However, when he tries to assault the Parisian writer, Flamel, alerted by his friend's cries, gains the upper hand and stabs the attacker in the side, causing him to abandon the dagger stamped with two revealing initials: N and F—Nicholas Flamel.

Devastated by the loss of his unfortunate partner and feeling responsible for his tragic fate, Flamel dedicates the rest of his life to distributing his immense fortune to the poor as a form of penance.

"Poor Sanches, what a horrible end," Madame Chamberlin finally admitted. "We will certainly never know the origin of this treasure."

"We don't know much more than you, ma'am," Isaac replied insincerely, making a considerable effort to suppress his laughter. "We prefer that a romantic legend spreads around the mysterious castle, which, let us not forget, belonged to Richard the Lionheart and later served as a prison and place of torture for the unfortunate Templars."

After all, Isaac continued, it is not forbidden to dream. This legend will provide excellent publicity for the village, and the castle will surely attract many curious visitors. What do you think, Mayor?

– I completely agree with your opinion, Isaac, and I thank you all, especially the young Dror. Thanks to you, our little town will become a prominent tourist destination in France.

Isaac and Ranzi had refrained from formulating a second hypothesis about the origin of the treasure. They both knew that a second enigma surrounded none other than Prince Abraham Lévi. The learned Jewish Kabbalist had painted the castle's facade of Chinon on the cover of his manuscript, where he may have been held captive. He inscribed a mysterious poem in Hebrew on this same cover, enabling our friends to discover, six centuries after Flamel, the secret passage to the laboratory and gain access to the treasure chamber.

But who really was Abraham the Jew?

We think he was an alchemist, a doctor, or perhaps a rabbi? In truth, he was all of these. It was common for intellectuals of that time, as long traditions prove. Was this scientist hosted and protected by the castle's owner, who remained unknown? Or was he forcibly detained to fill his host's coffers? Like many princes, lords, or kings of the Middle Ages, the castellan who hosted him likely enjoyed surrounding himself with scholars and doctors at his court. Had he struck a deal with Abraham, promising him protection in exchange for his special talents to replenish his empty coffers? In any event, he provided an outbuilding of his castle and all the necessary resources for the Jewish scholar to conduct his research on the Philosopher's Stone.

Clearly, the alchemist succeeded.

Additionally, Abraham was well aware of the massacres committed by the Inquisition in Gaul, a point he mentioned in the preamble of his manuscript dedicated to his brothers persecuted by Christianity. He likely entrusted his grimoire to a trustworthy individual, tasked with delivering it to a

Jewish authority, so that victims of the Inquisition could benefit from it.

Unfortunately, this emissary was surely caught, and the manuscript fell into the hands of those who, not understanding a single word, eventually sold it for a pittance to Nicolas Flamel for two florins—a miserable sum. Educated in the purest Hermetic tradition, Flamel recognized the significance of the parabolic figures and the accompanying Hebrew poems. However, he lacked the key!

The rest is well-known.

During this time, alone in the mayor's opulent private office, Martine and Dror had engaged in a long and serious discussion. The teenagers naturally sat opposite each other on either side of Charles Vedrin's imposing desk.

Martine was the first to initiate the dialogue. Blonde with incredibly blue eyes, she exhibited both admiration and curiosity, which made the young Yakobi very uncomfortable.

– Do you have a girlfriend in Khenchela, Dror, or a fiancée?

The boy was clearly unaccustomed to such flirtatious discussions with girls his age; in his remote village in the Aurès, boys and girls did not mingle. He was taken aback by Martine's direct question and hesitated briefly before confessing.

– Uh, no, what a funny idea. Most of all, I have great friends. And you?

– I have lots of them, she replied, laughing, but none seems interesting to me; they are so stupid, you would think you were dealing with babies. You need a real girlfriend! I have an idea, she said finally, if you and I became good friends, would you come and spend your next summer vacation here at Château Chinon?

Dror was immediately taken with this proposition, which his father would surely disapprove of. He responded honestly:

– I can't decide anything, Martine, but of course I would like to. And you, he proposed in a very solemn tone, would you come to my house in Khenchela if I invited you?

"I'm sure my mother would approve," Martine replied, staring Dror straight in the eye. "In the meantime, let's maintain a correspondence. What do you think? Let's exchange our addresses, and then we'll join our parents so they don't notice our absence."

CHAPTER 19

Thursday, April 22, 1954

After a brief detour to greet Superintendent Boulin at the Tours police station, our four heroes arrived at the Tours flying club around eight-thirty, carrying their precious cargo.

A twin-engine aircraft awaited them. The necessary revisions had been completed the day before, including a full tank of fuel. With the flight plan finalized, all that remained was to return the rental car, settle the flying club bill, and take off.

As Isaac entered the cabin, he called out to Ranzi, who was just about to buckle his seatbelt.

"There is something that intrigues me. What did Amrouche say before he died, Ranzi?"

"Long live the Algerian revolution."

"That's all?" Isaac replied, sounding disappointed.

"Yes, that's all! And you, damn joker, what did you whisper in Charles' ear just before he offered to take all the vials?"

"First of all, that you were the last survivor of a race thought to be forever extinct, that of the blowers. Secondly, that you were convinced you could transform this powder into gold in your alchemical laboratory of Khenchela."

Ranzi burst out laughing. "Sacred joker," he repeated.

Isaac couldn't help but laugh too. "And you, big trickster, what possessed you to offer him his share of the treasure?"

"I would have liked to leave him all the gold in exchange for the vials, but he would've found my generosity suspicious," Ranzi replied, laughing even harder.

"What are we going to do with all this gold, Targui?"

"I propose we distribute it to the many needy people who, alas, populate our country."

"I agree, but on the condition that you leave some ingots with the Targis companions who helped you."

Ranzi and Isaac were true sages. Gold, silver, and power held no allure for them, no matter how extraordinary that might seem. They could have wielded all the earth's wealth if they desired. Through years of study and dedication, they had risen to the rank of Adept, just like the predecessors who had initiated them. As Philosophers by Fire, their only remaining desire was for immaterial wealth. They pursued an ancestral quest that had started decades earlier with the first learned philosophers: the search for the Absolute. The Philosopher's Stone was merely the first step in this long journey.

The twin-engine took off southward. Exceptional weather blanketed the southwestern region of France, as the Azores anticyclone seemed firmly established there.

The plane stopped in Marignane, landing on the reserved runway of the flying club at precisely nine forty-five. Ranzi entrusted the aircraft to the coordinator, whose dedication and skill he had already appreciated a few days earlier.

After a quick refueling, a few routine checks, and a zinc coffee from the club, the four Algerians found themselves soaring over the Mediterranean.

But Isaac looked worried. He isolated himself in the back of the cabin to think. He acknowledged that he and Targui had maneuvered skillfully, without needing to consult each other. By offering part of the treasure—a valuable gift of gold and silver bars—Ranzi had secured in return all the mysterious vials, which held more than merely scientific value.

Isaac congratulated himself on his young son's courage and composure during the attack and his remarkable ability to solve puzzles. Still, he felt a twinge of discomfort about having concealed the true nature of the vials' contents from the mayor. Those contents were worth more than all the gold in the castle, even more than the cargo that Flamel had recovered six centuries earlier. Did he and his brother even have a choice? They couldn't reveal such a heavy secret.

Upon reflection, he thought, all the contents of the secret chamber belong to us. It is indeed the three of us—Dror, Ranzi, and myself—who discovered it. We cannot reasonably let such a commodity go to waste, especially since no one but us can correctly exploit the properties that are so secret and powerful.

Moreover, the mayor would never have been able to accept that the gold and silver ingots—which were merely a tiny fraction of the treasure—were the result of alchemical transmutations conducted six centuries earlier.

"We still have work to do," Isaac concluded, just before succumbing to fatigue and falling asleep.

It was two-thirty when the plane parked in the hangar of the aero-club in Constantine, following a perfect landing.

Ramirez, alerted by radio during the crossing, awaited them at the edge of the runway. He let the four passengers disembark, noting that their load seemed larger and heavier than on the outward journey. He saluted the pilot.

"Did you have a good trip, Sheikh Ahmed?"

"Excellent, Mr. Ramirez," replied Targui, who was not at all resentful. "You entrusted me with a powerful, well-adjusted, and reliable aircraft. Despite some disturbances from the low pressures over the sea, we were able to appreciate the excellent stability and maneuverability of the twin engine. Here are the flight papers; please refuel. I'll meet you at your office in an hour for the return formalities."

The four friends took advantage of this brief respite to relax and eat in the club cafeteria. They relished the special atmosphere that filled their wonderful country. Their country! Though they had enjoyed the brief stay in the small town in France along the Loire, Algeria was undeniably different.

While his companions ordered two more coffees and a soda at the bar, Ranzi went to the coordinator's office to sign various flight documents, collect his deposit check, and pay the flying club bill. He asked Ramirez for permission to use the phone and isolated himself for a few minutes in the adjacent office. Once the communication was complete and the formalities finalized, he rejoined his friends, who waited impatiently at the checkpoint.

Isaac felt delighted to locate his DS19. He helped Khaled and Ranzi stow the precious cargo and luggage in the large trunk, which, despite its size, proved insufficient, necessitating the neutralization of part of the rear seat.

The doors finally slammed shut, and the car roared to life, heading due south.

Now it was Ranzi's turn to rest. The journey over the Mediterranean had completely exhausted him due to the strong turbulence for three-quarters of the route. He thoroughly appreciated the comfort and silence of the DS19. Isaac, Khaled, and Dror maintained a respectful silence throughout the ride, fearful of waking their companion.

There were just one hundred and fifty kilometers of road left. This road again! This treacherous national route, narrow and winding, was prone to frequent landslides from the destabilized slopes of the mountain. It was risky to exceed the authorized speed limits, even with a high-performance vehicle. Nevertheless, Isaac managed the remarkable feat of returning to Khenchela just two and a half hours after leaving the Constantine flying club. Ranzi had just awakened when the car pulled up in front of the villa gate.

"So Targui, did we have sweet dreams?" Isaac joked.

"This little nap did me the greatest good," Ranzi assured. "Come in, my friends; I'll offer you some very cold lemonade while Ali unloads our things."

As soon as they heard the bell ring at the gate, Leila and Rachida rushed to the front door of the villa, closely followed by Mahmoud, Saïd, and Aïcha. Welcoming ululations rang out as they spotted the quartet climbing the front steps. Rachida kissed her brother, then Isaac and Dror, before authoritatively grabbing Ranzi's arm. As they crossed the hall, the you-yous resumed even louder. This time, Rachel and Sarah were quietly seated on ottomans alongside the coffee table.

An outpouring of joy and excitement filled the air. It was like this every time the two families reunited.

Good reunion, Ranzi thought, as Isaac and Dror settled between Rachel and Sarah after tenderly kissing them. He knew the questions would soon come from all sides, and he would do his best to answer them with the patience he had cultivated for such occasions. He was about to speak when Isaac asked Rachel, "How come you two are here?"

"Rachida received a phone call from Ranzi at the Constantine flying club. He informed her of your return about three hours ago. His Highness asked him to let us know to welcome you here."

"Ah, ah, ha! Sacred Ranzi. He will spend his life astonishing me. But he was absolutely right; we won't have to recount our Chinon epic twice in a row. And Dror, I don't see him. Where is he?"

"He sped toward the library like a meteor," Leila answered. "I'll ask Ali to go get him."

"No need, Aunt Leila. I'm here, and I'm finally done," Dror said proudly as he entered the living room, triumphantly brandishing a sheaf of handwritten sheets.

"What have you finished, my disciple?"

"The complete translation of the manuscript, Uncle Ranzi, on the plane, on the flight home. I just got my first notes."

"But that's wonderful! We're going to need you again to decrypt the coded message from the grimoire."

Ranzi then took the teenager's right hand and lifted it as high as he could.

"Well, my friends," he said, "here is the real hero of the day, my disciple, and I am proud of him. Do you realize? Thanks to Dror, we were able to solve the riddle of Chinon Castle, Isaac, Khaled, and I got our hands on Nicolas Flamel's treasure, and we eliminated a gang of criminals! But Isaac will tell you about our adventures better than anyone."

CHAPTER 20

Friday, April 24, 1954.

Very early in the morning, Ranzi and Isaac had undertaken long and meticulous preparations in the large laboratory, with the goal of analyzing the products recovered from the secret cache of the Château de Chinon.

The vials were now neatly cleaned, stored, and labeled on a shelf above the bench; there were exactly twenty-two small vials. Each vial had a numbered label that mentioned the gross and net weights, the aspect, the color of the contents, and sometimes even the name of the contents, if the composition was already written on the vial.

The black ore recovered from the underground room of the Château de Chinon was stored in a wooden box near the athanor; it had been carefully dusted beforehand by passing it through a fine sieve under the extractor hood.

The two friends had divided the tasks to save time; they had already carried out a whole series of simple but necessary physical measurements, and were now tackling chemical analyses, which were more delicate and time-consuming. The work was carried out in an almost religious silence, in this modern and over-equipped laboratory where two unorthodox researchers were studying alchemy in secret.

They belonged to a race of dreamers who had never died out; they were the last representatives of a long line of initiates who had been cultivating the old philosophy for three thousand years. Alchemy, the ancestor of our modern sciences, had been their lifelong passion. In the middle of the twentieth century, two men were manipulating the Secret Fire or the Spirit, the Philosophical Mercury, and the Quintessence on a daily basis, substances that were indeed mysterious but of which they knew all the properties perfectly. There was only one last test left for them to face to finally reach the Absolute.

They spent the whole day working out the tests and analyses of the twenty-two samples identified in the vials, as well as the black ore. When Leila came to serve them an iced tea late in the day, they seemed exhausted; they had finally completed all the analyses they could undertake with the equipment at their disposal.

Ranzi spread his notes on the large desk and asked Isaac to do the same with his, in order to achieve the long-awaited summary. On a large sheet of paper, Isaac, in flawless calligraphy, wrote under Ranzi's dictation:

Ore: premium kohl, origin unknown, possibly Hungary, inexplicably high 90% metal sulphide content. Impurities detected: gold, potassium, bismuth, lead, and arsenic.

Vial No. 1: Potassium nitrate from the covering mixed with lime, ammonium, and sodium nitrate, ultra-fine particle size, purity 92%, slight residual moisture.

"How can you tell it's dustpan, Ranzi? The content of ammonium nitrate and lime, Isaac. Synthetic nitrate contains practically no calcium."

Vial No. 2: likely residue of accidental fermentation (poor sealing of the wax), contains mainly potassium. Symbol appearing on the vial: that of Tartar. It must have been potassium bitartrate, an organic salt that can ferment.

Flask No. 3: iron slag with a high content of ferric sulphide, 98%, mixed with a saline complex of potassium carbonate and lime. Coarse grain size 0.1-0.5 mm. Symbol on the vial: a triangle surmounted by a cross (Sulfur).

Vial No. 4: salt complex of potassium carbonate and lime, amorphous. Calcium content 2-3% approximately. Symbol appearing on the vial: circle crossed out diametrically, that of Salt.

Vial No. 5: mixture of potassium carbonates, calcium, and potassium nitrate.

Vial No. 6: pulverulent antimony sulphide, particle size 50 to 100 microns, purity 98%. Symbol on the vial: crossed out circle surmounted by a cross.

Vials N° 7 to 10: product of greenish color, complete analysis difficult, contains a NOx radical. Density 2. Melting point 70°C. Symbol on the vial: fire triangle.

Vials Nos. 11 to 20: amorphous powder, crimson color, specific gravity 38. Melting point 64°C. Analysis not possible, does not react with bases or acids, soluble in water and alcohol. Symbol on the vial: three royal crowns.

Vials N° 21 to 22: metallic powder, silver color. Density 6.69. Melting point 631°C. Very pure antimony. No symbol on the vial.

"What do you think of all this?" Isaac asked, once the long list had been written down in the analysis notebook.

"All these parameters are consistent and the analyses show us that these samples resemble in all respects the products resulting from our own experiments. There is no doubt that the Adept who filled all these vials was working in "art brevi"—the short way. Same process, same materials, with one exception, he had access to an ore of extraordinary quality, the equivalent of which, alas, cannot be found today. The mine from which this ore was extracted has certainly been exhausted for a long time. It is therefore a royal gift that Abraham the Jew gave us, posthumously, he urged to add."

"Regarding the samples numbered 11 to 20, Ranzi, how do you feel?"

"I am amazed at the quality of these samples." replied Ranzi, "You are aware that density is the index that best measures the transmuting power of the Stone. In general, transmutation powders hardly exceed a density of 33. At this level, already, there is no comparable natural or synthetic chemical element on Earth. The most extraordinary thing, you see, is that rare are the powders which have a transmuting power of 10,000 to 15,000 times their weight. However, this one, with 38 kg/dm^3 of specific mass, is certainly capable of phenomenal power, of the order of 40,000 times its weight, or even more. Yssic is fantastic."

"And the three crowns inscribed on the bottle, do you know what they represent?"

"Success, the culmination of the three works, of course. I confess that I still do not understand why Flamel did not appropriate the stock of powder. The vials were prominently displayed on the shelves, though," Isaac observed.

"Perhaps he was only looking for immediate gain: gold and silver. He found hundreds of kilograms of precious metals that he had to take on several trips. Imagine the colossal fortune that a ton of gold can represent, whether in the year of grace 1370 or today, in 1954, it is comparable to something close. So the powder was perhaps not his concern at the time... And then, if he had taken it into his head to open the vials numbered from 1 to 10, what do you think he would have concluded?"

"I would say even more," agreed Isaac, "he could never have guessed the importance and value of the contents of vials 11 to 20; he would have been unable to do so without knowledge of the proper mode of operation; Sacra fama auri – the thirst for gold – he had eyes bigger than his stomach!

"No, I don't think so," disapproved Ranzi, shaking his head several times. "Flamel used all this fortune to do good, don't forget it little brother. I especially believe that he didn't have much of time at the time of its incursion into the basement of the castle."

They still had a long way to go to properly exploit the precious contents of the vials. Isaac did not want to rush anything, in these circumstances, he always recommended extreme caution.

"I have a suggestion for you to avoid wasting our time and wasting our supply of powder, my prince."

"Go ahead, Yssic, I'm listening to you," replied the Targui, visibly interested.

"Let us first study the grimoire of Abraham, we will perhaps find there all the instructions necessary to avoid failing.

"Yssic, I've thought about it before, figure you, and I totally agree. But not tonight, I remind you that today is Friday; go home for Shabbat. Let's meet Sunday morning, say eight o'clock. Ask Dror to accompany you; he will be of great help to us in analyzing and deciphering the original texts. And then, he added, it will give him a nice practical exercise."

CHAPTER 21

Sunday, April 25, 1954

City of Bougie, 7:00 a.m., Bordj cove.

The yacht, now renamed "Admiral," cautiously slowed as it entered the cove, skillfully avoiding the many rocks jutting out of the water. The sailor piloting the boat knew the area well.

As the boat approached the shore, the pilot stopped the engines and cast off the anchor. He slid down the hull and headed for the beach, straining to gain speed in the water that reached above his knees. He was acutely aware that he was expected by a man of rare cruelty, whose unpredictable mood swings he feared above all else.

The man in question stood on the beach, impatiently swinging his cane as if it were a metronome. He had a dull complexion and wore a dark gray hat. Thick-rimmed brown tortoiseshell glasses accentuated the hardness of his face.

"I hope I haven't disturbed myself for nothing," he growled in greeting as the sailor reached dry land.

"Sir…"

"Never say my name. I forbid you," the man replied curtly, his tone initially unsympathetic.

The sailor trembled, fully aware that his interlocutor was never joking.

"Yes, sir, please forgive me. There must have been a hitch in Chinon," the sailor suggested. "I was instructed to wait for the adviser to return to the agreed place for a maximum of three days, then to come back and meet you here, whatever happens, to return this envelope. Here it is, sir. Do you have any further instructions for me?"

The man was clearly dissatisfied, displaying an aggressiveness that bordered on hysteria. Nervously, he opened the envelope, took out a letter, and unfolded it. He cast an inquisitive look at the contents, thought for a few seconds, and finally took out his lighter to ignite the mysterious document, only letting go when he nearly burned his hand.

"It's okay," he said dryly. "You have been fairly remunerated, I believe. Leave the yacht here and return home to await my further instructions."

The interview lasted no more than three minutes. The two men parted without even saying goodbye.

Sunday, April 25, 1954

Khenchela 9:20 a.m

Ranzi stood in front of the blackboard, a stick of chalk in his hand. He wore a white blouse that he had neglected to button. On the dais, he resembled a distracted chemistry teacher, laboriously writing abstract formulas on the board.

Having finished the meticulously drawn synopsis, he finally turned around.

"I will try to establish a rational program to bring order and method to our approach," he said simply. "To start, we have different materials distributed in twenty-two labeled and numbered vials. Among these bottles, twelve contain intermediate products, and their state of conservation leaves much to be desired. We won't worry about that for now. The vials that interest us are those numbered from 11 to 20; they all contain the same product. Isaac, can you provide some clarification to our disciple?"

Isaac was visibly embarrassed to play the role of teacher, especially with his son. Dror had never needed outside help for his studies and was convinced he would make a poor teacher. The gaze of the Targui became increasingly insistent. Eventually, he made up his mind to speak.

"You have certainly begun to see what is very special in this basement, son. You must have even wondered, at one time or another, if your uncle Ranzi wasn't some kind of crazy wizard brewing magic potions in his secret lair, right?"

Dror wanted to answer, but his father waved him off.

"And you would have been absolutely right," Isaac said, winking at Ranzi. "Only, you quickly realized that it was not about magic, but about a very particular kind of chemistry, on the margins of official science. A chemistry whose teaching is provided oddly in the thousands of works of the immense library next door. Books that everyone can read, but whose content is only accessible to a very few chosen ones, only insiders.

You had the opportunity to study one of these books, the grimoire of Abraham, and, extraordinarily, you masterfully translated it from Hebrew into French. So I'm going to ask you a question: What particular things did you learn on this occasion?"

Intrigued, Dror began to think without haste. He reviewed the verses that made up the legends of the twelve illustrations. Part of the texts related to materials called philosophical sulfur and mercury, secret fire and water. The other part seemed to evoke mysterious chemical processes involving the union of the fixed and the volatile, sublimation, multiplication, and fermentation. It was all Chinese to him, he thought.

"Well, I'm very puzzled," the teenager finally replied. "A priori, one might think that it is poetry of a somewhat particular, hermetic style, and this applies to the text in Hebrew and its translation. But when you think about it, you can detect some sort of cooking recipes that call on ingredients with mysterious names, bodies that you have to react with the help of no less mysterious reactions in secret devices. It is therefore necessary, in order to decipher these texts, to have a perfect knowledge of the jargon used by the author—a particular jargon, which must be that of a well-defined corporation—and then to put all these words in their place in the time which is theirs, with their own meaning."

"Hey, not a bad answer, disciple!" Ranzi exclaimed. "You have perfectly defined in very few words what esotericism is. It is exactly that: a coded language whose keys are rather vague words but which have a very precise meaning in a particular context. It is indeed a jargon of a special style, that of the alchemists and spagyrists of the Middle Ages. In summary, to understand the grimoire of Abraham, it is the language and the meaning of the words of the alchemists that must be known. Imagine that your father and I think we know this jargon, in all modesty," concluded the Targui, signaling to his foster brother to continue the explanations.

"Let's get back to our vials numbered 11 to 20," Isaac said, more at ease now. "We believe they all contain the Universal Elixir. If that doesn't mean anything to you, know that it's the ultimate culmination of a long process that makes it possible to extract the quintessence of the material, according to a technique that is three thousand years old. This technique has been transmitted invariably from master to disciple to avoid any disclosure. But, to prove that this is indeed our elixir, it must undergo the last test, that of transmutation. To achieve this, the elixir must first be directed towards the metallic kingdom in order to prepare the projection powder. This final operation cannot be carried out haphazardly, and this is where the text that you were kind enough to translate comes in."

Dror couldn't believe his ears. This dense, scarlet red powder came from a provision made six centuries earlier by a learned alchemist, a rabbi named Abraham Levy. Today, Dror was going to have the singular privilege of participating in the very last transformation of the elixir to make it the Philosopher's Stone. It's amazing, he thought.

"Judging from what I have been able to gather from the contents of the grimoire," Dror said in response to his father's invitation, "fermentation is described as the last operation of the magisterium. The figure that relates to this operation consists of a pomegranate roasting on a brazier. Around the pomegranate, in a semicircle, the picture book has arranged five gleaming suns in the upper part, with a splendid phoenix with outstretched wings beneath this composition. The legend corresponding to the twelfth plate is as follows:

'When the jewel at last the night will shine,

Give him the king's body to eat,

Until you're full, make no mistake.

On a blazing brazier you will immolate him.

In the early morning, the Phoenix from its ashes will be reborn.'"

"Excellent, my disciple," cried Ranzi. "Good job. The legend fits perfectly with the illustration, but in my humble opinion, it is the carbuncle that is involved here and not a jewel. Definitely, this Hebrew word still poses a problem. Look at this vial."

Then, addressing his foster brother, he ordered, "Isaac, turn off the light just for a moment, will you?"

Immediately, the contents of the vial began to glow with a fluorescent green light, faintly illuminating the lab like a small candle.

"When the carbuncle finally the night will shine..." That's the meaning of the first verse, Dror thought in wonder; the symbolism can be seen in alchemy. The Carbuncle! The Philosopher's Stone, the Lantern.

"You can turn on the light now, Isaac," Ranzi ordered.

Then, addressing Dror again, he said, "You must know that the fluorescence we observed can be accentuated during the successive phases of multiplication of the Stone. Arriving at a certain stage of exaltation, the Stone no longer coagulates; it becomes liquid. At the final stage, a feat that only grandmasters can pull off without triggering a horrific explosion, it will become gassy. In this gaseous form, the Stone shines even during the day. Enclosed in a well-sealed glass bulb, it constitutes the famous perpetual lantern that is said to have sometimes been found in mysterious tombs.

"Let us return to our carbuncle," continued the master. "Unlike the other operational phases of the Great Work, which followers have shown themselves so reserved about, the last operation has been described in very loose terms by a large number of artists. Abraham's message is simple: we must melt together five parts of pure gold, which are our five suns, with one part of elixir, our carbuncle—the pomegranate in the illustration—all over high heat and for a dozen hours to complete the final fermentation."

"Why does the author warn us not to be mistaken?" Isaac questioned, puzzled by a recommendation that Ranzi had ignored.

"You are right to ask that question, Yssic. We must give him gold to eat and not silver. This is the red Stone made for gold and not the white one dedicated to silver. Have you also noticed that the proportion indicated by Abraham differs significantly from that traditionally recommended by the ancient Adepts?"

"From three to four parts of gold for one of powder, according to the majority of authors," replied Isaac. "I think

I understood that, the power of the Stone being extraordinary, the quantity of added gold must be proportionate to it. But this is not the only anomaly; the authors are also divided on the time required for the ultimate coction, and some do not hesitate to recommend a duration of up to forty-eight hours."

"It may also depend on the power of the Stone, Isaac, but if you want my opinion, it is better to strictly follow Abraham's indications. We do not have enough time today to start our tests; I suggest that we resume our discussion next Thursday, very early in the morning."

"No inconvenience for me or for Dror, I suppose. Rachel is expecting you all for lunch this afternoon; she absolutely wants to see Rachida again before leaving for El Goléa."

The Targui took leave of the Yakobi fairly late in the afternoon.

Ali ran to the gate of the villa as soon as he saw his master in the company of the entire Sahrawi family. He took his master aside.

"Sir Ahmed, you had a phone call just now; unfortunately, I just hung up. I can call back your correspondent if you wish; he left me his personal number. It's Commissar Petit," he added breathlessly.

"Perfect, Ali, call him and pass the communication in the small living room, please."

Ranzi slipped away into the small living room, which turned out to be an office. He didn't want Leila or Rachida to overhear this conversation regarding a call from Commissioner Petit, who, he thought, must have important revelations to make to him on a Sunday.

Ali returned after a few minutes with the handset, which he handed to his master.

"Hello, superintendent, Ahmed Ranzi here. Are you on duty this Sunday?"

"My respects, Si Ahmed. I was pulled out of my nap just now to send me a dispatch from HQ in Algiers. Amrouche's yacht was spotted around noon by a French Navy launch in a creek near Bougie."

"Was there anyone on board?"

"No, no one. Police are taking fingerprints and searching the yacht from top to bottom in the hope of finding clues. Ah, I forgot, the owner made up the name of the boat very roughly, but that would never have fooled the maritime authorities in the event of an inspection."

Ranzi was upset but tried to keep calm.

"What you have just told me is serious, commissioner. It means that the real sponsor of all these operations is still active. Amrouche was therefore only a second knife."

"It is for this reason that I took the liberty of warning you, Si Ahmed. You and your family are in danger. My superiors have ordered me to protect you, so I will organize a discreet but very muscular surveillance around your villa…"

The Targui reacted firmly, not giving Commissioner Petit time to continue his explanations.

"No, no, commissary, not my villa! I am very well kept; do not worry, especially for me, nor for my family either. My sister will return to El Goléa tomorrow with her children and her husband. On the other hand, rather exercise discreet surveillance on the Yakobi, rue de Paris. They are much more vulnerable than I am. But please, don't alarm them for the moment, if you know what I mean."

"I can possibly protect you both, with the help of the gendarmerie…"

"No, it's useless. My two collaborators have not yet returned to El Goléa; they will serve as my bodyguards until we have finally neutralized the head of this organization."

"Agreed, Si Ahmed. The device will be in place from the first hour tomorrow."

Ranzi took a moment to think. He was finally going to tell Isaac; it was better, he thought. He picked up the telephone receiver and asked the PTT switchboard to put him in communication with the Yakobi.

"Isaac, I have something new. Can you join me at the villa as soon as possible? No, not on the phone; I'm waiting for you."

Isaac, intrigued by the Targui's sudden attitude, hurried to the villa on rue Gérôme-Bertania. It took him less than ten minutes to walk there.

"You have something very serious to tell me," he said, entering the living room.

Ranzi kept thinking, still unsure how to approach the problem. After a few minutes of silence, he decided to speak.

"Amrouche has accomplices who will certainly soon be looking for us. Commissioner Petit has just informed me that his yacht has been found in the cove of Bordj, near Bougie. According to his assessments—and they agree with mine—the adviser was not the mastermind of the plot; there is certainly someone else who is orchestrating everything at the top level."

"Yeah," Isaac nodded. "I suspected that for a long time, and I think I can even guess that you know who…"

"You're right; I was not very objective in this case. You see, I never thought it would come to this. He is one of our own, you understand, an influential member of the Grand Council, someone above suspicion."

"It was naturally him whom you met in Mecca and who suggested that you join the revolutionaries, right?"

"I gave him my word that I would never mention his name. I couldn't believe for a moment that any of the members of the Grand Council could associate themselves with a criminal enterprise. He overstepped the bounds. It is about Doctor Boutelja," Ranzi said, disgusted.

"Incredible, austere, taciturn Boutelja! I never liked this guy, you know, but to think that he was plotting…"

Isaac, though very disturbed, continued his detailed analysis.

"There are several obscure points that must be clarified immediately. The first question I ask myself is this: why did he wait for your return to try to recover the grimoire that he knew had been in our possession for five years? You presided over the last assembly before your temporary exile, and during your closing speech, you informed the members of the discovery of the manuscript. If I remember correctly, you even asked me to circulate the famous photographs of Mustapha in the assembly."

"There was no question of revolution at that time. I think the movement was set up quite recently following the events in Indochina. Boutelja's membership in this movement must be quite recent, and he took the lead of a network of activists. When the photographer died, the councilor informed him of the existence of the photographs of the manuscript or their negatives. Amrouche recognizes the castle of Chinon in one of the pictures; he insists on the importance of the manuscript. Boutelja then remembers that I had the original and decides to do everything possible to recover it. He entrusts this mission to his accomplice, the adviser, although the latter does not have the culture required to decipher the grimoire."

"You seem to forget that Boutelja knew that the manuscript was written in Hebrew."

"You are once again right, Yssic. Amrouche may have acted as a maverick, without informing his leader, at least at the very beginning. He may have warned Boutelja later, perhaps when he was forced to remove the bachagha for fear that he would speak."

"My second question is the following, Ranzi: knowing this, what do we do now?"

"We will take the bull by the horns. Boutelja lives in Sétif; we are going there tomorrow."

"No, it's too risky. If Boutelja decides to send a new team here, imagine the consequences for our families. No one will be there to protect them. Let's consider other hypotheses, shall we?"

Ranzi nodded several times.

"Précipitatio e diabolico: rushing is diabolical," goes the old saying. "Let's wait for them on our land and organize a reception worthy of the name; give them a warm welcome. Khaled and Amin are still in Khenchela; we should be able to set a mousetrap."

"O.K. Ranzi. You take Amin, and I'll take Khaled. Do you see any downside?"

"But you are not there at all, Yssic. I'm almost certain that the adversary will try to attack me first; he knows that the manuscript is in my possession, so my men will be hidden near my villa and…"

"How, dare you… you're going to put my family in danger!" Isaac cried, taken aback by the Targui's sudden levity.

"Tst, tst. You disappoint me enormously, Yssic. Who do you take me for? You and your family will be entitled to the national guard and to all the honors due to your high rank!"

"But I don't understand anything anymore," Isaac blurted, completely bewildered.

"Petit offered me discreet babysitting. I told him it was better for him to watch your house than my villa. In addition, you live close to the police station; the presence of police in your area will not shock anyone."

"Well done, well done. Next time, ask me my opinion anyway instead of making decisions for me!"

The Targui ignored the remark. Something bothered him; he knew that the doctor would soon try an action against him, but would he intervene in person? That, he doubted.

"Isaac," he said, frowning, "I don't think Boutelja is so crazy or reckless as to come in person to oversee the operations. What do you say?"

"I say you are right for once. We are going to share the task, but I think it is better to put Petit and Guichard in the game, for Boutelja and for everything else."

"Decidedly, you become cautious with age," joked Ranzi. "Reason, again reason! You make me miss the time of camel raids, when I once crisscrossed the dunes of the Sahara."

"That's why I called you 'Prince of the Dunes' when we were still teenagers, remember?" Isaac replied, with a hint of lyricism in his voice.

Pretending to ignore his foster brother's last remark, the Targui called out to the chaouch passing through the hall.

"Ali, call Commissioner Petit, please."

Monday, April 26, 1954

It was still dark.

Leila woke up with a start. She was alone in the big bed, and her companion had already gotten up. Worried, she headed for the bathroom, which was lit. Through the half-open door, she saw Ranzi finishing his toilet.

"Already standing up?" she asked in a soft voice.

"I must have made a noise when I got up," he said, as if to apologize. "I didn't want to wake you up so early."

Leila approached the Targui, barefoot on the bathroom floor, looking falsely threatening as she pointed her right index finger in his direction.

"You have to go away again, don't you?"

"Not for long this time. I'm just going to Sétif. It's good that you're awake; I had important things to tell you before I left."

Puzzled, his companion frowned.

"Are you going to put your life in danger again, Ranzi?"

"No, not at all, Leila. I will be just, how can I put it, a witness, an observer. The police will do all the work this time."

"This affair frightens me, Ranzi. You have in front of you fanatics of the worst kind, without faith or law. I can't wait to see all this bunch of scoundrels locked up."

"This case scares me too, Leila. We are convinced, Isaac and I, that they will try to launch an operation here, today or tomorrow. So I'm going to ask you to go and take shelter with the Yakobi with Mahmoud. There you will fear nothing; the police have put several men on duty to ensure your protection. As for Rachida, she will hasten her departure with Bashir and her children and will leave Khenchela this very morning, at dawn. She should wake up soon."

Commissioner Petit had asked Inspector Giordano to take charge of Boutelja's arrest with the help of the main witness in this case, Prince Ahmed Ranzi. Divisional Guichard and a local team would provide them with logistical support in Sétif, he added.

As agreed, the policeman showed up at the gate of the villa at six o'clock sharp. Ali ushered him into the living room, where breakfast was waiting for him.

The Sahraoui family was complete around the coffee table.

"Hello, inspector," said Ranzi simply, beckoning him to approach. "Sit down and take your time; you have at least fifteen minutes to eat. We will not stop on our way for this excursion."

Around six-fifteen, the Targui kissed his sister and the two sleeping little ones who were going to board the Land Rover with Bashir at the wheel. He then headed for the DS19, once again borrowed from his foster brother. He got Leila and Mahmoud into the back of the vehicle and asked Giordano to sit in the front.

"We're going with them to Isaac Yakobi's; it's on our way," Ranzi said simply.

After dropping off the two passengers at their home on rue de Paris, the Citroën sped north.

It took three and a half hours to reach Sétif.

Sétif, a city in eastern Algeria, experienced dark days after the Second World War. There were riots that were suppressed very severely by the French government. People were struggling to find their new marks; too much blood had been shed.

Now that the doctor's involvement in the bloody attacks of recent times was no longer in doubt, Ranzi was convinced that Boutelja had certainly taken part in the events of May 1945, probably acting in the shadows. He's such a coward, the Targui thought to himself.

Arriving in the city center, the gray DS19 crossed the main street, passed in front of the railway station, and ended up stopping in the avenue de Suffren, just opposite the home of Doctor Boutelja. Divisionnaire Guichard's black front-wheel drive was already parked along the sidewalk, about ten meters away.

The divisional got out of his car as soon as he saw the silhouette of the Targui through the window of the DS19. He pretended to ignore his friend's presence and headed for a brasserie on the corner of the street.

Ranzi joined him at the bar a few minutes later.

"His Highness will have a coffee?" Guichard looked rather sleepy.

"Hello, André, thank you for waiting for me. Order some hot coffee and croissants for me, please. I don't think you got much sleep last night. How long have you been hiding in the street, you and your two assistants?"

"We arrived in Sétif around six o'clock this morning, and nothing has changed since. Do you know what day it is?"

"Monday?"

"Easter Monday, my friend, not just any Monday! I'm going to face terrible retaliation when I get home!"

"You will blame me for your misfortunes; your wife will forgive you! Have you planned all the necessary mandates?"

"Yes, Ranzi, all the formalities will be carried out according to the rules. It is important that no defect of form can hinder his indictment. Could you give me some additional explanations?"

"Nothing you don't already know, André. I have good reason to believe that Doctor Boutelja is at the head of this whole organization of arms traffickers, whose members have been put out of harm's way. As you know, this character is an influential member of the Grand College. He betrayed all the great principles to which he adhered when he was enthroned. You have to be ruthless with individuals of this ilk. I am convinced that the searches of his home and his office will bring you all the elements required to indict him. I can't tell you more; I'm sorry."

"It's heard. Do you still want to stop him with Giordano's help?"

"Yes, André, I want to participate in his arrest, and I will gladly handcuff him. Do not forget that this man ordered my assassination several times. Let's go back to the cars; I don't want to miss him when he comes out of his house."

Inspector Giordano was dozing soundly in the lower right-hand seat, but Ranzi had been watching every suspicious coming and going for two hours now, wondering if he had gotten it all wrong. He feared that the revolutionary leader had not gone in person to Khenchela.

The clock on the dashboard showed twelve-thirty when Giordano finally woke up.

"I think I dozed off a bit," he said apologetically. "My God, half past twelve already! I understand why my stomach is crying out for food. Sheikh Ahmed, will you allow me to go and buy a snack?"

"It's too late to walk away from here now, Inspector. I'll treat you and the divisional to a gourmet meal as soon as we arrest our man, I promise."

At twelve-forty-five, the door of the building finally opened, yielding passage to a figure dressed in a dark suit and wearing a dark gray hat. He wore wide-rimmed horn-rimmed glasses.

"It's him," said Ranzi. "Let's go."

The doors of the DS19 slammed as the suspect approached the car. The doctor was taken aback when he recognized the Targui in his traditional attire. He was stuck like a rat; his opponent hadn't given him a chance.

"You," he stammered, "you traitor...I'll...you..."

"No need to tire yourself," Ranzi replied. "It's over for you. We will stop you from doing harm once and for all. By now, your accomplices have certainly been arrested by the Khencheloise police."

"In the name of the law, Mr. Boutelja," said Giordano, "you are under arrest."

He carried out a thorough search of the accused to ensure that he was not carrying any weapon. He put handcuffs on her wrists unceremoniously.

Guichard and his two deputies came running as quickly as they could. They did not need to lend a hand; however, it was they who would take charge of the suspect to question him at the Setif police station.

"This arrest is abusive!" shouted the doctor, forced to sit in the back seat of the black car. "I will be free within seventy-two hours at the latest, after the legal period of police custody. No charges can be brought against me."

Ranzi then leaned toward the prisoner, staring him straight in the eye. He whispered to him in a low voice so as not to be heard by the police:

"It's over for you; you won't do any more harm, Boutelja. You have failed in all your duties as a member of the Grand Council, so I proclaim your definitive expulsion from the fraternity. That's not all; as soon as I return to

Khenchela, I will contact the members of the Grand Council one by one to inform them of your treachery."

When Ranzi was done with Boutelja, Guichard slipped a few words to one of his deputies just before the black Citroën drove off, then turned to his friend.

"I have given orders for the searches to be carried out by my men, assisted by the local police, as soon as the doctor is imprisoned. Are you satisfied?"

"Perfect, Andrew. Let's have lunch now." He sketched a smile and added, "Giordano is starving, aren't you?"

Khenchela

Monday, April 26, 1954, noon

The sun was at its zenith in a spotless sky. It was very hot and dry, with an intermittent south wind blowing, causing whirlwinds of dust or fine sand.

Khaled and Amin were waiting behind in the hooded Jeep, about twenty meters from Prince Targui's villa. With a good supply of fresh water in a jug, they could maintain a very long watch, especially since they did not seem to be bothered by the heat that reigned that day on the set of Nememchas.

Commissioner Petit was stashed inside the house, accompanied by a sergeant in uniform. They were both standing behind the gate of the villa, ready to intervene at the slightest alarm. The policeman had a walkie-talkie and maintained double contact with the Targuis, who were just opposite, as well as with the two policemen in discreet surveillance on rue de Paris. Ali, the chaouch, had carefully taken shelter in the basement of the villa.

The mousetrap on rue Gérôme-Bertania could operate without endangering the lives of innocent people.

Around one o'clock, in the scorching heat, a moderately-paced black Renault passed the villa twice in a row, a few minutes apart. The carousel alerted Khaled and Amin, who immediately informed Petit.

"I spotted her; don't worry," replied the policeman through the microphone of his radio. "Let's wait for them to stop and show up before reacting. Thank God," he added, "the street is completely empty. In this hellish heat, people have nothing better to do than nap."

A few minutes later, the vehicle reappeared and stopped along the sidewalk, less than ten meters from the gate of the villa. Three unsavory-looking individuals dismounted. They approached the house hastily, with the visible intention of entering it.

The gate was wide open, but that was not likely to arouse their suspicions. The one who had taken the lead, their leader perhaps, put his right hand to his belt, took his pistol, and signaled to the two other accomplices to follow him with a simple wave of the hand.

The bandits broke through the gate.

The two Targuis on the lookout got out of the Jeep at the same time and hid behind the off-roader, guns drawn.

In perfect synchronism, the door of the villa opened ajar, and the superintendent ordered in a dry voice through his megaphone:

"National Police. Surrender without resistance; you are surrounded."

The arrest surprised the gang leader, who pressed the trigger of his weapon several times, pointing it in the direction of the policeman. The shots did not reach their target; Petit, by reflex, had taken shelter behind the thick wall.

On the other side of the street, a revolver thundered once. The bandit who had just dropped his weapon gazed, dazed, at his bloodied hand.

Khaled had just hit the mark; he had disarmed the aggressor with a single shot from the Beretta he had recovered in the desert. He said a few words in Arabic aloud. The two accomplices, feeling surrounded, raised their arms in the air without consulting each other and threw their weapons on the ground, judging it more reasonable to surrender.

The voice of the megaphone was heard again:

"Lie face down on the floor, arms and legs outstretched. And no more gestures, or I shoot."

The brigadier appeared hesitant. He held three metal bracelets in one hand and a gun in the other. He was immediately followed by his leader, who was holding his regulation P38 in his hand.

"Disarm them and put the brigadier handcuffs on them; we don't risk anything now."

The policeman recovered the Beretta as well as the two other pistols that had fallen on the lawn, then approached the bandits lying on the ground to handcuff them. He took care to search them carefully under the approving gaze of the superintendent. The latter signaled to the Targuis to approach.

"Thank you very much, my friends; your help has been invaluable to me. It was you who disarmed the chief," he inquired, addressing Khaled. "My congratulations; it was an exceptionally accurate shot. You can go back now," he said with a wink. "You were never here today, were you?"

Khaled stepped forward to shake the policeman's hand.

"We don't know what you're talking about, commissioner," he said with a wink.

Petit pressed the button on his walkie-talkie several times until it sputtered. He immediately got in touch with the policeman who was providing close protection for the Yakobi.

"Hello, Commissioner Petit speaking. The party is over. Hello, I repeat, the party is over. Immediately notify Mr. Yakobi that everything is back to normal."

CHAPTER 22
Tuesday, April 27, 1954

The Jeep stopped on rue de Paris, right in front of the Aurès bazaar. Ranzi jumped out of the SUV and headed straight for the store, a leather briefcase in hand. As he entered, he greeted Nathan, who was stocking the window. He went behind the counter and made his way to the back room, where Isaac's office was located. Out of breath, he exclaimed, "Hello, Yssic! You'll never guess what's in my towel!"

"A courier from the honorable mayor of Chinon," replied the tradesman without flinching. "I just received a copy just now. Charles wrote us a long letter of thanks. He tells us that the administrative formalities are going well and that we will soon be able to recover our share of the treasure, minus the inevitable taxes and duties.

He adds that the recent discoveries in the basements of the Château de Chinon made headlines in the metropolitan newspapers, and he probably sent you some clippings so we can share the glory for which he claims to be indebted to us.

Finally, he invites us all to Chinon for the inauguration of the restoration works of the castle, planned for next month. Thanks to all the publicity surrounding the discovery of the treasure, he was able to secure an important subsidy from the Ministry of Culture."

"And I thought I was giving you a surprise," replied the Targui, disappointed to have missed his effect. "Well, after all, I didn't come just to tell you this news: Superintendent Petit wants to see us this morning, all business."

Commissioner Petit paced up and down the large office, appearing very agitated. He had asked Ranzi and Isaac to come and sign their depositions in his office. Their behavior surprised him; some points needed clarification.

"You helped us put an end to international arms trafficking, Sheikh Ahmed, and you too, Mr. Yakobi. I received congratulations from my superiors and even from the head of the DST himself. Thanks to you, we have arrested all the traffickers, both in mainland France, in Chinon, and in Algeria. We even imprisoned their leader, who will remain behind bars for a long time. These successes? We owe them to you, so why the hell do you want to stay in the shadows?"

"I have already told you, and I confirm it once again: we Sahrawis are simple people, and we have nothing to do with honors. As you know, someone tried to steal a precious object from me, and the worst thing is that it doesn't even belong to me. There were several attempts on my life, and by the grace of Allah, I got away with it. The police provided me with all the help I needed to put an end to these attacks, and fortunately, neither I nor my relatives were affected. I ask for nothing more, you see."

"Agreed, it's up to you," said the resigned policeman. "We will maintain confidentiality on all your interventions. While waiting to complete your statements, I will tell you what we were able to gather after hearing Boutelja's accomplices and following a long investigation."

He mechanically leafed through a few pages of a file open on his desk, taking a moment to organize his thoughts before beginning his story.

"Boutelja's accomplice, whom we intercepted and arrested in Khenchela, confessed everything; he will serve as a prosecution witness. His boss is behind this whole dark affair. Originally, there was a large arms trafficking operation between Italy, Eastern Europe, and North Africa, requiring enormous capital to develop.

Upon the death of his brother, the former adviser Amrouche, who was Boutelja's right-hand man, recovered the duplicates of the photographs of the manuscript of Abraham the Jew. He quickly realized that, on the cover, there was an illustration of a place he knew very well from having stayed there one summer: the Château de Chinon. Amrouche also knew the legends surrounding the treasure of the kings of France or the Templars, having perhaps heard them during a visit to the ruins. For him, there was no doubt that the famous grimoire would reveal the secret cache of the fabulous treasure.

Extraordinarily, Boutelja had already seen these photographs; he had held them during a meeting with members of a private circle in 1949 in Algiers. He knew that the inscriptions on the manuscript were indecipherable, while Amrouche was convinced of the contrary. It was therefore on his own initiative that the latter mounted the expedition that cost him his life in Chinon. Anyway, and by the doctor's own admission, the manuscript had enormous market value that he could have monetized very well with the help of another accomplice you also know: the Khenchelois bookseller, Kalifa.

But the story does not end there. Hold on tight. The searches ordered by Divisionnaire Guichard made it possible to seize important documents proving that a large-scale conspiracy was in preparation—a kind of reissue of the riots of Guelma and Sétif in 1945, but on a larger scale. It was to fuel this insurrection that weapons were purchased in Italy and certain Eastern countries.

Finally, and still according to the documents in our possession, it seems that the whole gang was neutralized."

Ranzi met Isaac's gaze and gave his foster brother a discreet wink. Like him, he did not believe that this case would end there; it must have far deeper ramifications than those the police had just uncovered. He refrained, however, from raising the slightest comment on this subject.

"Commissioner," he said in conclusion, "my brother and I are delighted with the happy outcome of this affair. Our dearest wish is to never hear about this story again. Allow us now to take our leave. We will meet again soon, if you wish, in a slightly less austere setting—perhaps for dinner at my house? I will phone you shortly."

CHAPTER 23
Thursday, April 29, 1954

Isaac looked excited. He had barely slept the night before, so obsessed was he with the experiments scheduled for the day. He woke Dror at five-thirty, and the two arrived a good half-hour early at the Targui villa, which was already hard at work.

Once in the laboratory, Isaac took charge of the operations.

"How much pure gold do we have, Ranzi?"

"Do not panic! I have several kilograms of precious metal in my safe, but it's better to be cautious. We will start with a kilogram of gold and two hundred grams of powder. Let's go?"

Using a long glass spatula, Isaac took a portion of powder from bottle No. 20 and delicately placed it on the Roberval tray. He had prepared two hundred-gram weights on the opposite platform. The amount of powder was excessive, so he took several small fractions before finally achieving balance.

The Targui then handed him a vial containing pure gold powder and a zirconium crucible. What a luxury, Isaac thought as he saw the crucible. But he agreed on the choice; it was not worth the risk of a piercing during a coction that would last twelve hours.

He grabbed the container with the precious metal and emptied its contents onto the Roberval plateau. He checked the weight again, then poured the gold powder into a tinned iron dish. He intimately mixed the gold and the scarlet powder with a glass spatula, praying that the choice of fixed proportions was correct.

Dror, in an almost religious silence, recorded the manipulations his father performed with a skill that disconcerted him. He held his breath with each operation, as if a rabbit were about to emerge from a test tube.

The teenager was amazed to discover a new father, one very different from the man he had known, and ultimately closer to his foster brother, the Targui.

"Ranzi, please light the oven and open the door of the middle hearth; I will introduce the crucible there."

The Targui complied and closed the door as soon as the flame of the burner seemed properly regulated. He walked over to the blackboard and wrote in fine, regular handwriting with white chalk:

This day, Thursday, April 27, 1954, at 7 a.m. sharp.

Test No. I

Sample No. 20: 200 grams of scarlet powder.

Powdered gold, purified three times: 1,000 grams.

Lighting the oven: 1 Bunsen burner no. 3, thermostat set at 900°C.

Natural draw.

"Uncle Ranzi," Dror interrupted curtly, "what does 'gold purified three times by cupellation' mean, and what is the reason for this choice of temperature? Is it arbitrary?"

"I am your master until the end of your apprenticeship; do not forget it, my dear disciple," said the Targui with a falsely offended air.

Dror, more teasing than ever, replied mockingly, "Yes, Uncle R… Uh, sorry, master."

Ranzi smirked and launched into a long explanation.

"The gold has been purified three times by cupellation; I am quite sure of its purity. Cupellation is a metallurgical method that involves heating gold alloyed with lead beyond the melting point of gold. Lead oxidizes and volatilizes, drawing various impurities through the porous wall of the dish, thus leaving a pellet of pure gold at the bottom of the crucible.

Now, regarding the choice of temperature, it's a bet that we make, your father and I. Logically, you should never reach the melting point of gold in this type of operation, but the temperature must still be very high to ensure the ingres— this is how the ancients referred to the penetrating power of the Stone. 900°C corresponds approximately to the fourth degree of the fire of the adepts, which rises to the melting point of gold, that is to say, 1064°C. We will know more around 7 p.m. when we test the powder obtained."

"If we took a break until tonight, what do you think?" Isaac suggested.

It was exactly seven o'clock when Ranzi and Isaac approached the athanor to extinguish the burner. The pyrometric rod indicated 904°C. Dror carefully watched all the manipulations that took place.

Isaac turned off the propane gas control valve while Ranzi activated the forced ventilation to cool the scorching hearth above the oven. Their gestures were synchronized by long-standing common practices.

As a precaution, they waited a quarter of an hour before entering the central chamber, which had sufficiently cooled. At the opportune moment, Ranzi seized the still slightly smoking crucible with a large steel tong, which he held with both hands.

He exclaimed in shock, "My friends, the time has finally come to experience this jewel that comes directly from the past. We will all soon know if Abraham the Jew was truly an Adept."

He overturned the crucible onto the all-white earthenware of the straw mattress.

Dror let out a cry. "Dad, Uncle Ranzi, look!" Dror observed, visibly disappointed. "The appearance of the powder has completely changed. It's crushed orange-red glass that we made; all the gold has disappeared—poof! Completely vanished!"

"It's true, my son. Gold has turned into glass, but what glass!" Isaac replied, amused. "A true Philosopher must know how to make Dror glass."

"Prostrate yourself before the Eternal, O disciple, and contemplate well the miraculous creation, in accordance with the teaching of Solomon in the Song of Songs and that, anonymous, of the Aesh Mezareph. You have the signal privilege of admiring the famous and true carbuncle, the Phoenix of Phoenixes, our King seated on his throne and proclaiming like Thoth-Hermes: 'As above, so below; just as below, so above, to work the miracle of a thing.'"

Then, changing his tone and burning with impatience, thus breaking with his usual calm, Ranzi called out to Isaac, "Yssi! Quick, quick, I need lead—fissa, fissa!"

His foster brother didn't take long to respond. He retrieved some deep gray shot as quickly as he could from a large bottle on the shelf of metallic substances. He weighed the metal and questioned Ranzi, "Saturn, 2,750 kilograms; is that okay with you?"

"Perfectly," said the Targui, visibly overexcited. "Take the thirty-thousandth part of this wonderful powder, please," he added, pointing to the orange product spread on the bench.

Dror did not understand what the two adults were about to do, but he mechanically made the calculation in his head.

"This is exactly 0.0916 grams. Well, I believe."

"Good," Isaac said, not bothering to check. "I will weigh 1 decigram; to hell with greed."

He carefully scooped out an amount roughly the size of a fingernail clipping from the still-warm heap on the bench. He weighed his sample on the trebuchet, removing the excess with tweezers. He seemed to be thinking hard and suddenly, raising his head, he looked around as if he had lost something.

"Oh, I found it!" he finally said, tearing a blank page from the notebook in front of the trebuchet. "Here is the appropriate envelope."

Dror understood less and less. Why make a sheet of paper? He noticed that his father was carefully wrapping the insignificant bit of the strange orange product in the sheet of paper, which he then rolled into a ball.

Guessing the question his son was asking, Isaac anticipated by revealing the secret reason: "If the tiny portion of the Philosopher's Stone is not protected when thrown into the molten metal, Dror, it may volatilize prematurely, and all will be ruined. Usually, when we have time, we coat it in wax, you see, but today we are in too much of a hurry."

He finally handed the crumpled dumpling to Ranzi. "It's up to you, highness."

The Targui complied. He immediately placed the supply of lead in an alundum crucible, which he set on a tripod above a Bunsen burner. He took the precaution of turning on the ventilation, lighting the flame, and adjusting it to an intense blue.

The lead began to melt slowly. Ranzi then plunged a steel rod into the molten mass and vigorously stirred the metal, which was beginning to smoke.

"Beelzebub, I almost forgot!" he exclaimed.

He opened the sliding door of the cupboard below the sorbonne with armoured glass and took out a varnished beechwood box the size of a shoebox. He flipped the lid, pulled out a tube that looked suspiciously like a microphone, and plugged it into the black dial device in the case. He placed the tube on its support, pointing its end toward the crucible about a foot away.

"It's a Geiger counter," he said, throwing the ball of paper into the liquefied lead.

A firework-like display erupted, with a spray of green color, followed by a very bright glow accompanied by a noise similar to strong bubbling, muffled by the protective glass of the Sorbonne and the hum of the exhaust fan. The surface of the molten metal began to swirl, taking on all the colors of the rainbow. A strong bluish glow flooded the entire room, setting the stage for a spectacle of multiple and mysterious manifestations.

As this spectacle unfolded, the black apparatus suddenly began to crackle, and the hand jumped from one end of the dial to the other before finally stabilizing, along with the frequency of the crackles. Ranzi approached the counter to note the value of the radiation once the needle of the counter stabilized, eager to understand the changing dynamics.

The transformations triggered by the Powder Fraction insignia seemed like magic, leaving the teenager amazed by the spectacle unfolding before his eyes. He still did not understand the purpose of all these operations, and his wonder was palpable.

"You have to wait at least fifteen minutes for everything to be homogeneous," explained Isaac very pragmatically. "Look, the temperature is certainly climbing at breakneck speed; it shows in the color of the molten metal that keeps changing. The lead has swapped its original dark silver color for a very bright orange and then green."

Meanwhile, the Geiger counter needle had dropped back to almost zero, indicating a significant change in the radiation levels.

"Ranzi," Isaac suddenly ordered, "don't stand there with your arms hanging idly by; let's get on with it. We're almost there; give me the ingot mold, please."

Ranzi complied with a good heart and a blissful smile, quite unusual for him, proof of intense emotion. He placed the ingot mold on the bench, under the Sorbonne, near the Bunsen. Isaac, on the other hand, seemed very calm, but in reality, he, like the other two witnesses, had great difficulty keeping his cool.

The tension had risen a notch since the start of the lead metamorphoses, and the air was thick with anticipation. Prince Targui put out the fire from the Bunsen burner without haste, skillfully seized the crucible with the long steel tongs, and spilled the contents in a single jet into the ingot mold.

The metal, greenish-yellow in the liquid state, became golden and shiny with a very characteristic luster as it solidified, a truly remarkable transformation.

Isaac didn't wait for the ingot to cool on its own. He filled the sink with water, grabbed the ingot mold again with the tongs he was still holding, and plunged everything into the sink. There was a plume of smoke accompanied by a dull hiss, then nothing, a sudden stillness.

Isaac still held the pliers in his hand. When the effervescence was over, he took the towel hanging over the sink and spread it on the bench, then turned the ingot mold over it.

The fine gold bar then appeared in all its glory, a dazzling sight.

Dror could not believe his eyes; he understood that an extraordinary phenomenon of which he was the privileged witness had just occurred: a transmutation of lead into gold.

Ranzi nearly burned himself grabbing the ingot, though it was wrapped in the towel. He was about to swear but stopped in time.

"I'll weigh it right away," he exclaimed with ill-contained impatience.

The weights piled up on the plateau of the little Roberval.

"3.365 kilograms," said Dror, calculating mentally and quickly adding up the weights on the tray. "It's inexplicable; we should have weighed 2,750 kilograms with more or less some dust. Where does this excess of 615 grams come from? That's almost 22% more than the mass of lead involved." He paused for a moment, as if he had just discovered something even more important than this increase in mass—something incredible, impossible…

"But," he noticed abruptly, "1 decigram of powder made it possible to manufacture 3.365 kilograms of gold! This powder therefore has a transmutatory power!"

"Wouaouh! Wouaaaaoooooooooooooooouh!"

"Two thousand two hundred and forty billion francs!" exclaimed the bewildered young Dror. "You must immediately buy a lead mine."

"Wait a minute; you must have made a mistake somewhere in your calculations, Dror," Isaac immediately challenged in bad faith. "And then, how do you know the price of gold?"

Dror, too engrossed in the results of the experiment that had just unfolded before his eyes, refrained from answering.

The Targui immediately came to the rescue of his young disciple. "Dror is unbeatable in mental arithmetic, Yssic; he was not mistaken, and his advice is sound. Let's buy lead before the prices of base metal soar."

Then, addressing the teenager, he made a surprising confession: "However, know, O disciple mathematician, that gold is accessory. It represents no value for the philosopher; the true secret of the Stone is elsewhere."

"What secrets? Could there be another secret?" asked the teenager, more intrigued than ever.

"The transmutation of gold is not an end in itself for the Adept, my son," Isaac replied. "It is only a test that verifies the maturity of the Stone and that the Adept has worked well. The one and only goal of our quest, Dror, is the Universal Elixir. The pure gold we have just produced is the only clue the Adept has to ensure that the final goal is finally achieved."

Ranzi nodded. "Your father has aptly summed up three millennia of Hermetic tradition and philosophy in these few words, my boy. The Elixir is the most precious thing in this world. It can cure many diseases and perhaps even prolong life. But we still have a long way to go to find the right conditions of use because the Elixir, if administered poorly, can become a dangerous and deadly poison."

"And it's not over yet, Dror," Isaac replied, no doubt wanting to further arouse the teenager's curiosity. "There is another particularity of the Stone that we have just highlighted: the Stone is an incredible reservoir of energy."

"How so? Not finished yet? An energy reservoir?" Dror repeated in disbelief.

Ranzi, more competent in physics than his partner, decided to reveal the last secret, the most incredible of all—the "Secret Secretorum," or the Secret of Secrets.

"You will learn that it takes 5,118.6 kilowatt hours to transmute one gram of lead into gold. But starting from pure energy, it would take 212,280 kilowatt hours to synthesize one gram of gold, i.e., the entire production of a 300 Megawatt coal-fired power plant, like that of Algiers, for about 42 and a half minutes.

Now you can calculate how much energy it took to bring the extra 615 grams of gold out of thin air!"

"All output from the same power plant for about 18 days, master," Dror replied unabashedly. "But I do not understand how these 615 grams of gold could arise from nothing? It's not magic, is it?"

"No, Dror," the Targui replied softly, "it's quantum mechanics. The Stone creates a bridge that allows access to another universe—a universe parallel to ours—from which it draws the antimatter or the energy necessary for transmutations. Perhaps it draws this mysterious energy from the void.

Fortunately, the intrusion of antimatter takes place gradually, according to a natural balance that dissipates energy as the reaction occurs. We can call it cold fusion.

The radioactivity values that I noted during the transmutation are very low, with the exception of a few emission peaks at the start of the process—an initialization period during which the system seeks a new equilibrium—thus confirming that the experiment we have just carried out is safe for the environment and living beings. But we already knew that during the tests we conducted with the powder that your father and I had developed."

The teenager had to make a considerable effort to contain himself so as not to let his surprise slip away. His father, his uncle—alchemists? So they had hidden their game forever. They could have flaunted their wealth if they had wanted to, but instead, they lived normally, like ordinary people.

Dror could not help but question his father, as if he still doubted the confidence that Ranzi had just let slip. "Did you two really craft the Philosopher's Stone in secret?"

"Yes, my son," Isaac confessed. "But its power was mediocre compared to that which we have just experienced, and its transmuting power scarcely exceeded ten thousand parts of lead for one part of the philosopher's stone. Abraham mastered the process better than anyone else, and thanks to your translations, we will be able to find his entire path."

"And what do you plan to do now?" asked the young teenager.

"Take a well-deserved rest and build a new world. A big task awaits us tomorrow, Dror…" answered Ranzi.

EPILOGUE

Sunday, 2 May 1954

In the heart of a magnificent oasis, on a soft spring morning, the camp of El Goléa was preparing to celebrate an exceptional event: the marriage of Leila, the beautiful Kabyle woman with a tender heart, and Cheikh Ranzi Ahmed, a man respected for his courage, wisdom, and generosity.s

Despite coming from different cultures, the two families had woven strong bonds of friendship and respect over the years.

The celebration lasted for three days, filled with music, dancing, and joyous gatherings among family and friends. The groom presented his bride with a generous dowry and numerous gifts—jewellery, clothing, and camels. Leila was adorned in a magnificent Kabyle dress of sheer fabric, embroidered with gold threads that shimmered in the sunlight. Her outfit was completed with a belt decorated with traditional patterns and a delicate scarf framing her radiant face. Her hands were adorned with henna, symbolising beauty and happiness.

Across the camp, Ranzi was preparing with the help of his friends. He wore a traditional Tuareg outfit, the *melhafa*, a long indigo robe that reflected the depth of the desert. Around his head, an indigo turban—symbolising pride and heritage—was carefully wrapped, lending him an air of distinction and mysticism. A magnificent golden Southern Cross, set with emeralds, adorned the turban.

The entire Jacobi family had gathered to witness this momentous occasion.

Isaac stood before his foster brother, his face etched with emotion, unable to hold back his tears of joy.

"My brother," he said, his hoarse voice trembling, "you have finally come back to life, like a phoenix rising from the ashes. My family wishes you an eternity of happiness. May Allah bless you with beautiful offspring."

He stepped forward and embraced the Tuareg prince for a long time. Ranzi, overcome with emotion, was unable to find words to reply.

Together, they made their way to the heart of the oasis, where the ceremony was to take place. The setting was adorned with flowers and vibrant draperies, a dazzling spectacle of colour.

The villagers, dressed in their finest attire, gathered to share in the joyous occasion. The melodies of flutes and drums filled the air, stirring hearts with excitement and happiness. Women in festive garments trilled their traditional *you-you*, their voices rising and falling in rhythm with the beat of drums and bagpipes.

As the sun began to set, painting the sky in hues of gold and pink, Ranzi stepped towards Leila, his eyes filled with admiration.

The traditional rites were observed: the ritual of sharing bread and salt—a sacred symbol of unity and solidarity—followed by the recitation of poetry celebrating love and devotion. The voices of ancestors seemed to echo in the songs, weaving together Kabyle and Tuareg traditions in perfect harmony.

The celebration continued under a canopy of stars. Guests danced through the night, blending the lively steps of Kabyle dance with the graceful movements of Saharan traditions. Laughter and song filled the air, while wooden tables were laden with lovingly prepared traditional dishes.

At dawn, as the first rays of sunlight caressed the dunes, Ranzi and Leila stood hand in hand, with Isaac and Rachida as their witnesses. They pledged to love and support one another, uniting their destinies beyond the borders of their respective cultures.

Their marriage was not only the union of two souls but also a symbol of harmony between Algeria's diverse traditions—a fusion of the desert's breath and the whisper of the mountains. This celebration would be remembered as a radiant testament to love and mutual respect, illuminating the path of their life together.

November 1, 1954: The Algerian War begins

Seventy attacks take place in about thirty locations across Algeria. The number is significantly higher in the Aurès region than in other regions. Attacks take place against military buildings in Biskra, Batna, and Khenchela.

The first victims of the revolution died in Khenchela:

- *André Markey, 21, a conscripted soldier from the 4th Artillery Regiment*
- *Lieutenant Roland Darneau, 37, an officer in the 13th Dragoon Regiment*

www.ingramcontent.com/pod-product-compliance
Lightning Source LLC
Chambersburg PA
CBHW071148060526
44107CB00133B/426